The Five-Minute Linguist

Bite-Sized Essays on Language and Languages

THIRD EDITION

Edited by
Caroline Myrick and Walt Wolfram

SHEFFIELD UK BRISTOL CT

Published by Equinox Publishing Ltd.

UK: Office 415, The Workstation, 15 Paternoster Row, Sheffield, South Yorkshire S1 2BX

USA: ISD, 70 Enterprise Drive, Bristol, CT 06010

www.equinoxpub.com

First edition edited by E. M. Rickerson and Barry Hilton published in 2006 by Equinox
Second edition edited by E. M. Rickerson and Barry Hilton published in 2012 by Equinox
Third edition edited by Caroline Myrick and Walt Wolfram published in 2019 by Equinox

ISBN-13 978 1 78179 854 6 (hardback)
         978 1 78179 855 3 (paperback)
         978 1 78179 856 0 (ePDF)

British Library Cataloguing-in-Publication Data

A catalogue record for this book is available from the British Library.

Library of Congress Cataloging-in-Publication Data

Names: Myrick, Caroline, editor. | Wolfram, Walt, 1941- editor.
Title: The five-minute linguist : bite-sized essays on language and languages
    / edited by Caroline Myrick and Walt Wolfram.
Description: Third edition. | Sheffield, South Yorkshire ; Bristol, CT :
    Equinox Publishing Ltd., [2019] | Includes bibliographical references and
    index.
Identifiers: LCCN 2018053608 (print) | LCCN 2018059640 (ebook) | ISBN
    9781781798560 (ePDF) | ISBN 9781781798546 | ISBN 9781781798546 q(hardback)
    | ISBN 9781781798553 q(paperback) | ISBN 9781781798560 q(ePDF)
Subjects: LCSH: Linguistics--Miscellanea. | Language and
    languages--Miscellanea.
Classification: LCC P107 (ebook) | LCC P107 .A15 2019 (print) | DDC 400--dc23
LC record available at https://lccn.loc.gov/2018053608

Typeset by JS Typesetting Ltd, Porthcawl, Mid Glamorgan

*In memory of our colleagues
who contributed to previous editions of this book:*

*Peter Ladefoged, 1925–2006
Frank Borchardt, 1938–2007
Dora Johnson, 1937–2012
Amelia Murdoch, 1923–2015
Paul Chapin, 1938–2015
Robert Rodman, 1940–2017
Robyn Holman, 1948–2018*

Contents

Language variation and change

Language learning

Language and society

Language in the United States

Foreword

Ben Zimmer

Soon after children begin stringing words together, they learn that this new tool at their disposal, language, gives them an exciting power: the power to ask questions. Questions, and the answers we receive, shape our reality from the start. Why are things the way they are? Who does what? How did we get here, and where are we going? By questioning the world around us, we create vast (and yet never completed) systems of knowledge, cobbled together through social exchanges, one communicative step at a time.

Because humans are born into a life of endless questioning, it's only natural to interrogate the very instrument that allows us to ask questions. What is this thing called language? How does it work? What makes it both inward-looking—a vehicle for expressing our deepest thoughts and feelings—and outward-looking—the key to interacting with every person in our social orbit? The simultaneous intimacy and gregariousness of language mean that our questions about it are never remote, hypothetical concerns. Striving to understand language is another way to understand ourselves and those around us.

This deeply felt nature of language puts linguistic scholars in a peculiar position of weighing in on matters about which all of us feel a certain measure of expertise, simply by being language users. Everyone is, more or less, an amateur linguist. Or perhaps it's more accurate to say that everyone is an amateur meta-linguist, because communicating by means of language lets us think about, and form opinions about, language itself.

The good news is that those opinions can be informed by experts who have devoted their careers to understanding the inner workings of language in all of its varied facets. And it doesn't require diving deep into esoteric and abstruse texts. You can start with the very text in front of you, which breaks down the most burning questions about language and provides accessible answers that don't require a Ph.D. to understand. And the answers in these pages aren't mere guesswork, either. Each one crystallizes a carefully worked-out body of scholarship, up to and including the latest avenues of research.

Because language never stays still, the study of language is always on the move. This edition of *The Five-Minute Linguist* (the third, following editions in 2006 and 2012) reflects the constantly shifting and expanding purview of linguistics. Among the many new or newly improved chapters in this edition, you'll find cutting-edge concerns about the intersections of language and technology, covering questions about social media, computer-aided language teaching, machine translation, and text-messaging. Linguistic diversity is likewise reflected in an increasingly diverse panoply of subjects. Gender, sexuality, race, and ethnicity are all explored in terms of how they shape our linguistic identities.

Each of these topics could itself support a book-length treatment, but the goal here is to convey authoritative answers to common questions about language in bite-sized informational nuggets. Of course, a reader who is suitably intrigued by the answers provided by the experts can use the book as an invitation to dig deeper into the wide-ranging subject matter that linguists study. If you like dipping your toes into language and linguistics, consider going for a full swim.

This latest edition of *The Five-Minute Linguist* is particularly heartening for me, since it's such a wonderful display of how linguists and language professionals can communicate their scholarship to a general audience. My own career has evolved from the academic study of linguistics and linguistic anthropology to more public-facing endeavors in language commentary. I'm gratified to see so many bright minds sharing their expertise in a format that is both entertaining and enlightening. The old image of knowledge being locked up in an ivory tower is increasingly inapt when it comes to the study of language, as more and more scholars seek to break down the communicative barriers of their discipline and bring linguistically informed understanding to the public at large.

This book owes its origins to an exercise in public outreach—the 2005 radio series *Talkin' about Talk*—that was a salutary effort in using mass media to convey linguistic knowledge in digestible chunks. Since then, linguists have grappled more and more with how they can communicate to the public more effectively. Recently, the Linguistic Society of America (LSA) has borrowed the 'five-minute' format of the radio series and the book it inspired, launching a competition at the LSA's annual meeting where scholars vie to create the most compelling presentation of their research under tight time constraints. It turns out that even complex linguistic topics can be boiled down into engaging and accessible summaries. This edition of *The Five-Minute Linguist* continues this worthy enterprise at a time when short-form journalism has demonstrated the value of concise 'explainers' for cutting through the clutter of a busy media landscape.

One takeaway that I hope that readers get from this book is that the study of language contains multitudes. Public discussion about language often veers into grammar and usage peeves, or narrowly constrained considerations of individual words and their semantics. Now, I'm a big fan of individual words—much of my own writing plumbs the history of word usage through what I like to think of as a form of narrative lexicography—but language is much more than a collection of words in a lexicon. The sixty-six mini-essays in this volume encompass so many ways of thinking about language: considerations of different structural levels, a diverse array of cultural and political angles, and the practical concerns of acquiring and maintaining linguistic knowledge. I hope you enjoy these forays into the multifarious landscape of language, and never stop questioning.

About the author

Ben Zimmer is a linguist, lexicographer and all-around word nut. He is the language columnist for *The Wall Street Journal* and a contributing editor to *The Atlantic*. He serves as chair of the New Words Committee of the American Dialect Society and is the recipient of the Linguistic Society of America's first-ever Linguistics Journalism Award.

Introduction

Caroline Myrick and Walt Wolfram

More than a century ago, one of the pioneers in the field of linguistics—Ferdinand de Saussure—observed that linguistics should not remain the focus of a handful of specialists. 'In practice,' he said, 'the study of language is in some degree or other the concern of everyone.' As the study of language has advanced into the twenty-first century, with so many specializations and technical advances that linguists can barely keep up with their own concentration, the need to make the field accessible to the public becomes more critical. What do linguistics do and how do they do it? Perhaps more important is the question of why they do it. We now live in an information age unimaginable only a few decades ago, with limitless networks of information only a keystroke away. One of the challenges of a highly specialized field like linguistics is to provide small bites of information for the public to digest. *The Five-Minute Linguist* is an attempt to offer this type of information about language to the public in an informative, entertaining, and accessible format.

The book is intended for non-specialists, an upbeat introduction to language and linguistics for general readers. The chapters are short (three to five pages), suitable for browsing or reading on the move, and its style is intentionally light—more like what used to be called 'fireside chats'—or, somewhat more currently, 'speed-dating events.' In fact, it was born as a series of radio chats called *Talkin' About Talk*, which in 2005 was part of a celebration of the 'Year of Languages' in the United States. The essays have an informal tone because of the on-air persona of the narrator, a knowledgeable and amiable guide whose task it was to de-mystify the sometimes complex subject of language for a wide range of listeners. Each week the narrator talked about a language-related topic in a relaxed, conversational style for *exactly five minutes*—thus the title of the book.

For the third edition, we have added a number of new topics covering contemporary subjects of interest that were not included in earlier editions of the book. Furthermore, chapters from previous editions have been updated. We hope that this expansion and updating have made the collection more comprehensive and current, while remaining faithful to its guiding principles: What do people who are *not* in the language field want to know about language? What are some of their major misconceptions? What do our readers want to know about *learning* or *using* languages? The resulting essays, each with a question as its title, are what we like to think of as a savory platter of linguistic *hors d'oeuvres,* something to whet your appetite and invite you to proceed to a more substantial dish of linguistics.

The authors of the essays represent an impressive array of talent, and we encourage the reader to look at their brief biographies at the end of each chapter. Many have written highly acclaimed books of their own that discuss, at greater length and with narrower focus, the topics discussed in this book. Most are prominent researchers on university faculties and organizations professionally engaged with language. They include *scientific linguists* (linguistics professors, field linguists, phoneticians, psycholinguists, and others primarily interested in linguistic theory and linguistic data); *language educators* (specialists in second language acquisition, and teachers of various languages); and *applied language professionals* (translators/interpreters, language officers in government agencies, lexicographers, anthropologists, directors of resource centers and language programs, and members of advocacy groups or professional organizations). We believe it to be a unique feature of the book that its contributors represent the entire breadth of the language profession.

How to read this book

The Five-Minute Linguist does not have to be read sequentially. Since the chapters are essentially free-standing, they may be read in any order. That does not mean, however, that each chapter is unconnected to the rest. Chapters may be related to adjacent chapters and to other parts of the book as well. To help readers access topical interests, this edition of the book has arranged the articles into convenient sections in order to help the reader better navigate the book. The sections include an introduction to linguistics and language (Chapters 1–6), the structure of language (Chapters 7–12), issues of communication (Chapters 13–17), language's relationship with brain function and thoughts (Chapters 18–21), the history of language and languages (Chapters 22–28), language diversity and change over time (Chapters 29–34), language learning (Chapters 35–41), the social context of language (Chapter 42–46), issues of language in the United States (Chapters 47–52), language and digital technologies (Chapters 53–56), and issues of language at school (Chapters 57–61). The final section (Chapters 62–66) includes topics of language 'applications,' including lexicography, translation, forensic investigation, and language preservation.

Acknowledgments

As new editors for the third edition, we stand on the accomplishments of those who imagined, created, and compiled the first two editions. Obviously, our debt of gratitude to the original compilers, E. M. 'Rick' Rickerson and Barry Hilton, is monumental. The second editor of this edition (the first editor was in high school at the time) remembers extended conversations with them in which he encouraged them to pursue this venture, guaranteeing that it would be highly useful for the people who wonder what linguists do for a living. Over a decade later, we are thrilled to have been given custody of Rickerson and Hilton's brainchild, and to carry on *The Five-Minute Linguist*'s legacy of bringing linguistic knowledge to the public!

The editors of this edition represent both emerging and long-time investments in the field of linguistics, with a focus on making the volume more inclusive, up-to-date, and representative. Caroline Myrick recently received her Ph.D. as an emerging scholar in the field, whereas Walt Wolfram has been a professional linguist for more than a half-century. We hope that our diverse chronological vantage points offer a complementary and authentic perspective on the field. But the real champions of this effort are the distinguished authors who so graciously assumed the challenge of writing meaningful explanations of often very-specialized topical areas for the public, including those who updated earlier essays. Special thanks, as well, to Ben Zimmer, who personifies the goals of this effort in his everyday writing, for doing the foreword.

We hope that the clarity and authority of the essays in *The Five-Minute Linguist* will be obvious to readers. Not observable, except to the editors, is the collegiality and selflessness that characterized the writing and shaping of the essays. Past and present contributors joined the project voluntarily for the benefit of the profession, and did so without reserve. They embraced the project so wholeheartedly that the modest goal of raising public awareness about language and linguistics became, ultimately, a celebration of language itself.

About the authors

Caroline Myrick holds a Ph.D. in sociology from North Carolina State University, where she specialized in sociolinguistics and social inequality. Her research has examined language and gender ideologies as well as language variation and change in the Caribbean. She is passionate about bringing linguistic information to the public.

Walt Wolfram is William C. Friday Distinguished University Professor at North Carolina State University, where he also directs the North Carolina Language and Life Project. He has pioneered research on social and ethnic dialects since the 1960s and published more than 20 books and over 300 articles.

What is linguistics?

1
Why learn about language?

Robert Rodman

Have you ever wondered which language is the oldest? Or how babies learn to talk?

Language is universal, and each of us is a kind of expert in using the language we were raised speaking, but there's a lot more to language than what we use in everyday life, and it raises a lot of fascinating questions. Whatever happened to Esperanto? Can machines translate languages? Are some ways of speaking or writing better than others? The chapters of this book will address all these questions and many more.

Let's start with a big question: what is it that makes us human? Is it walking on two legs? Or living in society? Is it our ability to love and hate? To some degree, all of those. But none is unique to the human species. Birds walk on two legs. Ants live in society. And my dog loves me, and hates the cat next door.

It's language that distinguishes us from all other creatures. Whatever else people do when they're together—whether they play, or fight, or make love, or serve hamburgers, or build houses—they talk. We're the only creatures on the planet with the power of speech.

Every human being, rich or poor, is capable of language. Every child learns his or her native tongue, be it English or Zulu, just by being exposed to the talk around them. Most children are fluent before they're ten years old, sometimes in more than one language. Equally impressive is that as they grow up they master different styles of speech: everything from formal, job-interview talk to street slang.

Among the questions to be taken up in this book is how something as complex as language can be so easy for children to learn, yet so difficult for adults. We do know that certain areas of the brain specialize in language, and that children are born with a capacity to learn any human language to which they are exposed. Moreover, as will be discussed later, a child who is isolated from language while growing up may never learn to speak well as an adult. Based on that evidence, many scientists believe that the capacity for language is genetic, but that much of that capacity is lost by adulthood.

Our discussion pertains to spoken and signed language. Learning to read and write—literacy—is another matter entirely. Writing—though it's closely related to spoken language and will be addressed in several chapters of this book—is a human invention, like the bicycle, and has to be studied. Talking is a biological trait, like walking, and comes naturally.

Something you'll see clearly in the course of the book is how much variety there is in the world's tongues, and how constantly they change over time. There are thousands of languages on the planet, all descended from earlier languages that spread and changed and split up into dialects as people moved. Given enough time, the separation of groups and the dialects they speak inevitably leads to the birth of new languages, the way French, Romanian and Spanish grew out of the Latin spoken by the Romans.

You'll also read what linguists have discovered about how and when language began. What do you think? Was there a 'first language' spoken by some brilliant ancestor? Did musical grunts evolve into language around a campfire? Or did aliens from another planet teach our forebears to speak in the recesses of history? There's no shortage of theories, ranging from the supernatural to the imitation of animal sounds.

Do animals talk? Clearly, apes and other animals communicate with each other, and can be taught to do some language-related tasks, but they lack the linguistic flexibility of humans—our amazing ability to express new thoughts, without limits on subject matter.

And what about computers? In some ways they seem very clever. But can we teach a machine to speak and understand like a human? Not quite. Although they're capable of some flashy simulations of human-like skills, computers are limited in their ability to understand and produce meaningful speech. And they certainly lack the spontaneity and creativity of human language.

Think about it: almost every time you speak or sign—except for a few set phrases such as exclamations of pain or anger, or words you recite from memory like poems or prayers—you're creating a sentence different from any other sentence you've ever heard or seen. Each one is unique. And every day you create hundreds, or even thousands, of them! One reason language is special is that it's a universal form of human creativity. Happily, even without being great poets, authors or orators, we can be creative every day of our life when we speak.

There is no human trait more pervasive, or in many ways more valuable, than language. It's capable of expressing all of human thought, even thoughts about itself—which is what this book is all about. So start reading!

About the author
Robert Rodman (1940–2017) was a UCLA-trained linguist and professor in the Department of Computer Science at North Carolina State University. He was co-author of a best-selling linguistics textbook, *An Introduction to Language*. Rodman was also a forensic linguist and consulted with the judiciary in matters involving language and the legal system. In 2009, he was elected into the American Academy of Social Sciences for his achievements in Computational Forensic Linguistics.

Suggestions for further reading
Fromkin, Victoria, Robert Rodman and Nina Hyams. *An Introduction to Language* (Cengage Learning, tenth edition 2013). This is a comprehensive book about language and linguistics written for persons with no

previous background in languages. It is written in a light, readable style and makes copious use of cartoons, pithy quotations, poems, and song lyrics to make its linguistic points. More than one million copies of this book have been bought.

Pinker, Steven. *The Language Instinct: How the Mind Creates Language* (Harper Perennial Modern Classics, revised third edition 2007). This is a fascinating, witty treatment of the nature of the human mind as it pertains to language. It is well written enough to be a page-turner despite its technical subject. It's a must-read for anybody in the language field, and a joyful read for the linguistically curious.

2
You're a linguist? How many languages do you speak?

Paul Chapin

What is linguistics really about? What do linguists actually do, anyway?

Every profession has its cocktail party moment, the stereotypical reaction you get when someone finds out what you do. Economists are complimented on their ability to balance their checkbooks, psychologists are asked to refrain from analyzing fellow guests. For linguists, it's the question in the title.

Most linguists have trained themselves not to wince visibly when asked this. Their answers reflect a variety of strategies, some less polite than others. One linguist would say, 'One, I think.' Another, 'All of them, at some underlying level.' But the question is asked in good faith, and offers an opportunity to explain what linguistics is really about. So a good answer is something like the following.

People who speak multiple languages are called 'polyglots.' (You can learn more about them in Chapter 36 of this book.) That's an admirable skill to have, but it's different from linguistics, which is the scientific study of natural human language. Native-level ability to speak a language being studied is generally useful and sometimes necessary, but by no means always. This is good, because otherwise the number and variety of languages that linguists could work on would be vastly reduced.

So linguists mostly don't learn to speak languages. What exactly do they do, then? Well, language is a big subject, and the answer has to be broken down into parts. Let's look at some of them.

Many linguists work on describing particular languages. Every spoken language has a structured system of sounds, called its phonology; a set of ways the sounds are combined into words: the morphology; a list of the words and their meanings: the vocabulary; and a set of rules for combining the words into sentences: the syntax. Describing a language means making a systematic report of all these components. If the linguist is not a native speaker of the language, he or she works with a native speaker as consultant. In these days when many of the world's languages are rapidly disappearing, as you will read elsewhere in this book, linguistic description is a particularly urgent task. If we cannot save all the endangered languages, we can at least try to document them.

Some linguists work at the more abstract level of linguistic theory. Most linguists today believe that all human languages have many fundamental features in common. Theoretical linguistics is the effort to identify those features and weave them together into a basic model of language, sometimes called a universal grammar. Contrary to what you might think, building a universal grammar is not a matter of somehow welding together all the grammars of all the world's languages. Any feature that's universal must appear in every language, so theoretical work often consists of very detailed analysis of a single language—just as modern genetics began with years of research concentrating on just a few organisms, such as fruit flies.

Most languages are spoken. The study of speech is a scientific field in itself, with two major components: phonetics and speech perception. Phoneticians study the various body parts involved in speaking and the intricate way they function together, as well as the acoustics of the sounds of speech. Speech-perception specialists study how the hearer translates the noises hitting the ear into meaningful messages. Since speech is a measurable physical phenomenon, unlike syntax or morphology, phoneticians are able to use the tools of the physical sciences in their research, including mathematics, the laws of physics, and sophisticated laboratory instruments. This gives their work an enviable rigor.

Language changes over time. Groups of people who start out speaking the same language, but are isolated from each other for centuries, eventually reach a point where they can no longer understand one another. Studying these processes of change, and reconstructing earlier stages of a present-day language by comparing it with other related languages, are the business of historical linguistics.

Because language is such a central aspect of being human, it is a necessary concern of other scientific fields that study human cognition and behavior. Interdisciplinary research is thus essential to understanding language better. Linguists team up with colleagues in psychology, neuroscience, child development, anthropology, or sociology, or become versed in those disciplines themselves, in order to explore the full range of what language is about. These efforts are sometimes called hyphenated linguistics, as in psycholinguistics, neurolinguistics, sociolinguistics, and so forth.

Psycholinguists study what goes on in our minds when we talk or read or listen to another talking. They have developed a number of very clever tricks for looking at this invisible process. What neurolinguists do can be described the same way, except substituting 'brains' for 'minds.' Research in neurolinguistics has advanced greatly since the appearance of new tools and techniques for brain imaging, especially functional magnetic resonance imaging (fMRI).

A fundamental mystery of language is how every child learns it so quickly and so completely, without any formal instruction, as easily and naturally as he or she learns to walk or recognize faces. Linguists interested in language acquisition have been studying this process for decades, and have learned a great deal, but there is still much mystery to solve.

Before the 1960s, language was generally considered a cultural phenomenon, so linguistics was a branch of anthropology. While the center of gravity of linguistic research has shifted to language as a component of cognition, it is still the case that language and culture are deeply interdependent, and anthropological linguistics continues to be a thriving enterprise. Anthropological linguists study how culture is expressed in language, and how language impacts culture. They used to focus primarily on pre-industrial societies, but today may apply their skills and perspectives in any setting.

We all know of other people who speak our language, whom we can understand and communicate with perfectly well, but who don't speak the same way we do. They may live in a different part of the country, or just elsewhere in town; sometimes they're of a different age. This variation in language is the central interest of sociolinguists. They have shown that social factors such as gender, ethnicity, and socioeconomic class influence linguistic variation profoundly. They have also shown that this variation plays a significant role in language change.

So now you know, when you run across a linguist, what not to ask. Ask instead, 'What's your specialty?' You will have an instant friend.

About the author
Paul Chapin (1938–2015) received his Ph.D. in linguistics from MIT in 1967. After eight years on the faculty at the University of California at San Diego, he went to the National Science Foundation in 1975, where he became the first National Science Foundation program director for linguistics. When he retired from the NSF in 2001, he received the Director's Superior Accomplishment Award. That same year, the LSA awarded him the first Victoria A. Fromkin Award for Distinguished Service to the Profession.

Suggestions for further reading
All the other chapters in this book. They give a good broad view of the whole field of linguistics.

See the list of current grants made by the Linguistics Program at NSF for a taste of what's going on right now at the frontiers of research in linguistics and the language sciences. Start at www.nsf.gov, and click 'Awards' on the home page. On the next page, type 'linguistics' in the search box and click 'Search.' A long list of grants will appear at the bottom of the screen. Click on any title that interests you to see a little more information about that project.

3

What is the difference between dialects and languages?

G. Tucker Childs

Is it better to speak a language or a dialect? Which do you speak?

Strange as it may seem, there is no generally agreed-upon way to distinguish between a 'language' and a 'dialect.' The two words are not objective, scientific terms, even among linguists. The lay community shares the same predicament, and people often use the terms to mean different things. As used by many people, language is what *we* speak and dialect is the linguistic variety spoken by *them*, usually someone thought of as inferior. In other contexts, language can mean the generally accepted standard, the variety sanctioned by the government and the media. Dialects, on the other hand, are homelier versions of the standard that vary from region to region and don't sound like the speech of radio announcers.

Language varieties, then, tend to be labeled dialects rather than languages for non-linguistic reasons, usually political or ideological. Dialects are spoken by people who don't run the country. They're generally considered to be not as 'good' as the standard language and consequently have little prestige. Oftentimes they're not even written. In short, the distinction is subjective. It depends on who you are and the perspective from which you judge the varieties.

From a linguistic perspective, no dialect is inherently better than any other and thus no dialect is more deserving of the title 'language' than any other dialect. A language can be seen as a group of related dialects. For example, the dominant position of the Parisian dialect in France is largely an accident of history. When the Count of Paris was elected king of France in the tenth century, the dialect of his court became the 'standard' French language. Other related varieties were disdained as well as other unrelated varieties (e.g., Basque in the southwest and Breton in the north). If things had gone differently, however, the dialect of Marseille or Dijon might have become the national language of France today.

Dialects can be *socially* determined, as Eliza Doolittle and the audience learn in *My Fair Lady*. In this play and film, as will be remembered, the snobby phonetics professor Henry Higgins wagers with fellow phonetician Col. Pickering that he can take an ordinary flower girl, change her speech, and make her presentable in high society. He succeeds, much to his own chagrin. (Higgins was based on the real-life phonetician Daniel Jones, no doubt a much more appealing person. Rex Harrison, who played Higgins in the film, was coached by the real-life phonetician Peter Ladefoged, who later contributed Chapter 7 of this book.)

Dialects can also be *politically* determined. The linguist Max Weinreich is often quoted as saying, 'A language is a dialect with an army and a navy.' His point was that political concerns often decide what will be called a 'dialect' and what will be called a 'language.' Powerful or historically significant groups have 'languages'; their smaller or weaker counterparts have 'dialects.'

Sometimes what are languages and what are dialects can be *arbitrarily* determined by a person or a government. In southern Africa an early twentieth-century missionary created a language now known as 'Tsonga' by declaring three separate languages to be dialects of a single tongue. Conversely, the government of South Africa created two languages by arbitrary declaration—Zulu and Xhosa—even though there is no clear linguistic boundary between them. Instead, the two lie at the ends of what is called a 'dialect continuum,' in which no two adjacent dialects are wildly different, but the dialects at the ends are mutually unintelligible.

Dialect differences are often relatively minor—sometimes just a matter of pronunciation ('You say tomayto, I say tomahto') or slight differences in vocabulary (Americans say 'elevator' and 'cookie,' the British say 'lift' and 'biscuit'). Such differences are crucial to understanding George Bernard Shaw's famous quip that America and Britain are 'two countries separated by a common language.' But dialects can also differ so greatly from one another that they are incomprehensible. German speakers from Cologne and German speakers from rural Bavaria can barely understand one another, if at all. And although German is one of Switzerland's national languages, the Swiss speak local dialects of it that few Germans can understand.

One of the tests people use to differentiate 'language' from 'dialect' is mutual intelligibility. Many would say that if people understand each other without too much difficulty, they're speaking the same language; if not, they're speaking different languages. That seems like a good rule. So why are Cologne German and Bavarian German, which are *not* mutually intelligible, not considered separate languages? Or why are Swedish and Norwegian considered separate languages, when Swedes and Norwegians have no trouble understanding one another?

Such questions become even more unanswerable when speakers of Dialect A just don't *want* to understand speakers of Dialect B, and sometimes vice versa. One or both groups insist that they speak separate tongues, even though they are speaking—judged by relatively objective linguistic criteria—mutually intelligible dialects of the same language.

It is easy to conclude from all this that the terms 'dialect' and 'language' are politically and socially *loaded*. You might want to ask yourself whether you speak a language or a dialect. It's a trick question, of course, because ultimately, *all* languages are dialects. You speak both at the same time.

About the author

G. Tucker Childs is a professor and chair in the Applied Linguistics Department of Portland State University in Portland, Oregon, where he teaches courses in phonetics, phonology, language variation, pidgins and creoles, African American English, and sociolinguistics. He and several of his students have done research on the dialects of Portland, realized as the 'Portland Dialect Study' (www.pds.pdx.edu). His interests, however, focus on African languages, including the pidgins and new urban varieties spoken on the continent, his most recent book in that area being *An Introduction to African Languages* (2003). More recently he has been documenting dying languages in Guinea (www.ling.pdx.edu/childs/ MDP.html) and Sierra Leone (www.pdx.edu/dkb), for which he recently received the Kenneth L. Hale Award from the LSA. He has taught at universities in the United States, Canada, Europe and Africa, and has been a visiting researcher at France's National Council for Scientific Research (CNRS) in Paris, at Fourah Bay College (Sierra Leone), and at the University of Conakry (Guinea).

Suggestions for further reading

In this book
Dialects are discussed in Chapters 31 (dialects of ASL), 44 (languages of India), 49 (U.S. dialect change), and 51 (African American English).

Elsewhere
Alvarez, Louis, and Andrew Kolker. *American Tongues* (Center for New American Media, 1987). Essential viewing—an entertaining video that illustrates the many dialects of American English with a sophisticated but straightforward (socio)linguistic message.

Lewis, M. Paul, ed. *Ethnologue: Languages of the World* (SIL International, sixteenth edition 2009). Online at www.ethnologue.com. A useful reference cataloging and classifying all known languages of the world, including some information on dialects.

Joseph, John E. and Talbot J. Taylor, eds. *Ideologies of Language* (Routledge, 1990). A collection of articles illustrating how power and ideology control the status of such languages as Afrikaans and French.

Trudgill, Peter. *Sociolinguistics: An Introduction to Language and Society* (Penguin Books, 2000). An informed and accessible introduction to languages and dialects written for those with little knowledge of linguistics.

4

Do all languages have the same grammar?

Mark C. Baker

Is there a universal grammar that underlies all languages? What do English, Japanese, and Mohawk have in common?

Probably nobody would claim that all languages have the same grammar. But many linguists believe that all languages have certain basic design features in common, and that it is worth looking seriously into a concept often called 'universal grammar.'

Suppose there did exist some set of rules underlying all languages. Might that help explain how children can so easily learn any language as their mother tongue—without graduate courses or government funds—even though language is one of the most complex systems of knowledge that any human being acquires?

Perhaps, but it's not easy to see what all languages might have in common—especially if we look beyond the western European languages, which have many similarities because they share a common history. Each language obviously uses different words, and it seems no less obvious that the rules and patterns for assembling words into phrases and sentences differ widely from language to language. Let's look at a couple of non-European examples.

In English one says 'John gave a book to Mary'; the Japanese equivalent is *John-ga Mary-ni hon-o yatta*. The words for 'book' (*hon-o*) and 'gave' (*yatta*) are different, of course, but so are their positions in the sentence. In English, the verb 'gave' is the second word of the sentence; in Japanese it is the last word. In English, 'book' comes after the verb; in Japanese it comes before the verb. In English the gift recipient 'Mary' comes after the preposition 'to'; in Japanese the recipient comes before *ni* (the equivalent of 'to'). To speak Japanese you need to learn not only a new set of words but a new set of rules for how to combine the words—a new grammar.

The Mohawk language differs from English in a different way. In Mohawk, the sentence 'The man gave a blanket to the baby' could be expressed as *Owira'a wa-sh-ako-hsir-u ne rukwe*. Word order is not grammatically important in Mohawk: you can put *owira'a* ('baby'), *wa-sh-ako-hsir-u* ('he-her-blanket-gave'), and *rukwe* ('man') wherever you like and still get the same meaning. What's crucial in Mohawk is the form of the verb: if you replace *wa-sh-ako-hsir-u* with *wa-h-uwa-hsir-u*, the sentence then means 'The baby gave a blanket to the man,' whatever order the words are put in. Stranger still, the direct object 'blanket' is not even a separate word in these sentences. It is indicated by *hsir*, which combines with the verb root *u* to make a compound verb ('blanket-gave')—something not usually possible in English or Japanese. Indeed, a Mohawk complex verb like *washakohsiru* can stand alone as a sentence: 'He gave a blanket to her.'

Despite contrasts like these, linguistic research is discovering that the grammars of different languages are much more similar than they appear at first.

The subject in Japanese is at the beginning of the sentence, as in English. Did you notice that apart from that, the order of the words in Japanese is the exact mirror-image of the English order? The recipient 'Mary' comes next to the word meaning 'to' in both languages. The direct object 'book' comes next to the word meaning 'gave' in both languages. Overall, the same kinds of words combine with each other to form the same kinds of phrases in English and Japanese. The only difference is a systematic difference in order—whether verbs and prepositions are put at the beginning of the phrases they form (as in English) or at the end of those phrases (as in Japanese). That's why it is right to say that the grammars are almost the same. After all, a picture and its mirror image are not completely different, even though none of the pixels match up. On the contrary, they are almost the same image—a truth we take advantage of when we brush our teeth or comb our hair.

What about Mohawk, where word order doesn't seem to matter? Such flexibility doesn't seem so strange if you've studied Spanish or Italian, where verbs change form to agree with their subjects; the subject can be various places in the sentence and you can still recognize it. But how about the way the direct object merges into the verb in Mohawk? Even this is not a completely alien feature. The direct object appears next to the verb in both English and Japanese, just as it does in Mohawk; the only difference is whether the verb and object combine loosely, into a verbal *phrase* (English and Japanese), or tightly, into a verbal *word* (Mohawk).

Indeed, even in English a verb and its object can sometimes combine to make a single word. Think of noun compounds like 'dish-washer' and 'man-eater,' each combining an ordinary noun ('dish,' 'man') with a noun formed from a verb ('wash,' 'eat'). Notice that 'man-eater' refers to something (like a shark or a tiger) that eats a man, not to a man who eats things. That is, the noun 'man' is always the object of the eating, not its subject. This characteristic of English word-formation parallels what we see in Mohawk compound verbs, and in English and Japanese verbal phrases.

The fact that verbs always combine more closely with direct objects than they do with subjects is a good example of a general law of grammar, which seems to hold for all human languages. It turns out that there are many such universal laws. In fact, over the past several decades, linguists have uncovered dozens of them. The laws provide the basic skeletal structure of language, which individual languages then flesh out in various ways.

We are finding that once we dig beneath the surface, languages seem to have as many similarities in their structure as they have differences. So, while it is not quite true that all languages have the same grammar, it is much closer to being true than you might have thought.

About the author

Mark Baker was trained in linguistics at MIT under Noam Chomsky. He is now professor of linguistics and cognitive science at Rutgers University, where he specializes in the word structure and sentence structure of less-studied languages, especially those spoken in Africa and the Americas.

Suggestions for further reading

In this book

Other chapters discussing grammar include 8 (prescriptive grammar), 13 (language deprivation), 25 (origins of grammar), 50 (Native American languages), and 58 (grammar in schools), as well as 12 and 14 (animal communication).

Elsewhere

Baker, Mark. *The Atoms of Language* (Basic Books, 2002). A non-technical book-length discussion of the similarities and differences among languages, showing in more detail than this chapter how different-looking languages can be derived from almost the same grammatical rules.

Pinker, Steven. *The Language Instinct* (Harper Collins, 1994). Chapter 8 addresses the question of how languages differ, putting this question in the context of the overall view that language is an instinct hard-wired into the human brain.

Whaley, Lindsey. *Introduction to Typology* (Sage Publications, 1996). An introductory textbook that gives some of the history and main results that come from comparing a wide range of historically unrelated languages.

5

How many languages are there in the world?

M. Paul Lewis

How many languages are there in the world? Who counts them? Where are they spoken? Which have the most speakers?

How many languages are there? That's one of those 'it all depends' questions: how you answer it depends on what you call a language, and deciding what is and what isn't a language is not as easy as you'd think.

Suppose your favorite breakfast food is thin round cakes of grilled batter with butter and syrup. You call them 'pancakes.' Your neighbor, who likes the same meal, might call them 'griddlecakes.' If either of you travelled to a restaurant in a nearby town you might find that you have to ask for 'flapjacks.' Now imagine that chain of contacts stretching out further and that there are many other words that differ from place to place. Even tiny differences wouldn't have to accumulate for more than a few hundred miles before it could become hard to understand people. Where do you draw the line between a dialect and a language? Where does one language end and another begin?

Sometimes it's not hard to figure out. People in Iraq speak Arabic; their neighbors in Iran speak Farsi, a completely unrelated language. At other times, though, the linguistic differences are small, and the answer becomes a matter of politics and sociology.

Swedes and Norwegians can understand each other fairly easily. But they have different histories, customs, and governments, and they see themselves as two nations, speaking two languages, not one. The same thing, more or less, goes for Malaysians and Indonesians; or Macedonians and Bulgarians (not to mention the complication that there is also a variety of Greek called 'Macedonian' which neither Macedonians nor Bulgarians can understand—so you can't just count language names!). Some groups go to great lengths to distinguish themselves from their linguistic cousins across a border: Serbs and Croatians understand each other's speech, but they use two different writing systems. Other groups do just the opposite: A billion people live in China, with at least seven mutually unintelligible forms of regional speech. But it has served them well to think of themselves as belonging to a single nation, so they've maintained a unique ancient writing system that can be used anywhere in the country and enables them all to use the same written materials. But this doesn't mean they understand each other's spoken language.

Another dimension that has to be considered in answering the question is socioeconomic. Generally people with more education and economic opportunity adopt certain ways of talking. Those with less education and fewer opportunities often aren't able or willing to learn these more prestigious forms. Frequently, educated folk have a difficult time understanding those who aren't part of their social class. And some of the people of a lower socioeconomic status might not want to sound snobbish. While this occurs much more often in societies where social differences are clearly marked and strongly enforced, a certain amount of it goes on in any society. What you call a 'flapjack,' someone else in your society might prefer to call a 'crepe.' You may go to the store to 'buy' a new shirt, while your neighbor would go there to make a 'purchase.' The differences may be subtle, but sometimes they are so marked that people have difficulty understanding one another, and one or the other group in the society won't accept the variety they don't speak as being 'their language.' Also, sometimes the less prestigious group reacts by adopting their linguistic variety as a marker of their identity and they may insist with great pride that they speak a different language

So it's not easy to define what is or isn't a language, and counting becomes a matter of definitions. How many languages there are also depends on *when* you count them. Languages, like people, are born, they change and grow and sometimes have offspring, and they eventually dwindle and die.

Another factor to consider is *why* you are counting. Linguists would like to know more about all the different ways in which languages are structured. An educator might be more interested in how many students won't be able to understand a textbook because it isn't written in their variety. The linguist and the educator may very well come up with different numbers based on the criteria that they use.

We'll never have an exact answer to the slippery question of how many languages there are, but among the most dedicated enumerators are the researchers at *Ethnologue*, a comprehensive directory of the world's languages that released its twenty-second edition in 2019. Their estimate, based largely on how well speakers can understand each other, is that a total of 7,097 languages are actively spoken or signed in the world today.

Some of those are just about extinct, with only a handful of speakers left. In fact, just over *a quarter* of the world's languages have fewer than a thousand speakers and about 70 percent of the languages in the world have fewer than ten thousand. Many of those small groups are using their languages quite vigorously, but keeping a language alive is harder when there are fewer people to speak it with and when another language is being picked up and used for communication with outsiders.

At the other end of the scale is a much smaller group of very dominant large languages. Over the next century linguists predict that they will drive hundreds, or even thousands, of the smaller languages to extinction, just as superstores drive small shopkeepers out of business. The largest spoken language by far is Mandarin—over 900 million people in China speak it as a native tongue. English and Spanish each have around 400 million native speakers. Some other leading languages—all of which have between one and 200 million native speakers—are Arabic, Hindi, Bengali, Portuguese, Russian, and Japanese.

In addition to simply counting how many languages there are, it is interesting to observe how those languages are distributed around the world. We often think of Europe as a very multilingual place. And it does have 288 different languages, but those only account for 4 percent of the living languages in the world. Compare that with Asia, which has 2,303 living languages—nearly a third of the world's languages—or with Africa, which has almost as many (2,140, about 30%). There are 1,058 languages, about 15 percent, in the Americas and another 1,322, about 19 percent, in the Pacific region.

These numbers are constantly changing as some languages disappear, some new languages emerge, and linguists learn more about languages in remote places. What is clear is that the *diversity* of the world's languages is amazing. *Every* language is a window into the culture (and environmental setting) in which it is spoken and a window into the human mind as well. In addition, and perhaps more importantly, every distinct language represents an identity—a group of people who see themselves as belonging together and as having a shared history and culture. There are good reasons not only to study them but to preserve what we can of *all* of them.

About the author

M. Paul Lewis is a senior consultant in sociolinguistics with SIL International (a nonprofit faith-based language development organization) and from 2005 to 2016 was the editor of *Ethnologue: Languages of the World*. He is the co-author, with Gary F. Simons, of *Sustaining Language Use: Perspectives on Community-Based Language Development* (2016, Dallas: SIL International). He holds a Ph.D. in linguistics from Georgetown University. The twenty-first edition of *Ethnologue* was published in 2018.

Suggestions for further reading

In this book

Various languages of the world are described in Chapters 28 (Latin), 39 (Chinese), 44 (languages of India), 50 (Native American languages), and 52 (Spanish), as well as 17 (Esperanto) and 11 (other invented languages). Also relevant are Chapters 34 (language death), 47 (languages of the U.S.), 64 (language rescue), and 66 (the Museum of Languages).

Elsewhere

Comrie, Bernard, ed. *The Atlas of Languages: The Origin and Development of Languages throughout the World* (New Burlington Books, 1996).

Crystal, David. *Language Death* (Cambridge University Press, 2000). A good overview of the dynamics of language maintenance and death and related issues.

Eberhard, David M., Gary F. Simons, and Charles D. Fennig, eds. *Ethnologue: Languages of the World.* (SIL International, 22nd edition 2019). Online at www.ethnologue.com.

Grenoble, Lenore A. and Lindsay J. Whaley. *Endangered Languages. Language Loss and Community Response* (Cambridge University Press, 1998). Looks at the ways in which various communities have responded to the endangerment of their languages.

6

Why is Chomsky such a big deal in linguistics?

Greg Carlson

Who is Noam Chomsky? Why is he so well-known? What are his contributions to the field of linguistics?

Quick, name a linguist. If any answer comes out, it's a near certainty it will be 'Chomsky'. Okay, you're now asked, name another one. If you've never had a linguistics course, your answer is likely *a blank stare*. Noam Chomsky really is the dominant figure in linguistics and has been since the mid-twentieth century, and is possibly the world's most famous linguist of all time. How come?

In part, it's because Chomsky is famous for other reasons—as a public intellectual and political activist. But he is also a really big deal in linguistics, too. In the 1950s, around the time he became a professor at MIT, Chomsky formulated a novel approach to the study of language with his theory of transformational-generative grammar.

It is called 'generative' because it is a formal set of rules which—when followed explicitly—will generate expressions that are part of a language, while *not* generating expressions that *aren't* part of that language. This formal set of rules can be applied to artificial languages (like logic or arithmetic) or natural languages (like English, Japanese, Arabic, etc.). In the case of natural language, the expressions generated are grammatical sentences of the language! So an adequate set of rules for English will not give you things like 'The man are funny,' but *will* generate things like 'The men are funny.'

The 'transformational' part concerns the kinds of rules that are required. Chomsky argued that much more powerful rules than those required for arithmetic (e.g., formulas like $3 \times 9 + 6 = 33$) are required to generate the expressions of a natural language. He called these rules 'transformational rules.' The present-day study of sentence structure—or syntax—stemmed from this novel approach. Along the way, Chomsky ranked a series of types according to their 'power' (e.g., arithmetic only needs a V4 putt-putt engine, but natural language requires a top-of-the-line roaring V12).

But these impressive technical innovations are only a part of the reason Chomsky is a big deal. Rather, it is his ability to articulate a much larger world-view of the nature of language itself that gets people intrigued (or riled up!).

One of them has to do with a definition of a 'grammatical' sentence of a language. Chomsky argues that *form* alone—and not anything about *meaning*—defines grammaticality. He famously used the example 'Colorless green ideas sleep furiously' to illustrate that point. The phrase seems to be of the right form, even if its meaning (if it has one at all) is obscure at best. In other words, despite the nonsensicalness of the sentences, we know that 'Colorless green ideas sleep furiously' sounds right—it's grammatical. Chomsky argues, the *correct form* alone makes it a sentence of the English language.

Furthermore, a sentence can be a sentence of the language even if it has never been used, and never will be. This view does not sit well with those who insist one needs to document linguistic data through actual use (e.g., hear it during an interview, find it in a corpus); but it serves to illuminate another point Chomsky makes. The proper study of linguistics is not what we hear or see, but is rather the knowledge of a language that people carry around with them. Chomsky puts this in terms of 'competence' vs. 'performance,' with competence being the largely unconscious knowledge underlying our ability to use a language (which is with us when we are asleep and when we are not speaking or listening), and performance is something we do with that knowledge in listening and speaking (or watching and signing).

Up until Chomsky, the leading view of language—led by behaviorist psychologist B. F. Skinner—was of language as strictly behavioral. According to Skinner, language is a result of environmental control and training by caregivers; children learn the 'rights' and 'wrongs' of language via the rewards and punishments they receive for their verbal feats. Chomsky disagreed and, in a famous critique, railed against Skinner's theory.

In Chomsky's view, the performance of language indirectly at best reflects this linguistic competence—so why not study competence more directly? We can do this by asking people to directly tap their intuitions about language via linguistic intuitions. Even if you have never heard 'I have eating that bananas' before, you know it's a bad sentence; and 'I have been eating those bananas' is a good one—if you know English of course.

But Chomsky really ups the ante when he moves the debate to yet another level by connecting the theorizing of language with language learning (chiefly, by very young children). It goes something like this: Humans are the only creatures that can learn human-type languages, and humans can learn any of them provided that's what they are exposed to growing up. Furthermore, he argues, learning an entire language is done on the basis of being exposed to a remarkably small body of data by present-day computer standards.

So there must be some special capacity humans have that other creatures do not to achieve this. Chomsky calls this 'universal grammar'—our innate capacity to learn any languages of the type humans speak. This means that among the huge differences we find among human languages, they all share something in common, and getting at those underlying organizing principles is what his research program is all about.

At each step along the way, there are skeptics and critics who question this chain of thought. For instance, Daniel Everett has challenged several aspects of Chomsky's universal grammar theory based on his study of the Pirahã people of the Amazon basin. He argues that grammar is circumstantial, not innate. During his time living with and studying the Pirahã, Everett noticed an absence of language characteristics that Chomsky claims to be universal—such as *recursion*, or the embedding of clauses into other clauses. Nonetheless, no one (not even Everett) has come as close to igniting the kinds of debates about language that have taken place in linguistics and the psychological sciences as Chomsky.

Chomsky is also a widely known public intellectual renowned for his social and political views and analyses. Many have wondered over the years how his linguistics and political views might be connected. There seems no 'silver bullet' answer to this, and Chomsky himself has been known to say there isn't much connection, but his political views emerged well before he started in linguistics. What we *do* know for sure is that Chomsky is one of the most important contributors to linguistics, and his theories of transformational generative grammar and universal grammar are still central to the field today!

About the author

Greg Carlson is professor emeritus of linguistics, philosophy, and brain and cognitive sciences at the University of Rochester, where he has been since 1987. He has taught at the University of California at Irvine, the University of Iowa, Wayne State University, the LSA Summer Institute, the European Summer School, the University of Wisconsin, and the University of Trondheim (Norway), and visited at the Max Planck Institute (Netherlands). His research interests focus on natural language semantics with a special interest in generics; he also conducts research in experimental psycholinguistics, with other strong interests in philosophy and computer science. Publications include *Reference to Kinds in English* (Garland, 1980), *The Generic Book* (Chicago, 1995), and *Sold on Language: How Advertisers Talk to You and What This Says about You* (Wiley-Blackwell, 2010). He served as editor in chief of *Linguistics and Philosophy* (1992–1997) and editor of *Language* (2009–2017). His dissertation advisor at the University of Massachusetts at Amherst, Prof. Barbara Partee, was one of Chomsky's earliest students.

Suggestions for further reading

In this book
Further discussion of universal grammar appears in Chapter 4. Other chapters addressing relationships between language and mental processes include 18, 20, and 21 (language and the brain), 10 and 46 (gender and grammar), 13 (language deprivation), and 35 (babies and language), as well as 12 and 14 (animal communication).

Elsewhere
Lyons, John. *Noam Chomsky* (Penguin Books, revised edition 1979). Written for a general audience, this book chronicles Chomsky's linguistic theories their impact on other fields.

Pinker, Steven. *The Language Instinct: How the Mind Creates Language* (Penguin UK, 2003). A popular classic, this book supports the Chomskian argument that language is a hard-wired human instinct, using humor, wordplay, and entertaining stories.

Tomalin, Marcus. *Linguistics and the Formal Sciences: The Origins of Generative Grammar* (Cambridge University Press, 2006). A scholarly text overviewing the influence of mathematics, logic, and philosophy on the work of linguists during the twentieth century.

Antony, Louise M., and Norbert Hornstein, eds. *Chomsky and His Critics* (John Wiley & Sons, 2008). Part of a ten-part series devoted to famous 'thinkers' of our time, this book delves deeply into Chomsky's theoretical contributions to study of language and the mind.

Language structure

7

How are the sounds of language made?

Peter Ladefoged

What kind of sounds make up languages? Do all languages have consonants and vowels? Do they all have the same ones?

Everyone knows that when you talk you use your tongue and lips. You probably also know that speech sounds often involve the action of the vocal cords—nowadays more usually called vocal folds, as they are two thin folds of muscle in the throat that vibrate when air is blown between them. To get the vocal folds to vibrate you have to push air out of your lungs. To talk, we then move parts of the vocal tract and, in various ways, alter its shape to produce consonants and vowels. Here are some examples of how it all works.

The lips are used to make the consonants at the beginning of the English words *pea, bee, me*. In the *p* sound, pressure is built up behind the closed lips. The vocal folds do not vibrate and there is usually a little puff of air (called aspiration) when the lips open and before any following vowel begins. This puff of air is missing when you say *b*, and there may even be some voicing (vocal fold vibration) while the lips are closed. There is always voicing during the lip closure for *m* in which the air comes out through the nose.

The English consonants *t, d, n* and *k, g, ng* are pronounced in ways similar to *p, b, m*, except that for *t, d, n* the air is stopped from owing out of the mouth by raising the tip of the tongue to form a closure just behind the teeth; and for *k*, *g*, *ng* the closure is made by raising the back of the tongue to contact the soft palate, the fleshy part at the back of the roof of the mouth. Other consonant sounds, such as those in the words *the*, *thigh*, *sigh*, *shy*, don't have a complete closure stopping air from owing out of the mouth but are produced by forming a narrow gap through which the air hisses and hushes as it escapes. In these sounds the vocal folds are not vibrating. There is, however, another set of fricative sounds in which there *is* voicing, as in the sounds at the ends of the words *move*, *smooth*, *ooze*, *rouge*.

Most forms of English have twenty-two consonant sounds and anywhere from thirteen to twenty-one different vowel sounds. You can hear many of the different vowel sounds between the consonants *b* and *d* in the words *bead*, *bid*, *bayed*, *bed*, *bad*, *bawd*, *booed*, *bide*, *bowed*, *bode*, *Boyd*, *bud*, *bird*. It is very difficult to make accurate descriptions of vowels in terms of their tongue and lip positions, but they can easily be specified in terms of their acoustic overtones.

So how do languages differ with respect to the sounds they use? All spoken languages have consonants and vowels, but the sounds of the world's languages vary so extensively that altogether they may have as many as 600 different consonant sounds and 200 different vowels as modified by different pitches and voice qualities.

Sounds like *p*, *t*, *k* occur in 98 percent of all the languages in the world. Hawaiian is one of the languages that does not have all three; it lacks *t*. Interestingly, Hawaiian has only eight consonants, *p*, *k*, *m*, *n*, *w*, *l*, *h*, and a glottal stop (a closure of the vocal folds), written with an apostrophe, as in the word *Hawai'i*.

Other languages have consonants that don't occur in English. Spanish and Italian, for example, have trilled *r* sounds. Trills made with the lips occur in a number of small, endangered languages such as Melpa and Kele in Papua New Guinea. Lip trills preceded by a special kind of *t* occur in Oro Win, a language spoken by only half a dozen people living near the border between Brazil and Bolivia. American Indian languages have a wealth of sounds not found in English, sometimes including long strings of complex consonants. In Montana Salish the word for 'wood tick' in an English spelling would be something like *chchts'elshchen.*

The only speech sounds that can be made without using air from the lungs are the clicks that occur in languages spoken in central and southern Africa. These sounds are made by sucking air into your mouth, much as you might do when dropping a kiss on your grandmother's cheek. A language called !Xóõ, spoken in the Kalahari Desert, has eighty-three different ways of beginning a word with a click sound. Zulu, a more well-known language, spoken in South Africa, has three basic clicks, each of which has five variants.

Where European languages stand out is in their number of vowels. French has vowels, not found in English, in which the lips are rounded while the tongue is in the position for the English words *tea* and *day*, forming the French words *tu* 'you' and *deux* 'two.' The largest number of vowels occur in Dutch and German dialects.

It falls to phoneticians to be concerned with describing the sounds of the world's languages: what sounds there are, how they fall into patterns, and how they change in different circumstances. Because there are so many languages and dialects, because the vocal apparatus can produce such a wide variety of sounds, and because each of us has a different way of speaking our own language, it is an infinitely challenging task—and one of the most fascinating aspects of the study of language.

About the author

Peter Ladefoged (1925–2006), professor of phonetics emeritus at UCLA, was the world's foremost linguistic phonetician and one of the most important figures in linguistics in the twentieth century. He published 10 books and 130 scholarly articles on various aspects of the theory and practice of phonetics and the phonetic properties of specific languages. The essay above was one of the last pieces he wrote before his death in early 2006.

Suggestions for further reading

In this book
Other chapters that talk about the sounds of language include 29 (language change), 37 (foreign accents), 39 (Chinese), 50 (Native American languages), and 51 (African American English).

Elsewhere
Ladefoged, Peter. *A Course in Phonetics* (Harcourt Brace, 1975; fifth edition, Thomson/Wadsworth 2006). The standard textbook in the field, which has been used to train generations of linguists.

Maddieson, Ian. *Patterns of Sounds* (Cambridge University Press, 1984). A useful reference text that describes the distribution of sounds in more than 300 languages of the world. Readers can look up a sound and find which languages contain it, or they can look up a language and find its particular phonetic inventory.

International Phonetic Association. *Handbook of the International Phonetic Association* (Cambridge University Press, 1999). A comprehensive guide to the phonetic alphabet used by linguists all over the world. The principles of phonetic analysis are described and examples of each phonetic symbol are given.

Some of the sounds of the hundreds of languages Dr. Ladefoged studied can be heard at www.phonetics.ucla.edu

8

What is the right way to put words together?

Dennis R. Preston

Is there a 'right' way to use a language? What authority determines it?

The U.S. has no shortage of linguistic gatekeepers. Language pundits warn in the press, on the air, and even on the inside of matchbook covers that if we don't clean up our linguistic acts, the doors of opportunity will be closed. Fear of not saying things the 'right' way causes some of us to break out in a sweat when choosing whether to say 'between you and me' or 'between you and I.'*

What makes us so linguistically insecure? It's the idea that a language has only one correct form, and the fear that we're not in step with it. But let's remember that the choice of the 'best' or 'most correct' way of speaking is just a matter of history. Saying 'between you and me'—like not wearing sneakers with a coat and tie—is a convention, not a divine law. Power, money, and prestige cause one variety of language to be preferred. In England, the focus of wealth, commerce, and government in London caused a variety of southern British English to be thought of as the best. In the U.S.,

---

* 'Between you and I' is said to be wrong by prescriptivists, who point out that the 'I' should be 'me,' since it is the object of the preposition 'between.' They forget to tell us that such constructions have an ancient and glorious history. It was after all Shakespeare who wrote 'All debts are cleared between you and I.'

where there was no such center, the language of the well-educated, higher classes became the preferred variety. Over time, that variety came to be seen as the only acceptable way for people to express themselves.

There will always be people who prescribe how we should talk, and who point out what they see as flaws in other people's speech. Because they think the preferred language is the only one that's acceptable, prescriptivists try to prove that other varieties of language are deficient.

If you say 'I don't have no money,' for example, one of them may tell you that 'two negatives make a positive,' but even in simple arithmetic, minus two plus minus two equals *minus* four. Besides, does anybody really believe that people who say 'I don't have no money' mean that they *do* have some money? Are people who say such things frequently misunderstood? Not likely. The test of a language's effectiveness is not whether its arbitrary noises or scribbles meet a standard but whether it communicates. A speaker of impeccable English may say silly and illogical things; a speaker of a down-home variety may be logical and precise.

One must feel sorry for the watchdog pundits who try to tell us when to use 'whom' instead of 'who.' Such attempts are a losing battle, because how language will be used can't be legislated. Words and combinations of words don't have a 'real' meaning. They only mean what we agree they'll mean, and different groups may come to different agreements. Besides, language isn't a fixed system. It evolves. Some of yesterday's poorly-thought-of language may become today's preferred variety. You may deplore this if you're a speaker of yesterday's preferred variety, but most often, as language evolves, it adjusts in the direction of how lower-status speakers use it. That doesn't make it wrong or deficient. It's just what language does.

That said, another aspect of language is that it happens in societies, and societies always make judgments. It's a reality in English-speaking countries that speakers who use double negatives will earn disapproval from certain people, some of whom have power over what we hope for in life. If you're not a native speaker of the preferred variety of language, there are social and economic advantages to learning it, even though it's only a historical convention, no more logical or beautiful than the way you already speak.

Prescriptivists even want us to give up our native varieties. But we shouldn't let ourselves be bullied. Prescriptivism comes out of a desire for uniformity in behavior, in language as in other areas. It can lead to elitism, racism, and even silliness. When told not to end sentences with prepositions, Winston Churchill is said to have remarked, 'This is arrant pedantry, up with which I shall not put.' So should we all.

About the author

Dennis R. Preston is Regents Professor, Oklahoma State University and University Distinguished Professor Emeritus, Michigan State University. He served as visiting professor at several U.S. universities and in Poland, Brazil, New Zealand, and Denmark. He was president of the American Dialect Society and served on the board of that society and the Linguistic Society of America, as well as the editorial boards of *Language* and others. His work focused on sociolinguistics, dialectology, and minority varieties and education. He revitalized folk linguistics and has provided variationist accounts of second-language acquisition. Some publications are, with Nancy Niedzielski, *Folk Linguistics* (2000), with Daniel Long, *A Handbook of Perceptual Dialectology* II (2002), *Needed Research in American Dialects* (2003), with Brian Joseph and Carol Preston, *Linguistic Diversity in Michigan and Ohio* (2005), with James Stanford, *Variation in Indigenous Minority Languages* (2009), and, with Nancy Niedzielski, *A Reader in Sociophonetics* (2010). He is a fellow of the Japan Society for the Promotion of Science and holds the Officer's Cross of the Order of Merit of the Polish Republic.

Suggestions for further reading

In this book

Other chapters touching on language standards include 9 (what makes a word 'real'), 25 (grammatical change), 29 (language change), 56 (text messaging), and 62 (dictionaries).

Elsewhere

For non-linguists, the belief that there is simply a right and a wrong way to use language is a very strongly held notion. There are a number of excellent books that document the history of this prescriptivism and its current status. The ones recommended here should require no specialized knowledge of linguistics.

Battistella, Edwin L. *Bad Language* (Oxford, 2005). A catalog of how 'bad language' even gets its users labeled as 'bad citizens,' highlighted in media reflections of popular attitudes to language.

Bauer, Laurie, and Peter Trudgill, eds. *Language Myths* (Penguin Books, 1998). Professional comment on twenty-one popular beliefs about language—all of which turn out to be false.

Bolinger, Dwight. *Language: The Loaded Weapon* (Longman, 1980). A book by one of America's most insightful linguists on matters of language and public usage. Bolinger tells you what bad language really is.

Cameron, Deborah. *Verbal Hygiene* (Routledge, 1995). A vigorous exposé of numbskull commentary on language use.

Finegan, Edward. *Attitudes toward English Usage* (Teachers College Press, 1980). A thorough investigation of the nastiness that ensued in the early 1960s when professional lexicographers dared to tell the public what was really going on in language.

Lippi-Green, Rosina. *English with an Accent* (Routledge, second edition 2011). Use bad language; go directly to jail (lose your job, go to the back of the line, etc. …).

Milroy, James, and Lesley Milroy. *Authority in Language* (Routledge, 1985). Who gets to say what's right and wrong? Why?

Niedzielski, Nancy, and Dennis R. Preston. *Folk Linguistics* (Mouton de Gruyter, 2000). A survey and analysis of what real people (i.e., not linguists) had to say about language in America in the waning days of the twentieth century.

9
What makes a word 'real'?

Anne Curzan

Are some words more 'real' than others? Can a word be 'real' if a word doesn't appear in a dictionary? Who decides which words are real and which aren't?

Facepalm, both noun and verb, refers to the act of covering one's face with one's hand to show embarrassment, exasperation or dismay. Evocative, a little slangy or informal, this word does some useful work in the language. But is it a 'real' word?

What about *unfollow*, to refer to unsubscribing from some-one's Twitter feed (or other social media), or now also to refer to cutting off a friend? Perhaps you have already unfollowed people on Twitter—or been unfollowed. It is clearly a real thing, and we need a word for it. *Unfollow* helpfully and transparently fills the gap.

When I drafted this essay in 2017, the spellchecker in my word processing program did not like either of these newish words, underlining them with a red squiggle. The online edi-tions of both *Merriam-Webster* and the *American Heritage Dictionary of the English Language* have added entries for *facepalm* (Merriam-Webster has it dated back to 1996) but have yet to add *unfollow*. Does this make *unfollow* any less of a real word?

Unfollow is functioning the way a word functions: conveying conventional or shared meaning from one speaker to another. So when does a word like *unfollow* become a 'real' word?

When people say a word isn't a 'real word,' they often mean it doesn't appear in a standard dictionary. That definition then raises a host of other questions, such as who writes dictionaries? And how did they get the authority to make official decisions about the status of words?

Even the most critically astute people tend to turn to 'the dictionary' for answers, not distinguishing among dictionaries or asking who edited them—or when they were written. Just think about the phrase 'look it up in the dictionary,' as if dictionaries were all the same (or there is only one) and equally authoritative. In libraries we put dictionaries on pedestals in the reference room. In English classes, we teach students to question every text they read, every website they visit—except dictionaries. As if dictionaries are unauthored works.

Dictionaries, though, are made by real people, whose job it is to document the language as it is used. If you ask dictionary makers, they'll say that they are trying to keep up with us as we change the language. And change the language we do. Change is part of any living language, and new words come as part of that package. The words may be borrowed (e.g., *emoji*) or, more often, made from words, prefixes, and suffixes already in the language (e.g., *bromance, BFF, to friend, cyberbully*).

Dictionary editors are tracking our speech and our writing, trying to see which words will stick and which won't. They have to gamble: they want to include new words that are going to make it (e.g., *cool, lol*) but not include words that will later appear faddish (e.g., *jiggy*). In the United States, dictionary makers are not trying to be the Académie Française, laying down the law about what is and isn't good American English.

Many dictionaries provide guidance about whether a word is slang or informal or offensive through usage labels. They mean these descriptively—that is, the word tends to be used informally or seems to be slang. We can sometimes mistakenly read the usage label as a judgment on the word's legitimacy. Dictionaries like the *American Heritage Dictionary of the English Language* include usage notes, created in large part to satisfy the public's desire to know more about how to use words appropriately or 'well.' The usage notes typically occur with words that are 'troublesome' in some way—they are often confused or they are changing meaning. Let's look at an example to illustrate the human process behind usage notes as well.

The word *peruse* is undergoing a radical shift in meaning. Many speakers now use it to mean 'skim, scan, browse.' You may be surprised to learn that most standard dictionaries still have the primary definition as 'read carefully.' American Heritage includes 'skim' as a second definition and calls it 'a usage problem.' The usage note reads:

> *Peruse* has long meant 'to read thoroughly,' ... But the word is often used more loosely, to mean simply 'to read,' ... Further extension of the word to mean 'to glance over, skim' has traditionally been considered an error, but our ballot results suggest that it is becoming somewhat more acceptable. When asked about the sentence *I only had a moment to peruse the manual quickly*, 66 percent of the Panel found it unacceptable in 1988, 58 percent in 1999, and 48 percent in 2011.

Who is on this Usage Panel? And should we trust them? If you look in the front matter of an *American Heritage Dictionary*, you can find their names. It's about 200 people: well-known writers, academicians, journalists, radio personalities, and a few linguists, including me. About once a year, I get a usage ballot asking me about the acceptability of various meanings and pronunciations of words.

To complete the ballot, I listen and watch what speakers and writers are actually doing. I don't listen to my own likes and dislikes about language. I personally don't like the word *impactful*, but that is neither here nor there in terms of whether the word should be considered acceptable in more formal edited writing. My opinion is not what determines whether a word is becoming common usage. It is the collective, usually unconscious decision of the group. And *impactful* has gained momentum over the past couple of decades.

Not everyone is going to like every new word, and that has been true historically too. The late nineteenth-century grammarian Richard Grant White thought the relatively new verb *donate* (derived from the noun *donation*) was an 'abomination,' and around the same time Dean Henry Alford harshly criticized the lexical newcomers *reliable* and *desirability*. Benjamin Franklin, a century earlier, described the newish -*ize* verb *colonize* as 'low,' and he rejected the nouns *notice, progress,* and *advocate* becoming verbs.

These concerns seem quaint now. New words like *donate* and *reliable*, which were generating such concern if not downright disgust a century or two ago, are now standard parts of the lexicon. It's easy to think, 'What was their problem?' Yet new words can generate equally strong reactions today. The verb *impact* continues to be rejected by many language sticklers, even though it is arguably a more efficient way to say 'have an impact on' and follows exactly the same process as functional shifts like *to progress* and *to notice*. People have similarly lamented *defriend* and *incentivize* as verbs (new -*ize* verbs have a history of meeting with hostility before they become standard—*finalize* did not fare well in the mid-twentieth century either), *invite* as a noun, and *verse* as a new verb meaning 'to play against' (back-formed from *versus*).

The fact that any one of us doesn't like a new word doesn't make it any less of a word. Some new words may be short-lived and others may last for centuries; some may arrive in the language amid criticism and some pop up unnoticed. We, all of us together, are the authorities about what words mean. Dictionaries then provide us helpful guidance about words we don't know or words that may be changing meaning under our noses. But there is not an objective 'dictionary authority' out there that determines the meaning of words and decides which words are 'real.' Slang and other informal words are very 'real,' even if we might choose not to use them in some formal contexts. If a community of speakers is using a word and knows what it means, that word is real.

Acknowledgment

This chapter expands on a TED Talk by Anne Curzan at TEDxUofM in March 2014 (see www.ted.com/talks/anne_curzan_what_makes_a_word_real).

About the author

Anne Curzan is Geneva Smitherman Collegiate Professor of English, Linguistics, and Education at the University of Michigan. Her research focuses on the history of the English language, language and gender, lexicography, and pedagogy; her most recent book is *Fixing English: Prescriptivism and Language History* (2014). She also appears weekly on the segment 'That's What They Say' on local NPR station Michigan Radio.

Suggestions for further reading

In this book

Other chapters specifically focusing on language change include 8 (prescriptivism), 25 (grammar), 27 (origins of English), 28 (Latin), 29 (language change), and 49 (U.S. dialect change), as well as Chapters 53 (social media) and 56 (text messaging). More about dictionaries and how they are made can be found in Chapter 62.

Elsewhere

Lynch, Jack. *The Lexicographer's Dilemma: The Evolution of 'Proper' English from Shakespeare to South Park* (Walker & Co., 2009).

Skinner, David. *The Story of Ain't: America, Its Language, and the Most Controversial Dictionary Ever Published* (Harper, 2012).

Stamper, Korey. *Word by Word: The Secret Life of Dictionaries* (Pantheon, 2017).

Winchester, Simon. *The Professor and the Madman: A Tale of Murder, Inanity, and the Making of the Oxford English Dictionary* (HarperCollins, 1998).

10

What is grammatical gender?

Caroline Myrick

Do all languages have grammatical gender? Are there different types of grammatical gender? Is grammatical gender purely arbitrary, or are there social implications?

If you speak multiple languages or have taken a foreign language, you are probably familiar with the reference to 'gender' in language. Hundreds of languages around the world have grammatical gender, including Bantu, French, German, Hindi, Portuguese, Russian, Spanish, Swahili, and Tamil. But not all languages do. In fact, grammatical gender is absent from hundreds of languages. Chinese, Japanese, Korean, Malay, Mongolian, Persian, and Tagalog all lack grammatical gender, as do most Native American language families.

For the languages that do have grammatical gender, not all of them organize or conceptualize gender the same way. While many of us might tend to think about gender binarily, many languages have systems with more than two genders. Icelandic and German, for instance, have three genders, while many Nakh-Daghestanian languages (e.g., Archi, Lak, and Tsez) have four genders. It has been reported that the Mountain Arapesh language in Papau New Guinea has 13 genders, and the Australian Aboriginal language of Ngan'gityemerri has 15 genders. Many of the Niger-Congo languages have over five genders—and as many as twenty!

So what is grammatical gender? To fully understand, it is helpful to distinguish the two broad types of grammatical gender. Some languages assign gender to nouns arbitrarily—referred to as formal gender. For example, in German, 'pencil' is masculine (*der bleistift*), 'pen' is feminine (*die feder*), and 'knife' is neuter (*das messer*). Other languages assign gender based on sex-based divisions in society for humans and animals—referred to as natural gender. In Italian, a male child is masculine (*il ragazzo*) as is a male cat (*il gatto*), and a female child is feminine (*la ragazza*), just like a female cat (*la gatta*).

Many languages have both formal and natural gender—and English used to be one of them! In Old English (spoken between 500 and 1200 CE), nouns, pronouns, adjectives, determiners, and demonstratives all had formal gender. There were a lot of suffixes to keep track of, and over 20 different pronouns! Today, the only English words that are inflected for gender are the 3rd-person singular personal pronouns (*she*, *he*, etc.), which have natural gender (with the exception of feminine pronouns being used to refer to ships and storms which, of course, do not have natural gender).

Many debates currently surround the social implications of natural gender as a linguistic barrier to inclusivity. For instance, languages that employ what's called the *generic masculine* often use the 'he/him' pronoun to represent an unknown or generalized person (e.g., '*A student should proofread before he submits his paper*'), or a masculine suffix being used when referring to a group of men and women (e.g., '*ciudadanos Americanos*' for 'American citizens'). See chapter 46 for more on 'gendered language.' However, the generally held opinion on arbitrary formal gender has been just that: that it's arbitrary. ... *But is it?*

Researchers who study language and cognition have made arguments that formal gender may have important social implications!

In a well-known 2003 study, German speakers described a 'key,' which is masculine in German (*der schlüssel*) with adjectives like *heavy*, *hard*, and *jagged*, while Spanish speakers described the key, which is feminine in Spanish (*la llave*) as *intricate*, *little*, and *lovely*. The researchers argued that this patterning shows influence of natural gender stereotypes on formal gender—that is, that notion of tough/rugged men and delicate/dainty women may have been influencing how these German and Spanish speakers were conceptualizing keys!

Not everyone is sold on the idea that grammatical gender influences the way we conceptualize inanimate objects. Some studies, for instance, have only seen speakers extending natural-gender-related characteristics to animals (based on whether the animal name is masculine or feminine in their language)—but not to inanimate objects like keys. Furthermore, many past hypotheses about language *determining* our thoughts have been largely rejected or complicated (see Chapter 19 for more about language and thought).

The jury is still out on how influential formal gender is on our conceptualization of the world—if at all. Some argue that it varies by language. Some believe it may vary by individual, based on personality type. Others maintain that formal gender is completely arbitrary (and that any connections to natural gender that researchers *think* they found are just flaws of their experiments). Nonetheless, it's always important to consider and question the ways in which language influences our social world!

About the author

Caroline Myrick, co-editor of this book, holds a Ph.D. from the Department of Sociology at North Carolina State University, where she specialized in sociolinguistics and social inequality. Her research has examined language and gender ideologies as well as language variation and change in the Caribbean. Her doctoral dissertation examined gender inequality as it relates to language ideologies in higher education. She has numerous publications based on the sociolinguistic fieldwork she carried out on the Caribbean island of Saba. Recently, she helped publish the first Saban English dictionary, *A Lee Chip* (NCLLP, 2016).

Suggestions for further reading

In this book
For further discussion of language influencing thought, see Chapter 19 (language and thought). Additional issues of language and gender are discussed in Chapters 32 (men's and women's language), 33 (gay speech), and 46 (gendered language).

Elsewhere
Corbett, Greville G. 2013. 'Number of genders' [map]. *The World Atlas of Language Structures Online*. Available online at http://wals.info/chapter/30. For a nice visual resource, click 'Go to Map'; this interactive map shows the location of spoken languages that have 0, 1, 2, 3, 4 and 5+ genders in their grammar.

Boroditsky, Lera et al. 'Sex, syntax, and semantics,' in Dedre Gentner and Susan Goldin-Meadow, eds., *Language in Mind: Advances in the Study of Language and Thought* (MIT Press, 2003), pp. 61–79. This is the famous 'key study,' in which Spanish speakers and German speakers were asked to associate adjectives with objects, such as keys and bridges. Participants associated stereotypically 'feminine' adjectives (e.g., *beautiful*) with grammatically feminine nouns, and 'masculine' adjectives (e.g., *sturdy*) with masculine nouns. The authors argue that this supports the notion of grammar influencing cognition.

Mickan, Anne, et al. 'Key is a llave is a Schlüssel: A failure to replicate an experiment from Boroditsky et al. 2003,' in Anatol Stefanowitsch and Doris Schoenefeld, eds., *Yearbook of the German Cognitive Linguistics Association* vol. 2, no. 1 (2014), pp. 39–50. This paper reports two attempts at replicating the findings of Boroditsky et al's 'key study.' The authors were not able to replicate the findings and suggest that the results of the original experiment were caused by a non-documented aspect of the experiment, or were a mere statistical coincidence.

11
What is an artificial language?

Christopher Moseley

Why do people invent artificial languages? Do people actually speak them? Can these invented languages be more scientific than natural languages?

With nearly 7,000 languages already in the world, what possesses people to make up new ones? For some, the motive seems to be idealistic, to create a single language to unite humankind in mutual understanding. But there may be a flaw in that reasoning: some of the bloodiest conflicts in history have been fought among people who speak the same language. Think of Vietnam or, for that matter, the English Civil War, the American Civil War, and the two British–American wars in-between!

Another motive seems to be to create an exclusive secret society. Children make up languages all the time to do that.

Then there are languages created as backdrops for fictional civilizations. Good examples are the Klingon language in the *Star Trek* television series, and more recently the Dothraki language created especially for the world of the HBO series *Game of Thrones*. Then there are films such as *Avatar*, with the language specially created to represent an alien civilization. And of course there are the languages Tolkien devised for the elves, dwarves and other inhabitants of Middle Earth in *The Lord of the Rings*.

Still another reason is that thinkers have been frustrated at how imperfectly natural languages represent the world. Beginning at least as early as the seventeenth century there have been attempts to create a 'logical' language, using symbols—as in mathematics—that could be understood regardless of what language the user spoke. Though the invented languages were logical, they were also complicated, arbitrary, and hard for anyone but the inventor to learn.

The late nineteenth century saw a great flowering of attempts at a universal language, starting in 1880 with a language called Volapük. Then came Esperanto, and languages with names like Novial, Interlingua, and dozens of others. Almost all of them were based on western European tongues, usually German, French, English, or Spanish. And most of them are extinct. Once an invented language is launched onto the stormy seas of language *usage* it rarely survives the death of its inventor, no matter how clever or systematic it may be.

Of these idealistic nineteenth-century ventures, Esperanto became the best-known and the most widespread; it now has a body of literature of its own and still has many enthusiastic speakers around the world today. Present-day artificial languages, however, at least those that come to the attention of the media and the public, tend to be created for specific entertainment purposes. In the nineteenth and early twentieth centuries, the heyday of Esperanto, the emphasis was on international communication. This was only natural in a world where different European languages dominated different spheres: German for science, French for diplomacy, English for commerce—and so these mixed European-based languages came to be created. But not all created languages were based on European structures and vocabularies.

One of those invented in the nineteenth century might remind you of the film *Close Encounters of the Third Kind*. You may remember the scenes in which an alien spacecraft begins its efforts to open communications with Earthlings by teaching them to reproduce a haunting series of five tones. The invented language Solresol was based on a very similar principle: starting with the do-re-mi system used to teach singing, it created words by combining the seven notes of the scale in particular sequences. For example, *fa-fa-do-fa* was the word for 'doctor' and *fa-fa-do-la* meant 'dentist.' Solresol was relatively easy to learn, and what made the language unique was that it could be sung, played or whistled as well as spoken! It was popular for quite a long time.

There have also been languages created for a scientific purpose, such as Loglan, which was invented in 1960 to test whether grammar rules based on mathematical logic would make a language's speakers more precise thinkers. And a language invented in 1962 called 'BABM' (pronounced 'Bo-A-Bo-Mu'), with a writing system in which each letter represents a syllable. Or one from 1979 that uses a system of icons instead of letters to represent concepts and sounds. The list goes on.

Dr. Zamenhof's creation, Esperanto, and the languages like Ido and Novial that competed with it in the late nineteenth century were all created on the basis of natural European languages. European empires encircled the globe at the time, and it was only natural for Latin and its daughter languages to be taken as the basis for these languages. They are what linguists call 'a posteriori' languages—created out of a blend of languages already existing. Solresol, Klingon, and a host of others, some using familiar alphabets, some with scripts of their own, are what we call 'a priori' languages—created from scratch.

Nowadays, in the world of the internet and social media, language creators no longer need to work in isolation. They can compare their efforts and encourage each other, and a new concept, the 'conlanger' has been born. 'Conlangs' (constructed languages) are the main concern of the Language Creation Society, an international organization for language creators, which has an active membership and a website: www.conlang.org. Would you like to create your own language, better than the ones we already have? If so, join the club. Among people who like languages, it seems to be a universal urge.

About the author

Christopher Moseley (Chrismoseley50@yahoo.com) is a university lecturer, writer and freelance translator, editor of the *Encyclopedia of the*

World's Endangered Languages (2006) and the *UNESCO Atlas of the World's Languages in Danger* (2009), as well as co-editor of the *Atlas of the World's Languages* (1993). He has a special interest in artificial languages (and has created one himself).

Suggestions for further reading

In this book
Other chapters on languages consciously created by humans include 17 (Esperanto) and 31 (sign languages).

Elsewhere
Large, Andrew. *The Artificial Language Movement* (Blackwell, 1985). Large's book is the most comprehensive overview of this complicated story in one volume. If you want to explore the individual languages further, you must seek out the textbooks and manuals of their authors and propagators. These can be very hard to find; hardly any are still in print.

Okrent, Arika. *In the Land of Invented Languages: Esperanto Rock Stars, Klingon Poets, Loglan Lovers, and the Mad Dreamers Who Tried to Build a Perfect Language* (Spiegel & Grau, 2009). Less encyclopedic than Large's book, but academically sound; also highly readable and entertaining.

Website of the Language Creation Society: www.conlang.org

12
Do animals use language?

Donna Jo Napoli

Do animals use language? And if they do, do they mean by it the sorts of things humans mean by it? Do they make models of the world with it, like we do?

Parrots talk. So the answer is yes, right? Not so fast. There are two issues here. One is whether animals use language among themselves; the other is whether animals can learn human language. Before addressing them, we must decide what counts as language.

Human languages have well-defined characteristics: First, they are *systematic*, with rules we call grammar. ('Chased dog the nasty a cat' is English words, but not a sentence—the words come randomly, rather than according to rules of syntax.)

Human language is also *innate*. Babies are hard-wired to acquire an accessible language. No one need teach them.

A third characteristic is *displacement*—humans can talk about objects that aren't present, like the man in this sentence: 'The weird man wrote an exposé of existentialism.'

Another feature of human language is the ability to talk about *abstractions*—like weirdness, exposé and existentialism.

Finally, the weird-man sentence is one I never used before. You probably never heard it before, either. Human languages have the ability to *create* new expressions.

Note that I don't include arbitrariness between form and meaning among the criteria, because significant iconicity occurs in sign languages and (less so in) spoken languages. So the word *book* in English and its counterpart *hon* in Japanese don't 'sound like' what they mean or like each other, but the signs for *book* in the sign languages of North America and Japan (and many other sign languages) are identical and do, in fact, 'look like' what they mean.

Animals communicate with one another in ways that meet some, but not all five, criteria. Most linguists agree this means animals don't use language.

Bees dance to convey location and quality of food sources. The paths and speeds of dances follow rules—the orientation of the dancer's head and the vigor of its waggle are significant. Dances are about food that isn't present (so we have displacement) and about food quality (so we have abstraction). And dancing appears to be innate. But creativity is lacking; information is limited. Bees can't communicate, for example, that a new food source is near another well-known one, or that other bees are approaching the source so the hive had better hurry.

Birdsong also has rules. Robin song motifs, for example, must occur in a certain order (a kind of grammar) to be intelligible. The ability to sing is innate, and birds not exposed to song within the first months of life never develop typical courtship-territorial song. Birdsong conveys emotion, so it refers to abstractions. We have no evidence, however, that it allows displacement (birds never seem to communicate that something scary happened behind the barn); nor do they make up new songs.

Whales and dolphins sing and whistle. Song form follows rules, and songs can convey limited meaning (distress or warning calls). In the wild, dolphins use whistles particular to their pods that they teach their offspring. But there's no evidence of the creativity characteristic of human language.

Chimpanzees grunt, bark, pant, wail, laugh, squeak, hoot, and call to alert others to the location of food sources, announce a kill, express alarm, identify themselves, or express satisfaction. Postures, facial expressions, and limb gestures play an even greater role in communication. But nothing indicates grammar-like rules.

Campbell's monkeys (also called Campbell's mona monkeys or Campbell's guenons) combine sounds to yield different meanings.

A certain screech warns a leopard is nearby; that screech plus a 'suffix' indicates general alarm; that screech plus suffix preceded by *boom* sounds indicates danger from falling branches. So we have grammar-like rules, but no evidence of displacement.

Prairie dogs exhibit meaningful calls that can be combined in novel ways to describe unfamiliar objects, but researchers note nothing about displacement.

Turning to the question of whether or not animals can learn human language, people have attempted to teach human language to birds, sea mammals, and primates. Alex, an African grey parrot, could identify objects with English words by their material, color, shape, and number. He could ask for food that wasn't present. He apologized when he misbehaved. But his verbal behavior was erratic in ways unlike even very young human behavior.

Dolphins have been taught to respond to hand gestures and are able to interpret new utterances. For example, dolphins who learned that the sequence of gestures PERSON SURFBOARD FETCH means 'bring the surfboard to the person' easily understood SURFBOARD PERSON FETCH as 'bring the person to the surfboard.' Some have been taught to mimic computer-generated whistles that they then used as names for toys (balls and hoops).

Chimpanzees, gorillas, and bonobos have been taught to use and respond to a sign language. The famous chimp Washoe, who learned signs from her trainers, adopted a baby named Loulis and taught him those signs. A gorilla named Koko amassed a vocabulary of over a thousand signs. A bonobo named Kanzi communicated using a keyboard with about 200 symbols for words. He could understand over 500 spoken English words.

Border collies have been reported to respond appropriately to language, some showing recognition of over a thousand words.

Such experiments suggest that in laboratory settings or with rigorous training some animals can learn language-like behavior to some extent; but there's no evidence that their ordinary communication with each other in the wild makes significant use of this capacity.

Could we be missing something? Could there be animals that achieve five-featured language-like communication with means like seismic thumping, olfactory spraying, electrical signaling, or dynamic skin patterns? Not impossible. But decades of research have found nothing among animals comparable to human language for pervasive systematicity, extensive creativity, and displacement. Language remains the most profound distinction between animals and humans. Importantly, this is not to say that human intelligence is a priori superior to that of other creatures. The recent move away from anthropomorphized study of animals in laboratory settings toward more holistic study of their communicative and other interactions in the wild already promises to change our understanding of intelligence in general.

About the author
Donna Jo Napoli is professor of linguistics at Swarthmore College. She publishes primarily on the structure of Italian and of sign languages. She also writes children's fiction: see www.swarthmore.edu/donna-jo-napoli.

Suggestions for further reading

In this book
Chapters discussing grammar as a distinguishing feature of human language include 4 and 6 (universal grammar), 13 (language deprivation), 14 (human-to-animal communication), and 25 (grammar in general).

Elsewhere
Anderson, Steve. *Dr. Doolittle's Delusion: Animals and the Uniqueness of Human Language* (Yale University Press, 2004). Distinction between communication and language.

Bradbury, Jack and Sandra Vehrencamp. *Principles of Animal Communication* (Sinauer Press, 1998). Communication between animals across various senses.

Hauser, Marc and Mark Konishi, eds. *The Design of Animal Communication* (MIT, 1999). Development of animal signals and responses.

Jabr, Ferris. 'Can prairie dogs talk?' *The New York Times* (May 12, 2017), www.nytimes.com/2017/05/12/magazine/can-prairie-dogs-talk. html?emc=eta1&_r=0

McGregor, Peter, ed. *Animal Communication Networks* (Cambridge University Press, 2005). Network perspective to communication between animals, including eavesdropping.

Perniss, Pamela, Robin L. Thompson, and Gabriella Vigliocco. 'Iconicity as a general property of language: Evidence from spoken and signed languages.' *Frontiers in Psychology* vol. 1 (2010), p. 227. Non-arbitrary mappings between articulation and meaning.

Language and communication

13
What happens if you are raised without language?

Susan Curtiss

Are there really people raised without language? Can such a person ever develop language? When is it too late to do so? What happens to such a person socially, cognitively, neurally?

It is almost impossible for most of us to imagine growing up without language—which develops in our minds so effortlessly in early childhood and plays such a central role in defining us as human and allowing us to participate in our culture. Nevertheless, being deprived of language occasionally happens in some exceptional circumstances. In recent centuries children have been found living in the wild, reportedly raised by wolves or other animals and deprived of human contact. One of the most famous cases is that of Victor, the 'wild boy of Aveyron,' immortalized in a film by Francois Truffaut, called *The Wild Child* (*L'Enfant Sauvage*).

It is hard to know the real stories behind these cases, but they are all strikingly similar with respect to language. The pattern from all these cases is that only those rescued *early* in childhood developed any fluency or grammar. Those found after about nine years of age learned only a few words or failed to learn language at all.

We also know cases in which children grew up in social or linguistic isolation because of tragic family circumstances. One of the best-known of these is the case of Genie, whose childhood was one of extreme neglect, deprivation, and abuse. For over twelve years, her father shut her away in a small bedroom, tied with a harness to an infant potty seat. When her blind mother finally escaped with Genie in the early 1970s and applied for welfare, the police intervened, and Genie was put in the rehabilitation ward of a children's hospital. She was thirteen and a half years old and knew no language.

Genie was studied by linguists and other professionals for almost a decade. She was of normal intelligence; she rapidly learned words within a few months after her discovery, and soon began to combine them. However, she failed to use grammatical elements like tense or agreement markers, articles, pronouns, or question words—the pieces of English that turn a string of words into grammatical speech. Most of her linguistic development consisted of learning more words and stringing them together into longer, semantically coherent utterances. In context, she could make herself understood. However, her speech did not adhere to standard English subject–verb–object word order. She appeared to comprehend more than she could produce, but even after many years, she developed little knowledge of grammar. Interestingly, Genie was a powerful non-verbal communicator, providing strong evidence that language is not the same as communication.

In contrast, children without hearing are not as handicapped as Genie. They can develop language and relate normally to others through signing—as long as language development starts early. There are a number of studies that show that the sooner a deaf child is exposed to a natural sign language, such as American Sign Language, the more proficient a signer he or she will become. As in other cases of linguistic isolation, the ability of deaf people to learn new words is not affected by the age at which they are exposed to language. But their ability to learn grammar is dramatically affected. Studies of deaf children first exposed to sign language after the pre-school years show that there is a critical window for grammatical development, which ends, perhaps, in the early school-age years.

Exciting evidence that a child brings something unique and necessary to language development comes from the creation of a sign language in Nicaragua. After the Sandinista movement came to power there in 1979, for the first time deaf teenagers and adults had the opportunity to form a Deaf community (Deaf with a capital 'D' indicates a connection to Deaf culture and identity; deaf with a small 'd' refers to hearing loss not connected to Deaf identity).

This first generation created a rudimentary system of gestures for communication. But when young children, under the age of ten, joined this community, they transformed this system into a real language, embodying the structural elements and characteristics that define all human grammars. Over a very few years, that language has become increasingly rich and complex grammatically.

Like other cases of linguistic isolation after early childhood is the case of Chelsea, a deaf woman from a loving, *hearing* family who used no signs. Chelsea was first exposed to language (signed and spoken English) in her thirties. She is normal psycho-socially, reflecting her loving family, but despite decades of teaching and exposure, she learned only vocabulary and never developed any grammar at all.

Provocatively, grammar acquisition may be crucial for triggering normal organization of higher cognition in the brain. Genie, Chelsea, and other late learners of a first language failed to develop a normal pattern of neural organization for language and other mental faculties, suggesting a crucial role for grammar, perhaps *the* trigger for the way the brain organizes cognition in humans.

About the author

Susan Curtiss is professor emerita of linguistics at UCLA. She is the author of *Genie: A Psycholinguistic Study of a Modern-Day 'Wild Child'*, as well as of close to a hundred journal articles and book chapters. She has also authored numerous language tests, including the Curtiss-Yamada Comprehensive Language Evaluation (the CYCLE), used by researchers across the U.S. and overseas. Her research spans the study of language and mind, the 'critical period' for first language acquisition, Specific Language Impairment (SLI), mental retardation, epilepsy, adult aphasia, progressive dementia, the genetics of language, and language develop-ment following hemispherectomy (removal of one hemisphere of the brain) in childhood. Her current work focuses on mapping grammar onto the brain in normal and epileptic adults.

Suggestions for further reading

In this book
Other chapters discussing language acquisition by children include 30 (pidgins and creoles), 35 (babies and language), 31 (sign languages), and 59 (children and second languages). Chapters 18–21 all deal with issues of language and the brain. The importance of grammar as a part of full language capability is discussed in Chapters 25 (grammar in general), 4 (universal grammar), and 12 (animal communication).

Elsewhere
Curtiss, Susan. *Genie: A Psycholinguistic Study of a Modern-Day 'Wild Child'* (Academic Press, 1977). A fascinating account of Curtiss's experi-ences and research with Genie and the implications of this work.

Curtiss, Susan. 'The case of Chelsea,' in Carson T. Schütze and Linnaea Stockall, eds., *Connectedness: Papers by and for Sarah van Wagenen* (Lulu Press, 2015), pp. 115–146. A detailed account of the case of Chelsea, what she has and has not been able to learn, and the implications of the case.

Hitchcock, Andrew. 'A language unlike any other: What is Nicaraguan Sign Language?' United Language Group editorial (June 8, 2017). A non-technical, highly readable description of the history and develop-ments in the creation of NSL, which can be found on the web at http://daily.unitedlanguagegroup.com/stories/editorials/nicaraguan-sign-language

Newport, Elissa L. 'Maturational constraints on language learning,' *Cognitive Science* vol. 14. (1990). A description of research on the effects of age on the acquisition of the grammar of American Sign Language (ASL) by Deaf individuals who were exposed to ASL at different ages, some not until adulthood.

14
Can animals understand us?

Robin Queen

Can animals understand humans? How do we know what they understand? Why don't they understand more?

Animals understand a lot more than we might think, but they don't understand as much as we often wish they did. Many humans believe animals understand us so completely that we interact with them using all our communication resources, including language. And animals respond to our interaction in ways that make sense to us. They cock their heads, look at us, purr, and snuggle with us.

Although many of us talk frequently with the animals in our lives, we also have an intuitive sense of what they can and can't actually understand. We don't ask them open-ended questions and we don't ask them their political opinions. In this chapter, we ask what non-human animals can and can't understand when we use language with them.

Every species has its own, innate communication system. The primary human communication system is language. By 'language', linguists mean the systematic organization of sounds, words, and grammatical elements that allows us to interact so richly with one another. Linguists don't typically include body language, facial expressions, non-language gestures, or emotional expressions (e.g., sighs, laughter, snorts) in the linguistic definition of language even though these are clearly connected to how humans communicate.

Notably, animals often understand these non-linguistic modes of communication reasonably well.

The words that make up languages consist largely of symbolic, arbitrary connections between something used to represent and something being represented. There is nothing, for instance, about the string of sounds in the word 'cat' that would allow someone who didn't know English already to deduce what the word stood for.

Many different species, including dogs, parrots, dolphins, and several species of primates, are able to make symbolic connections. Consider the commands we often teach our pets and how they respond. For example, dogs learn relatively quickly how to 'play dead.' They understand that the arbitrary string of sounds stands in for a particular action. Some dogs and some primates have learned over 1,000 different words/phrases and are able to figure out the meaning of a new word through mechanisms of deduction that resemble what young humans do as they start to learn the words of their language.

The same species that have learned to interpret these kinds of meaning relationships have also demonstrated that they can understand that putting words in different orders changes the meaning. A border collie named Chaser, for instance, understands the difference between 'to X, take Y' and 'to Y, take X.' And the bonobo Kanzi can interpret prepositions like 'in,' 'on,' and 'through' and distinguish between phrases like 'put the glitter in the bottle' and 'put the bottle in the glitter.'

These examples can start to make it seem like animals understand quite a bit of language, but we need to be cautious about this assumption. Importantly, animals' ability to interpret words and word order is rudimentary and limited to relatively few words. It also requires a lot of dedicated training by humans to emerge. While humans understand novel and complex uses of language almost immediately, even the most well-trained animals don't seem able to do so. These limitations make it nearly impossible for animals to fully understand our linguistic communications.

Three broad observations illustrate what animals can't understand. First, they don't understand that words can be broken down into component parts like individual sounds, prefixes, suffixes and stems and then that those elements can be recombined to create new words. In the 'play dead' example, dogs don't understand that 'play' can be combined with a different word like 'ball' to capture a new meaning.

Second, they don't understand complex relationships between words. For example, they can't understand the differences or similarities between utterances like 'You hear me' and 'Do you hear me?'. For humans, this seems really simple but it is in fact pretty tricky to understand because of the pronouns and the underlying relationship between statements and questions.

Third, animals don't seem to understand complex references to time (e.g., past and future) and space (e.g., 'here', 'there', and 'everywhere'). Even animals who understand many words can't be told, 'Repeat what you did yesterday!' Understanding that depends minimally on understanding the differences signaled by past and present.

Certainly some animals, like dogs and primates, are pretty impressive in what they can be trained to do with language. Yet, it is abundantly clear that humans and non-humans differ in the ability to make full use of the resources available through language. In short, human brains and minds differ from those of other species, and those differences involve the capacity for language in its fullest, richest expression.

Understanding what non-humans can and can't understand about language helps humans know how to communicate with other species. This understanding gives us insight into what aspects of language are unique among the world's communication systems. And perhaps most importantly, using language with the animals who share our lives helps humans feel closer to those animals and reminds us every day how amazing it is that we can bond to another species so intensely.

About the author

Robin Queen is an Arthur F. Thurnau Professor and Professor of Linguistics, German, English and the Honors Program at the University of Michigan. She is the author of *Vox Popular: The Surprising Life of Language and the Media* (2015), co-author of *Through the Golden Door: Educational Approaches for Immigrant Adolescents* (1998), and author or co-author of publications in the areas of language contact, language, gender and sexuality, and language in the mass media. She was the co-editor with Anne Curzan of the *Journal of English Linguistics* (2006–2012) and is a Fellow of the Linguistic Society of America. She has been researching, documenting and theorizing shepherds' communication with sheepdogs since 2012 and competes in sheep herding competitions with her border collies. She lives on a small hobby farm with a merry band of cats, dogs, chickens, and sheep.

Suggestions for further reading

In this book

More information about whether or not animals use language appears in Chapter 12 (animal communication). Other chapters focusing on the structure of language can be found in Chapters 4 (universal grammar), 7 (sounds of language), and 25 (grammar).

Elsewhere

Anderson, Stephen R. *Doctor Dolittle's Delusion: Animals and the Uniqueness of Human Language* (Yale University Press, 2006).

Andics, Attila, et al. 'Neural mechanisms for lexical processing in dogs,' *Science* vol. 353, no. 6303 (2016), pp. 1030–1032.

Berns, Gregory. *What It's Like to Be a Dog: And Other Adventures in Animal Neuroscience* (Basic Books, 2017).

Kaminiski, Juliane, and Sarah Marshall-Pescini, eds. *The Social Dog: Behavior and Cognition* (Academic Press, 2014).

Pilley, John, and Heather Hinzeman. *Chaser: Unlocking the Genius of the Dog Who Knows a Thousand Words* (Houghton Mifflin, 2013).

Rogers, Adam. 'What a border collie taught a linguist about language,' *Wired Online* (2017), www.wired.com/story/what-a-border-collie-taught-a-linguist-about-language/.

Savage-Rumbaugh, E. Sue, and Roger Lewin. *Kanzi: The Ape At the Brink of the Human Mind.* (Wiley, 1994).

15

What is 'speaking in tongues'?

Walt Wolfram

What happens when religious people 'speak in tongues'? Is their speech a real language? What is its relationship to natural language?

The utterances flowed effortlessly from his mouth: 'La horiya la hariya, la hayneekeechee aleekeechi arateeli haya.' It sounded like poetry in a foreign language, but no one else spoke the language or understood it. That didn't make any difference; the speaker who uttered these words in his private prayers considered them a special language for talking to God. Although it seems esoteric and mysterious to those who encounter it for the first time, 'speaking in tongues,' or, more technically, 'glossolalia,' is not an uncommon linguistic phenomenon. Millions of English speakers around the world have spoken in tongues and speakers of many other languages have experienced a similar form of linguistic expression. Glossolalia has a long history in Christianity and in other religions as well, perhaps as long as humans have had language. In Christianity, it has been well documented since the Day of Pentecost, with the last century witnessing a significant revival in its use, especially in so-called holiness churches but also in some more liturgical churches such as Catholic and Anglican congregations.

Glossolalia has also been documented in other religions and in some non-religious practices. For example, practitioners of

Peyotism among Native American Indians, shamans exercising witchcraft in Haiti, and Tibetan monks uttering various chants may also use a type of glossolalia. What exactly is it? Is it language? If not, what is its relationship to natural language? And how does it function in religious expression and in society?

Linguists have been studying the structure of glossolalia for some time now using the methods applied to the analysis of natural language. Studies include identifying the sounds, the sequencing of sounds into syllables, and the arrangement of segments into larger units similar to words and syntax in natural language. Glossolalic fluency may range from minimally organized, barely formed grunt-like sounds to highly organized streams of consonants and vowels that sound like highly expressive natural language.

The majority of sounds used in glossolalia come from a person's native language, though some speakers are capable of using other sounds as well. When compared with a speaker's native language, however, the inventory of sounds is restricted in ways that make it somewhat comparable to the speech of young children. For example, if a language has forty significant vowel and consonant sounds, only ten to twenty of those sounds might be used in the glossolalia. And syllables also tend to be somewhat simpler than in natural language, so that alternating sequences of a single consonant and single vowel are repeated. For example, notice how *lahoriya* in the sample alternates between a simple consonant and vowel. Glossolalia may, however, also exhibit traits of expressive or poetic language: rhyming and alliteration are found in some speakers' utterances. Notice, for example, the rhyming in phrases like *la horiya la hariya* or *haneekeechi aleekeechi*.

In some worship traditions within Christianity, after one person utters glossolalia in a public meeting, another person will follow with a prophetic 'interpretation' into a natural language such as English or Spanish. Usually these interpretations reinforce religious themes shared by the group. An analysis of utterances and the interpretations using the techniques of translation theory, however, reveals that such interpretations are not literal translations. There are also reports of knowledgeable audience members recognizing the utterances of glossolalists as particular foreign languages ('xenoglossia'), but recorded documentation of such cases has proven to be elusive.

Linguistically, glossolalia is a kind of 'pseudolanguage'—nonsense syllables of a familiar language that are reminiscent of an earlier, prelanguage babbling stage. While most people stop using nonsense syllables in childhood, once they have acquired a natural language, glossolalists return to a stage in which sounds are used for purposes other than the communication of specific thoughts. Of course, not all adult language users completely give up uttering nonsense syllables. The writer J. R. R. Tolkien had a proclivity for speaking nonsense syllables throughout his life, and some modern music genres (think of 'scat' singing in jazz) are also characterized by the use of nonsense syllables. Speaking in tongues may also be an acquired capability, in which regular practice results in more fluently constructed strings of syllables. Tolkien, for example, apparently practiced his production of nonsense syllables regularly in order to refine the expressive effect of his utterances.

Though some psychologists have connected speaking in tongues with hypnotic trance, hysteria, or even schizophrenia, such assessments seem far too severe and judgmental. In fact, normal, well-adjusted people may speak in tongues in socially specified situations such as personal prayer, religious ritual, or public worship. The religious significance of speaking in tongues lies mostly in its demonstration that in such situations a speaker is able to transcend ordinary speech.

About the author

Walt Wolfram is a William C. Friday Distinguished Professor of English Linguistics at North Carolina State University. Although he is most noted for his research on American dialects, his sociolinguistic career started with the study of speaking in tongues. In the mid-1960s, he conducted one of the first linguistic analyses of glossolalia based on an extensive set of tape recordings of its public and private use. He wrote a master's thesis on glossolalia in 1966. Decades later he still thinks that the collection of naturally occurring samples of glossolalia was the most sensitive fieldwork situation he ever encountered.

Suggestions for further reading

In this book
The topic of how social contexts influence the way languages function and interact is addressed in Chapters 30 (pidgins and creoles), 45 (language conflict), 32 and 46 (language and gender), and 42 (language and society).

Elsewhere
Goodman, Felicitas D. *Speaking in Tongues: A Cross-Cultural Study of Glossolalia* (University of Chicago Press, 1972). A comparison of speaking in tongues in different cultures that explains it as a kind of hypnotic trance. Though this psychological explanation does not hold up, the comparison of glossolalia across cultures is useful.

Nickell, Joe. *Looking for a Miracle: Weeping Icons, Relics, Stigmata, Visions, and Healing Cures* (Prometheus, 1993). A historical, forensic discussion of speaking in tongues along with other kinds of paranormal religious behavior. The focus is on explaining the need for the establishment of supernatural events within Christian religious tradition.

Samarin, William J. *Tongues of Men and Angels: The Religious Language of Pentecostalism* (Macmillan, 1972). Though somewhat dated, this still remains the most comprehensive linguistic description of glossolalia, which is presented as a kind of pseudolanguage comparable to pre-language babbling.

Samarin, William J. 'Variation and variables in religious glossolalia,' *Language in Society* vol. 1 (1972), pp. 121–130. A concise, technical linguistic description of glossolalia written primarily for linguists and sociolinguists.

16

How many kinds of writing system are there?

Peter T. Daniels

How do writing systems differ? Which one is used the most? Could we use a system other than an alphabet to write English?

Around the world, a little over thirty different writing systems are in official or widespread use today (counting all the different Roman alphabets, like English and French and even Vietnamese, as variants of a single one; likewise for all the varieties of Cyrillic and Arabic and so on). These systems, together with some used in the past to write languages now extinct, fall into about half a dozen different *kinds* of system that have been devised over the past 5,000 years.

Most familiar, and most widespread, is the *alphabet*. In an alphabet, each letter represents one consonant or one vowel, and (theoretically) all the consonants and vowels in a word are written down, one by one, from left to right. But since you read and write English, you know that we are very far from that ideal! Why should *though, through, tough,* and *cough* all be spelled with *o-u-g-h*? Because we've been spelling pretty much the same way since printing got started in England in 1475, while English pronunciation has been changing gradually over the centuries. Spanish and Finnish and Czech do a lot better at keeping the spelling the same as the sounds. The first language to be written with an alphabet was Greek—and to this day, Greek is written with the Greek alphabet. Every other alphabet in the world is descended from the Greek! Russian and many languages of the former Soviet Union are written with the Cyrillic alphabet, and the languages of western Europe are written with the Roman alphabet.

So, too, are many languages that have only recently started being written. Hundreds and hundreds of them, such as Massachusett and Maori, Zulu and Zomi, have had alphabets created for them, usually the Roman alphabet with maybe a few extra letters or some accent marks, by missionaries translating the Bible. These alphabets usually don't have much use outside the Bible texts and related materials. But sometimes they also get used for personal correspondence, newspapers, and even books and the internet—and a literate culture has been created.

Before there were alphabets, there were scripts of the kind I call *abjad*s. This seemingly simpler kind of writing can be seen in news photos from the Middle East. If you open a Hebrew Bible or a Qur'an, you'll see the letters surrounded by dots and dashes and curls, but if you look at billboards and placards, you'll just see the letters—Hebrew ones all squared up separate in a row, Arabic ones gracefully joined together to make whole words without lifting the pen. (These two scripts happen to be written from right to left.) The difference between the holy texts and the street signs, or ordinary books, is that ordinary writing in Hebrew and Arabic includes only the consonant letters; if you know one of these languages, you can fill in the vowels on your own as you read. But in holy books, getting the pronunciation exactly right is very important, and devout scholars in the early Middle Ages wanted to add helps to the reader. They wouldn't change the spellings they inherited, so they added in the vowels using dots and dashes around the letters.

The Greek alphabet developed out of the Phoenician abjad. The scripts of India developed out of the closely related Aramaic abjad—but with a difference. By the third century BCE, Indian linguists had improved upon the abjad by inventing a very sophisticated way of writing the vowels (I call the resulting type of writing system the *abugida*). For languages of India and its neighbors in south and southeast Asia, such as Sanskrit and Hindi and Bengali,

Tamil and Thai, you write a plain letter and it reads as a consonant plus 'ah.' If you want it to read as the consonant plus a different vowel, you add a mark to it; and if you want it to read as two consonants in a row with no vowel in between, as in *chakra* or *Mahatma*, you attach a piece of the letter for the first consonant in front of the whole letter for the second consonant. It can get complicated!

If we go back before the Phoenician abjad, back to the very beginning of writing, we find that the first writing systems are always *logographic*—instead of individual sounds (consonants or vowels), entire words (or word elements, called 'morphemes') are represented by a single syllable-sign. The one writing system based on the logographic principle that's still used today is the Chinese. Look closely at the characters on a Chinese menu. If you compare them with the English names for foods, you might see which ones correspond to 'kung pao' and which ones correspond to 'chicken' or 'shrimp.' With a logographic system you don't 'spell' words, because each character corresponds to a whole word or part of a word. It works very well, but it takes a *lot* of characters, and all languages have tens of thousands of words. In the case of Chinese, you can read almost anything published in the language today if you learn about 3,000–4,000 characters. If you look in a Chinese–English dictionary, you'll see that most of the words are two characters long, so the 3,000-odd characters are quite enough for writing almost everything one ordinarily needs to write.

Now look at a Japanese menu. Alongside the complicated characters that look like Chinese characters (in fact, they *are* Chinese characters, but each one stands for a whole Japanese word), you'll mostly see simpler characters. These represent the endings on the words, and each of these simpler characters stands for a whole syllable, a consonant plus a vowel. There are just fifty of these symbols, because Japanese syllables are just that simple: a consonant plus a vowel. *Su-shi, sa-shi-mi, ki-mo-no.*

Other languages are written with this kind of syllable-character, such as the American Indian language Cherokee and the Liberian language Vai. It would be hard to use syllable-writing for English, because the syllables of English can be very complicated, like 'strengths' and 'splint.' You'd need thousands of characters to write them all!

What may be the best writing system ever devised combines the syllable approach learned from China with the consonant- and vowel-letter approach learned from India: Korean writing, or *han'gul*. On a Korean menu, you'll see squarish shapes that look like simple Chinese characters—but look at them closely and you'll see just forty simple designs (the letters) combined into blocks (the syllables). A great deal of information in a small space!

Different types of writing system work more or less well with different languages; but languages change over time, while spelling systems tend not to, so over time a writing system works less and less well. You will find a glimpse of the history of writing in my later chapter, 'Where did writing come from?'

About the author

Peter T. Daniels is one of the few linguists in the world specializing in the study of writing systems. He has published articles in a variety of journals and edited volumes, and contributed to several encyclopedias. He co-edited *The World's Writing Systems* (1996) with William Bright and was section editor for writing systems for the *Encyclopedia of Language and Linguistics* (2006). His book *An Exploration of Writing* was published by Equinox in 2018.

Suggestions for further reading

In this book

Other chapters that talk about written language include 26 (origins of writing), 29 (language change), and 39 (Chinese), as well as 53 (social media) and 56 (text messaging).

Elsewhere

Daniels, Peter T. *An Exploration of Writing* (Equinox, 2018). Sets forth the author's ideas about the nature and history of writing systems, addressed to the general reader.

Daniels, Peter T., and William Bright, eds. *The World's Writing Systems* (Oxford University Press, 1996). A standard reference for facts about writing systems, past and present.

DeFrancis, John. *Visible Speech: The Diverse Oneness of Writing Systems* (University of Hawaii Press, 1989). Stresses that all writing is based on the *sounds* of languages.

Diringer, David. *The Alphabet* (Funk & Wagnalls, third edition 1968). Jensen, Hans. *Sign, Symbol and Script* (George Allen & Unwin, 1969). These two books may take some effort to find, but each offers a very full history of writing. Diringer is more readable, Jensen more reliable and scholarly.

Gnanadesikan, Amalia. *The Writing Revolution: From Cuneiform to the Internet* (Wiley-Blackwell, 2009). A well-written, compact summary of the important writing systems of the world.

Nakanishi, Akira. *Writing Systems of the World* (Tuttle, 1980). One-page descriptions of 29 current scripts, illustrated with newspaper front pages, and over 100 illustrations of other scripts, ancient and modern.

Rogers, Henry. *Writing Systems: A Linguistic Approach* (Blackwell, 2005). Preferable among the small number of textbooks on writing.

17

Whatever happened to Esperanto?

Arika Okrent and E. M. Rickerson

Whatever happened to the idea of a universal language? Is Esperanto still alive? And if so, who speaks it?

Wouldn't it be wonderful if everyone in the world spoke the same language? Or wouldn't it be almost as good if everyone could speak their own language at home but agree to learn the same *second* language for international communication; a language that didn't belong to any one country; and so easy you could learn it in just a few weeks?

If you like that idea, you're in good company. Starting as early as the seventeenth century with philosophers such as Bacon, Descartes, and Leibniz, there have been hundreds of proposals for an international language—and people are still trying to create one. For a variety of reasons, however, the only one that had lasting success was Esperanto, invented in Poland in the late nineteenth century by Ludwig Zamenhof, an idealist who understood the power of language to unite or divide.

What kind of a language is Esperanto? People who have heard of it but never heard it spoken are sometimes led to believe that it is based on Spanish, which is not true. The name 'Esperanto' has a Spanish flavor, but the vocabulary of the language is a mix of European tongues; it includes Slavic and Germanic word roots, as well as roots from Latin and Romance languages. The name of the language is formed from the Romance root for 'hope' (*esper-*) and the endings *-ant-* (indicating that the action is taking place) and *-o* (making it a noun). It means 'one who hopes.'

The endings used to form Esperanto words are completely regular. Nouns always end in *-o*, adjectives in *-a*, present tense verbs in *-as*, past tense verbs in *-is*; once you know the endings, you know how to add them to any root to make a word. This means that with a minimal amount of memorization, you can be up and running pretty quickly. Esperanto is much easier to learn than natural languages, with their pesky irregularities and exceptions. It is not, however, completely predictable. There are expressions, idioms, and ways of putting phrases together that must simply be learned. The rules of Esperanto are defined, but not too well defined. This is one of the reasons it has flourished while hundreds of competitors never gained any traction. Esperanto allows room for change and growth, and for a community of speakers to define its standards through usage.

So whatever happened to Esperanto? It was created in 1887, got a big boost in popularity from the war-weariness of the 1920s, even became a serious candidate to be the official language of the League of Nations—and then seemed to fade away. But it did not, in fact, disappear. Although it had ups and downs throughout the twentieth century, the language quietly survived. And as the twenty-first century gets under way, Esperanto has emerged again, robust and gaining in popularity—in part because of the internet. Where Esperantists once had to travel to meetings and conferences to find other people to speak with, now they can sit down at the computer to chat with their fellow Esperantists anywhere in the world.

That said, the meetings and conferences are still an important part of the Esperanto scene. While many invented languages have been presented to the world as mere useful tools for commerce, science, or international diplomacy, Esperanto gained its appeal by focusing on the wide range of other things that humans do with language. When Esperantists get together they perform Esperanto songs, comedy skits, and poetry readings. There are Esperanto novels and magazines. There's a translation of the Bible, as well as *The Lord of the Rings*. There are Esperanto jokes, puns, and swear words. There is even a feature-length film with a soundtrack entirely in Esperanto: *Incubus*, which stars a young, pre-*Star Trek* William Shatner.

There are also a few hundred people in the world for whom Esperanto is a native tongue. Since a native language is one you learn at your mother's knee, and Esperanto is a language *constructed* for people who already have a native tongue, you may wonder how anyone could speak it natively. Answer: mother and father meet at an Esperanto conference, but don't speak each other's native languages. So they use Esperanto with each other at home, and raise their children speaking it. These new native Esperanto speakers are *not* monolingual—they also speak the majority language outside the home. Their linguistic situation is not much different from that of children who grow up in a home where immigrant parents speak a language different from the majority language.

Esperanto speakers are dispersed, so it's hard to get an exact count of them. It's also hard to tell what level of fluency one should reach to be called an Esperanto speaker. But there are at least tens of thousands—50,000 seems a reasonable estimate—with some conversational ability. The annual Universal Congress—which is most often held in Europe, but has also taken place in China, Korea, Japan, Brazil, Australia, and Israel—usually has a couple of thousand attendees.

Esperanto is by far the most successful artificial language in the long history of language invention. It isn't a universal language, and it's unlikely to become one, but it has become a living language.

About the authors

Arika Okrent received a joint Ph.D. in the Department of Linguistics and the Department of Psychology's Cognition and Cognitive Neuroscience Program at the University of Chicago. She has written about language for *The American Scholar*, *Tin House*, and *Slate*. In the course of writing her 2009 book *In the Land of Invented Languages*, she earned a first-level certification in Klingon. She is editor-at-large of *The Week*, and is a frequent contributor to *Mental Floss*. In 2015 she received LSA Linguistics Journalism Award.

E. M. ('Rick') Rickerson served as the general editor of the first and second editions of this book. He is professor emeritus of German, director emeritus of the award-winning language program at the College of Charleston (South Carolina), a former deputy director of the U.S. government's Center for the Advancement of Language Learning, and an associate of the National Museum of Language. In 2005 he created the radio series on languages (*Talkin' about Talk*) from which *The Five-Minute Linguist* was adapted. He is currently retired in the mountains of North Carolina.

Suggestions for further reading

In this book
Other chapters on languages consciously created by humans include 11 (survey of artificial languages) and 31 (sign languages). Languages that have served as 'bridges' between groups that would otherwise be unable to communicate are discussed in Chapters 28 (Latin), 30 (pidgins), and 43 (lingua francas).

Elsewhere
Jordan, David. *Being Colloquial in Esperanto* (Esperanto League for North America, second edition 2004). A complete overview of Esperanto grammar.

Okrent, Arika. *In the Land of Invented Languages: Esperanto Rock Stars, Klingon Poets, Loglan Lovers, and the Mad Dreamers Who Tried to Build a Perfect Language* (Spiegel & Grau, 2009). A popular history of the many attempts to overcome Babel by creating artificial languages.

Richardson, David. *Esperanto: Learning and Using the International Language* (Esperanto League for North America, third edition 2004). Includes chapters on the history of Esperanto, a complete course in the language, an annotated reader, and a bibliography.

www.Esperanto.net. General information about Esperanto, in 62 different languages, with links to other relevant sites.

www.lernu.net. A multilingual site that will help you learn the language, free of charge.

Language and thought

18
Why do linguists study brains?

Lise Menn

How would you persuade a linguist that brains are worth studying?
Is there any practical value to studying how our brains store and
process language? Do neurolinguists know how our language is
stored in our brains, or are they still working on it? Is it changes in
our brains that make new languages harder to learn after childhood?

Most linguists don't study brains. But some do, and most of the
others are curious about the results of those studies. After all,
everything you know and everything you know how to do (even a
movement skill like whistling) must be stored in your brain somehow. We usually speak, understand, and read so quickly that it
seems effortless. Skilled speakers know how to pronounce words,
what they mean, how to put them together to make phrases and
sentences, and how to use words and their combinations, plus tone
of voice and the rise and fall of the melody of speech, to communicate with other people. How is this possible? And how does all this
language knowledge and skill get into our heads in the first place?

Some linguists study brains to find out whether our brains
have a single system for learning, speaking and understanding, or
whether we have two systems—one for 'knowledge' and the other
for 'mechanisms for speaking and understanding'—that are kept in
separate parts of the brain. They could be separate if your brain is
like a digital computer, which has programs that are separate from

the circuits that carry out the programs. But your language ability might work more like an analog computer, which doesn't have a program that's separate from its mechanism. A simple example of analog computing is a mechanical clock. It doesn't have a program; instead, the springs, gears, and other moving parts behind its face control its hands directly to show the time. Maybe what you know about language and how you use it are completely integrated, like a clock that grows inside your head! Or maybe your brain somehow uses both digital and analog computations. Linguists who study brains, *neurolinguists*, don't know the answer yet.

Many neurolinguists also care about brains because we belong to educational or clinical research teams trying to answer questions about everyday language problems or about serious language disorders like stuttering, dyslexia, and aphasia. But answering questions about disorders requires more than studying brains and language. We also have to figure out the automatic processing steps that our brains use when we express our ideas in words and when we understand what we hear or read, because language problems always involve language processing difficulties. In people without brain injuries, these processes are so unconscious that they have to be studied by experiments; the people who do these experiments are called experimental *psycholinguists*.

Clinical neurolinguists try to help people who have brain-based problems in using language—for example, developmental language disorders (specific language impairment, stuttering, dyslexia), language disorders caused by injuries to particular parts of our brains (aphasia), and language disorders that are part of diseases that affect all of our brain functions (like Alzheimer's disease or traumatic brain injury). Clinical neurolinguists work in teams alongside speech-language pathologists, psycholinguists, neurologists, and neuropsychologists, because many different kinds of skills are needed to figure out how brain problems cause language problems. Clinical teams have to decide how to educate or re-educate their clients. They also have to educate their clients' families—and sometimes their clients' doctors! Some specialists are still prescribing eye exercises for children with dyslexia, although almost all kinds of dyslexia are caused by differences in how someone's brain analyzes speech sounds and connects those sounds to meanings, so eye exercises won't help. Lots of people still believe that deaf children should be taught to speak before they are taught to use sign language, but in fact, communicating with people who use sign language fluently will give deaf children the early language exposure that they need. And Grandpa might not have Alzheimer's—his problem might be that he has a severe aphasia and can't tell when he has used the wrong words for what he means.

Research on the way human brains learn, store, and fetch our language knowledge when we need it helps us to figure out better explanations for everyday questions, too. Why is it so much work to learn a language in middle school? An older, purely neurolinguistic answer to this question is that language learning becomes harder with increasing age because children's brain fibers become better insulated as they reach puberty. A very different kind of answer is motivational: middle school language-learning is hard because, while small children can and do spend a huge amount of their time figuring out what the people around them are saying and how to do it themselves, nobody in middle school puts that kind of effort into classroom language learning. A more recent neurolinguistic approach suggests that learning to process just one language early changes connections in our brain that are hard to reorganize for a second language, but that learning two (or more) languages early leaves more possibilities open, so that more languages become easier to add.

In short, some linguists study brains for varied reasons, ranging from fundamental research questions about storage, usage, and development to clinical applications that help humans cope with brain-based language problems.

About the author

Lise Menn is a linguist who worked as a neuropsychology technician and research neurolinguist at the Harold Goodglass Aphasia Research Center of the Boston University School of Medicine before starting her teaching career in the Linguistics Department at the University of Colorado, Boulder, in 1986. Her research has focused on normal language development in young children and on the psycholinguistics of adult aphasia caused by strokes. Many of her books and research papers have been co-authored with psychologists and speech-language pathologists.

Suggestions for further reading

In this book
Other chapters that focus on language and the brain include 13 (language deprivation), 19 (language affecting thought), 21 (language loss), and 20 and 38 (multilingualism).

Elsewhere

Crago, Martha, Johanne Paradis and Lise Menn. 'Cross-linguistic perspectives on the syntax and semantics of language disorders,' in Martin J. Ball et al., eds., *The Handbook of Clinical Linguistics* (Blackwell, 2008), pp. 275–289.

Kroll, Judith F., and Christine Chiarello. 'Language experience and the brain: Variability, neuroplasticity, and bilingualism,' *Language, Cognition, and Neuroscience* vol. 31, no. 3 (2015), pp. 345–348.

Huber, Elizabeth, et al. 'Rapid and widespread white matter plasticity during an intensive reading intervention,' *Nature Communications* vol. 9, no. 1 (2018), www.nature.com/articles/s41467-018-04627-5.

Menn, Lise, and Nina Dronkers. *Psycholinguistics: Introduction and Applications* (Plural Publishing, second edition 2016). See ch. 2, which focuses on the brain and language, and ch. 6, which focuses on psycholinguistics and adult acquired language disorders.

Menn, Lise, and Cecily Jill Duffield. 'Aphasias and theories of linguistic representation: Representing frequency, hierarchy, constructions, and sequential structure,' *WIREs Cognitive Science* vol. 4 (2013), pp. 651–663.

19
Does our language influence the way we think?

Geoffrey K. Pullum

How are language and thought related? Do you think the way you do because of the language you speak? What's the real story on Eskimo words for 'snow'?

Some of the remarks people make that seem superficially to be about language must, if you think about it, be intended as comments about thinking. You may say 'We don't speak the same language' when talking about someone you can't work with, but that nearly always means that the other person's *thoughts* run along different lines. 'I was speechless' nearly always means that I was astonished, not that my vocal folds seized up. And so on.

Of course, language and thought are quite closely related. Language helps us to represent thought explicitly in our minds. It helps us reason, plan, remember and communicate. Communication with others gets most of the press when people talk about language. But could it be that the language we use actually causes us to *think* in certain ways? Could the language we speak make our internal representations of ideas different from those of people who speak a different language?

It's true that different languages phrase things differently. But does that mean it is possible to have thoughts in one language that can't be translated into another? Unfortunately, most of the people who answer 'yes' to this question turn out to have nothing in mind other than single basic word meanings.

It is pretty easy to find words in one language that don't have exact single-word equivalents in another. *Schadenfreude* in German is a famous example. It refers to a kind of malicious pleasure some people find in other people's misfortunes. But does the lack of an exact single-word English equivalent mean that English speakers aren't able to experience that feeling themselves or recognize it in others? Surely not. I believe I just explained in English what *Schadenfreude* means.

Another familiar example concerns color. Some languages have far fewer words than English for naming fairly basic colors. While some (like Greek and Russian) have more than one basic word for shades of blue, quite a few others use the same word for both green and blue. Some languages have hardly any color-name words. Does this mean their speakers can't physically distinguish multiple colors? Apparently not. An experiment in the 1960s found that members of a New Guinea tribe (the Dani) whose language named only two colors were just as good at matching a full spectrum of color chips as English speakers.

And lest we forget, I'd better mention the tired old claim that Eskimos (the Inuit and Yup'ik peoples of arctic Siberia, Alaska, Canada, and Greenland) see the world differently because they have some huge number of words for different varieties of snow. You may be disappointed to learn that there's hardly any truth to the linguistic claim: the eight languages of the Eskimoan family have only a modest number of snow terms. Four were mentioned in a 1911 description of a Canadian Eskimo language by the great anthropologist Franz Boas: a general word for snow on the ground; and words roughly corresponding to 'snowflake,' 'blizzard,' and '(snow)drift.' That was it. The remarkable compounding capabilities of Eskimoan languages make it possible to coin a virtually unbounded array of descriptive words for anything at all, just as English can build descriptions using phrases; but there seem to be very few basic simple words denoting snow types.

Boas was making a point that had nothing to do with numbers of words or their influence on thinking. It was about the way different languages draw slightly different distinctions when naming things. But years of exaggeration and embellishment led to a seductive myth that people with no knowledge of Eskimoan languages repeat over and over in magazines and newspapers. They report with wonder that the Eskimos have some amazing number of words for snow, a number that differs wildly from writer to writer: some say dozens or scores while others say hundreds or thousands. They offer no evidence, and they usually ignore the fact that English, too, has plenty of words for snow—words like 'slush,' 'sleet,' 'avalanche,' 'blizzard' and 'flurry.'

Do the vocabularies of Eskimoan languages really give their speakers a unique way of perceiving, unshared by English speakers? The possibility seems to have been grossly exaggerated. Some writers go as far as claiming that your language *creates* your world for you, and thus that speakers of different languages live in different worlds. This is conceptual relativism taken to an extreme.

The idea that our language inexorably shapes or determines how we think is pure speculation, and it's hard to imagine what could possibly support that speculation even in principle. For one thing, there is surely some thought (e.g., among animals) that is done without the aid of language. But notice also that in order for you to know there was a thought that was understandable for a speaker of (say) Hindi but not for you as an English speaker, you'd need to have that Hindi thought explained to you. If that couldn't be done, no Hindi speaker could convince you that the incomprehensible thought really existed.

In reality, things don't seem to be that way at all. Take as an example the Hindi word *kal*. It picks out a particular region of time: surprisingly, *kal* refers to both yesterday and tomorrow. You understand it whichever way is appropriate in the context. Does that give Hindi speakers a unique and special sense of time that you can never share? Surely not. Because I have just explained it to you perfectly well, so you can understand it after all.

Certainly, it is not impossible that your view of the world may be subtly influenced by the way your native language tempts you to classify the world; but that doesn't mean that your language defines a shell within which your thought is confined, or that there are untranslatable thoughts that only a speaker of some other language can have. If you find yourself trying to grasp a difficult thought, don't give up and blame your language. Just think a little harder.

About the author

Geoffrey K. Pullum was a professional rock musician for five years before doing a B.A. degree in language at the University of York and earning the Ph.D. in general linguistics at the University of London. For many years he worked as a professor of linguistics at the University of California, Santa Cruz. He was elected a fellow of the American Academy of Arts and Sciences in 2003. After moving to the University of Edinburgh in 2007, he became head of linguistics and English language, and was elected a fellow of the British Academy in 2009. He has published about 280 articles and books on many topics in linguistics, including a major reference grammar of English, *The Cambridge Grammar of the English Language* (2002, co-authored with Rodney Huddleston), which was awarded the LSA's Leonard Bloomfield Book Award in January 2004. His latest book is *Linguistics: Why It Matters* (Polity, 2018).

Suggestions for further reading

In this book

Other chapters that suggest questions about relationships between language and mental processes include 35 (babies and language), 18, 20, and 21 (language and the brain), 15 (glossolalia), 13 (language deprivation), 10 and 46 (gendered words and grammar), as well as 12 and 14 (animal communication. More information about Hindi appears in Chapter 44 (official languages of India).

Elsewhere

Lucy, John Arthur. *Language Diversity and Thought: A Reformulation of the Linguistic Relativity Hypothesis* (Cambridge University Press, 1992).

Major book-length study of the 'linguistic relativity' hypothesis that the grammar of our native language affects the way we think about reality; it contrasts English with the Yucatec Maya language of Mexico.

Martin, Laura. '"Eskimo words for snow": A case study in the genesis and decay of an anthropological example,' *American Anthropologist* vol. 88, no. 2 (1986), pp. 419–423. A critique of the absurdly exaggerated stories that have arisen concerning Eskimoan snow terminology.

Preston, John, ed. *Thought and Language* (Royal Institute of Philosophy Supplement 42, Cambridge University Press, 1997). A collection of serious papers on language/thought relations by some important modern philosophers.

Whorf, Benjamin Lee., ed. by John B. Carroll. *Language, Thought, and Reality: Selected Writings* (MIT Press, 1964). Edited collection of the (fairly accessible) writings of Whorf, who was perhaps the most important popularizer of the idea that language shapes thought.

20

How does the brain handle multiple languages?

Judith F. Kroll and Kinsey Bice

How does the bilingual brain juggle two languages? What does language mixing tell us about bilingualism? Does speaking more than one language change the brain?

You are sitting at a cafe sipping an espresso when your attention is drawn to a conversation taking place at the next table. The people are switching from English to Spanish and back to English again. They are speaking quickly and, despite your best attempt to politely ignore them, you can't help but try to understand how they can be mixing languages so easily. Until recently, many thought that code-switching—the act of mixing two languages in the middle of an utterance—reflected lack of knowledge of one language or laziness on the part of the bilingual speaker. What we now know is that code-switching may be a form of linguistic athleticism, revealing the skilled ability of proficient bilinguals to speak each language, mix the two languages, and rarely make an error of speaking a language with someone who doesn't know that language.

How do bilingual brains juggle the presence of two languages? Contrary to the view that the two languages might reside in separate places in the brain, many recent studies suggest that the same brain networks support both languages. Experiments conducted in the last twenty years show that when bilinguals read, speak, or listen to one language alone, the other language comes online, sometimes to the point where that language is on the tip of the bilingual speaker's tongue. The constant activity of the two languages means that they begin to influence each other, even at early stages of new language learning and also after individuals become highly proficient bilingual speakers. We might have thought that all of these interactions across the bilingual's two languages would confuse them and make understanding and speaking difficult. Our cafe speakers suggest otherwise. Learning to choose the language to speak appears to create a set of new skills that benefit bilinguals.

What are the consequences of a life of using two languages frequently? The constant juggling of the two languages leads to the development of control abilities that reduce errors in language but that also spillover into cognition more generally. Bilinguals become expert jugglers, able to use each language at will while also mixing them easily. That expertise may become especially important when a situation in daily life requires that a person quickly resolve a situation that is ambiguous (with two alternatives in conflict), switch from one task to another, or take multiple perspectives in decision making. Bilinguals may use the same brain structures as monolinguals to solve real-life problems, but recent studies suggest that the bilinguals use them more efficiently.

Perhaps the most provocative recent finding is that, as individuals age, a life of being a bilingual juggler appears to protect them against the severity of cognitive decline. Cognitive decline occurs in all healthy older adults, bilingual and monolingual alike, with increased word-finding difficulties and increased difficulty in resolving conflict and switching problems. Bilinguals seem to be advantaged in solving these problems relative to their monolingual peers, suggesting that a life of using two languages actively may come to create a level of mental fitness that better maintains these cognitive functions. For older adults facing pathology, such as developing dementia, the effects of bilingualism are even more dramatic, delaying the onset of dementia symptoms by four to five years. Bilinguals are able to compensate for the loss of cognitive function for longer than monolinguals. Although bilingualism does not protect against dementia itself, it prolongs the independence of bilingual speakers beyond the ability of any known drugs.

When is it too late to benefit from bilingualism? We used to think that true bilingualism described only individuals who were exposed to two languages from early childhood and who maintained the two languages throughout their lives. While early bilingualism may have some special benefits, we now know that it is never too late to begin learning a second language and to observe benefits for even older adult learners. New research reveals a level of flexibility in new learning that extends past early childhood and that illuminates not only language learning but mechanisms of brain function and learning more generally.

And what is the effect of language mixing and bilingual exposure for the youngest infants who come into the world in a dual-language environment from the start? Contrary to the concern that dual language exposure will confuse them or disrupt language and cognitive development, the evidence suggests that bilingually exposed babies develop a speech system that is more open to new language learning. Early bilingual development may differ from the monolingual norm, but the consequence is to enhance language abilities and change how they pay attention to their environment and how they are able to control their attention.

We see signs across the entire lifespan to suggest that bilingualism is a model of plasticity that creates a level of openness to new language experiences and new learning. Understanding the cognitive and neural mechanisms that enable these changes is the challenge for the next stage of research.

About the authors

Judith F. Kroll is distinguished professor of psychology at the University of California, Riverside and the former director of the Center for Language Science at Pennsylvania State University. The research that she and her students conduct concerns the way that bilinguals juggle the presence of two languages in one mind and brain. Their work, supported by NSF and NIH, shows that bilingualism provides a tool for revealing the interplay between language and cognition that is otherwise obscure in speakers of one language alone. She is a fellow of the AAAS, the APA, the APS, the Psychonomic Society, and the Society of Experimental Psychologists. She was one of the founding editors of the journal *Bilingualism: Language and Cognition* (Cambridge University Press), a founding organizer of *Women in Cognitive Science*, a group developed to promote the advancement of women in the cognitive sciences and supported by NSF (http://womenincogsci.org), and a co-founder of *Bilingualism Matters* at UC Riverside (www.bilingualismmatters.ucr.edu).

Kinsey Bice is a post-doctoral researcher in the Department of Psychology at the University of Washington. Her research considers what individual differences make it easier or better to learn a new language later in life, and also how to put people into the right state of mind to maximize language learning. She received her Ph.D. from the Department of Psychology at Pennsylvania State University with a dual title in Language Science and a specialization in Cognitive and Affective Neuroscience. Her work has been supported by the NSF, the Dingwall Foundation, and the Washington Research Foundation. As a member of *Bilingualism Matters*, she seeks to dispel myths about bilingualism and language learning to illuminate how bilingualism is not only normal, but most likely beneficial for children, adults and society.

Suggestions for further reading

In this book
The development of multilingual individuals is discussed in Chapters 35 (babies and language), 18 (language and the brain), 38 (bilinguality), and 40 (adult language learning); multilingual societies are discussed in Chapters 43 (lingua francas) and 44 (official languages of India).

Elsewhere
Abutalebi, Jubin, et al. 'Bilingualism tunes the anterior cingulate cortex for conflict monitoring,' *Cerebral Cortex* vol. 22, no. 9 (2012), pp. 2076–2086.

Alladi, Suvarna, et al. 'Bilingualism delays age at onset of dementia, independent of education and immigration status,' *Neurology* vol. 81 (2013), pp. 1938–1944.

Bialystok, Ellen, et al. 'Bilingualism: Consequences for mind and brain,' *Trends in Cognitive Sciences* vol. 16 (2012), pp. 240–250.

Green, David W. and Li Wei. 'Code-switching and language control,' *Bilingualism: Language and Cognition* vol. 19 (2016), pp. 883–884.

Kroll, Judith F., and Paola E. Dussias. 'The benefits of multilingualism to the personal and professional development of residents of the U.S.,' *Foreign Language Annals* vol. 50 (2017), pp. 248–259.

Kroll, Judith F., et al. 'Bilingualism, mind, and brain,' *Annual Review of Linguistics* vol. 1 (2015), pp. 377–394.

Werker, Janet. 'Perceptual foundations of bilingual acquisition in infancy,' *Annals of the New York Academy of Sciences* vol. 1251 (2012), pp. 50–61.

21
Can you lose language?

Daniel Kempler and Mira Goral

Is it possible to forget language once you've learned it? What happens to language in cases of aphasia or dementia? Can bilinguals lose their first language?

People typically develop their native language without direct instruction or conscious effort in childhood and their language ability remains stable throughout their lives. However, various neurological and social conditions can result in loss of language abilities. Language impairment in adulthood rarely involves total loss and generally affects certain aspects of the language system more than others.

Linguists are interested in how language impairments vary between individuals, and use the study of language impairment as a window onto the underlying organization and the brain bases of language. Examples of three distinct types of language impairment follow.

First, we'll discuss *aphasia*. This is a very common type of acquired language impairment. Aphasia is caused by damage to part of the brain. Brain injury can be caused by internal factors (a stroke, a tumor) or external forces (a fall, a car accident). Depending on the location and extent of brain damage, the language impairment might be mild or severe and can affect individual or multiple aspects of language (speaking, understanding, reading, writing). A person with aphasia will have trouble finding the words they want to say, and grammatical miscues may be apparent in their sentences. Multilingual speakers can experience comparable impairment in all their languages or different levels and patterns of impairment across their languages.

Anomia, the most common aphasia symptom, manifests as trouble coming up with words, similar to the normal tip-of-the-tongue phenomenon, only more frequent and more severe. Linguistic studies of anomia have revealed that aspects of word meaning and categories of words (e.g., nouns vs. verbs) can be differentially disrupted, leading to theories about how we organize words—and their various meanings—in our brains.

Another aphasia symptom, *agrammatism*, is characterized by difficulty producing and understanding sentences, particularly those with more complex grammar, such as passive voice sentences (e.g., 'The package was mailed by the man') or those with embeddings (clauses within clauses, e.g., 'The man mailed the package that contained an important document'). Agrammatism is particularly interesting to linguists because it suggests that grammar is conceptually and neurologically separable from other components of language, such as semantics (i.e., word meaning).

Other aphasia symptoms also highlight the ways in which components of language interact. For instance, occasionally an individual will have difficulty reading, but retain the ability to write, suggesting that those two systems (which are commonly impaired together) can be dissociated in aphasia, and therefore must rely on distinct brain mechanisms.

Most people with aphasia improve their language and communication abilities over time and with intervention, although most never regain their pre-aphasia abilities. Aphasia rehabilitation—facilitated by clinical speech-language therapists—consists of practice to improve speed and accuracy of language production and comprehension as well as learning compensatory strategies, including the use of technology, to improve communication.

Next, we'll discuss *dementia*. Other than a subtle increase in tip-of-the-tongue episodes and memory lapses that interfere with following a conversation or understanding a complex sentence, language generally persists through older adulthood relatively unscathed. The mild language impairments that people experience as they age are likely due to slowing of sensorimotor and cognitive processing that accompanies aging. This contrasts with *dementia*, the progressive degeneration of cognitive abilities, which affects a significant number of older adults.

In dementia, unlike aphasia, language loss happens in the context of cognitive impairments that change over time. Language impairment in dementia is slowly progressive and irreversible. Dementia has many different causes, including Alzheimer's disease, Frontotemporal dementia, and Parkinson's disease. Each dementia syndrome creates unique patterns of language and cognitive impairment associated with distinct patterns of brain deterioration.

For instance, in early Alzheimer's disease, word-finding difficulties occur alongside short-term memory deficits, followed by difficulty understanding complex language and disorientation to time and space. Interestingly, while the individual with moderate-severe Alzheimer's may have very little understanding of what is going on around them, they still produce grammatically well-formed (but often senseless) utterances. Individuals who acquire another dementia called Primary Progressive Aphasia experience language impairment before other cognitive declines are apparent. Linguists study the impairments associated with dementia to better understand the relationship between aspects of language and cognition and their neurological bases.

Finally, we'll discuss *first-language attrition*. Individuals may experience partial loss of a native language through lack of use and/or interference from another language in the absence of brain injury or neurological impairment. This type of language decline is called *language attrition*. The extent of decline in language abilities depends on the age at which language use changes. Extreme cases include children who were adopted at a young age and completely stop using their first language, leading to a near-complete loss of that language.

On the other end of the continuum are adults who become immersed in an environment in which they are primarily exposed to their second language—for instance, immigrants from Hungary, Brazil, or Japan living in an English-speaking country like the U.S. These individuals continue to use their first language to varying degrees. Here language attrition may be subtle and manifest as increased word finding difficulty, insecurity about the use of certain expressions and sayings, as well as interference from the second language into the first. Language attrition may be reversible if the individuals are re-immersed in their first-language environment.

Language is a very robust system, and people rarely lose their command of it. Nonetheless, language can be lost under specific physical and social circumstances—and the study of language loss is a vibrant area of research for linguists, speech-language pathologists, neurologists, and neuropsychologists.

About the authors

Daniel Kempler is professor emeritus at Emerson College, and trained as a linguist and speech-language pathologist. His research has focused on neurologically based communication disorders and he has published widely on aphasia, dementia, Parkinson's disease and is the author of *Neurocognitive Disorders in Aging* (2005). His teaching and clinical work has emphasized voice disorders. He has held the positions of Chief of Speech Pathology at USC and professor and chair of Communication Sciences and Disorders at Emerson College.

Mira Goral, Ph.D., CCC-SLP, is a professor of Speech-Language-Hearing Sciences at Lehman College and the executive officer of the Speech-Language-Hearing Sciences program at the Graduate Center of the City University of New York. She is also an adjunct professor at the Center for Multilingualism in Society across the Lifespan, the University of Oslo. She has published journal articles and book chapters in the areas of bilingualism, multilingualism, aphasia, language attrition, and language and cognition in aging, and has co-edited two books, *Aspects of Multilingual Aphasia* (2012) and *Bilingualism: A Framework for Understanding the Mental Lexicon* (2017).

Suggestions for further reading

In this book
For more information about why linguists study brains, see Chapter 18. Other chapters that focus on language and cognition include Chapters 13 (language deprivation), 19 (language affecting thought), 20 (the brain and multilingualism), and 36 (hyperglots). Further discussion of language attrition can be found in Chapters 38 (bilingualism) and 52 (future of Spanish).

Elsewhere
Bauby, Jean-Dominique. *The Diving Bell and the Butterfly: A Memoir of Life in Death* (Vintage 1998). Translated by Jeremy Leggatt. This memoir chronicles the important role of speech and language therapy during the author's recovery from stroke-induced paralysis.

Brookshire, Robert H., and Malcolm McNeil. *Introduction to Neurogenic Communication Disorders* (Elsevier, 8th edition 2014).

Köpke, Barbara, et al. *Language Attrition: Theoretical* Perspectives (John Benjamins, 2007).

History of language

22

What was the original language?

Barry Hilton

When did language begin, and how? What language did the earliest humans speak?

Questions like these were easier to answer back when supernatural explanations were in fashion. You could just say that language was a gift granted to humans when they first appeared in the world, like their senses and their limbs. The answer to 'when?' was 'when Adam and Eve lived in the Garden of Eden'; and as for identifying that first language, Chapter 24 of this book describes some of the theories advocated during that era.

Beginning in the eighteenth and nineteenth centuries, though, a different way of thinking about the history of languages began to develop: the science of historical linguistics. As described in more detail in Chapter 23, its practitioners have identified relationships among existing languages and shown how they fit into 'family trees' reflecting thousands of years of changing and splitting from previously existing languages.

In many cases, these language genealogies point back to ancestral languages that no longer exist. Historical linguists have developed a method of reconstructing those long-dead languages from clues surviving in their descendants, and almost all of them believe it allows valid deductions about languages whose descendants have been separated for up to about 7,000 years.

Some think that it's possible to look, cautiously, even further into the past. Most, though, believe that languages separated for 10,000 or more years have changed too much for the method to be reliable; and modern humans have been around five or ten times that long.

This leaves a large gap to bridge: what happened to change wordless early humans, or near-humans, into the talkers that we've since become? And what was their speech like? There's been no shortage of speculation on these subjects, beginning in the late nineteenth century. Maybe, it was suggested, early people invented speech by imitating animal calls or other natural sounds and, over time, attaching meaning to them; or by attaching meaning to their own inarticulate grunts of emotion or exertion. Guesses like these are a legitimate step in scientific inquiry if they generate hypotheses that can be verified, but there didn't seem to be any way of finding relevant concrete evidence. Critics, even friendly ones, applied mocking names like the 'bow-wow' theory, the 'ding-dong' theory, the 'pooh-pooh' theory, and the 'yo-he-ho' theory. For several decades, the Origin of Language was an unfashionable field of study.

Beginning around the last quarter of the twentieth century, though, increasing amounts of brainpower—and more and more *kinds* of brainpower—have been devoted to the question, and interest is picking up.

Paleontologists studying fossils and ancient artifacts have improved our chronology of humanity's early past, sharpening debate over *when* language is most likely to have emerged. With the first tool-using members of genus *Homo* some two million years ago? Or perhaps with the artistic flourishing that roughly coincided with the appearance of anatomically modern humans some fifty thousand years ago?

Other researchers have looked for modern analogs to the earliest human language origins: psychologists have intensively studied how infants make the transition from wordless creatures into talking children; primatologists have devised ingenious experiments to determine how much or how little human-like linguistic behavior apes can learn; and neurologists and anatomists making clearer to us just how extensively human language is enabled and limited by the human body and brain.

The anatomists, in particular, have suggested that language was impossible until humans had both the right kind of vocal tract to produce speech sounds and the right kind of nervous system to control them. One physical distinction between modern humans and all other animals, even chimpanzees and earlier humans, appears to be critical: a lowered larynx. Your dog can eat his food in a few quick gulps, but he can't talk. You can talk, but you can also choke from food lodged in your larynx. The human ability to make speech sounds is not a bonus provided by the body systems designed for breathing, chewing, and swallowing—it's just the opposite: the lowered larynx (and associated changes in the pharynx and mouth) is a handicap to the usual animal uses of mouth and throat, but on balance this handicap is far outweighed by the great survival value in speech. You can talk—and participate in civilization—because you *can't* wolf down your food.

It's unlikely that these multidisciplinary efforts will allow us to reconstruct what words our prehistoric ancestors said, or what their speech sounded like. But some interesting late twentieth-century research suggests that we may be able to know something about the *grammar* of the earliest languages—how words came together to form sentences. Within the past few centuries several new languages of a special kind have been born. European colonists arriving in the third world communicated with their local laborers using *pidgin* languages, a makeshift language using vocabulary from one or more languages, strung together with a grammar from another language or two. When children are raised speaking a pidgin as their native language, they turn it into a full-fledged language called a *creole*, with a broader vocabulary and a more elaborate grammar (see Chapter 30 for more details about pidgins and creoles). Now here's the fascinating part: unrelated creole languages in places as far apart as Suriname, Haiti, Hawai'i, and Papua New Guinea have radically different vocabularies, but some researchers find their grammars very similar, suggesting that the human brain may be hardwired to create particular patterns of speech. Could this be a clue to how the earliest languages worked?

About the author

Barry Hilton served as the associate editor of the first and second editions of this book and was a member of the review board of the radio series from which it was adapted. He is a freelance writer/editor and independent scholar living in Maine. He is an honors graduate of Harvard College who, after graduate studies at Cornell, Yale, and George Washington Universities and the Foreign Service Institute, has travelled extensively and lived in both Europe and Asia. In a variety of U.S. government assignments, he has made professional use of Vietnamese, Chinese, Japanese, French, and German. He describes himself as an 'armchair philologist and recovering polyglot.'

Suggestions for further reading

In this book

The origins and history of languages are discussed in the subsequent chapters of this section (Chapters 24–28), as well as 29 (language change) and 30 (pidgins and creoles).

Elsewhere

Bickerton, Derek. *Roots of Language* (Karoma, 1981). A readable, serious presentation of the by-no-means-mainstream theory that evidence relevant to the prehistoric origins of language can be found in creolization processes observable today.

Kenneally, Christine. *The First Word* (Viking, 2007). A comprehensive and highly readable overview of the multidisciplinary investigations that are revitalizing the study of how language began.

23

Do all languages come from the same source?

Allan R. Bomhard

What does it mean to say that two languages are related? Are all languages related?

Have you ever studied German, or Spanish, or French? If you have, you were probably grateful for cognates, foreign words that sound and look like English words with related meanings. In German, your parents are your *Mutter* and your *Vater*. In Spanish, they are your *madre* and *padre*. In French, they are your *mère* and *père*.

These resemblances not only make language learning easier, they tell us something about the history of languages. English and German share some similar vocabulary because they are both descendants of a language called Proto-West-Germanic, spoken by tribes in northern Europe well over 2,000 years ago. Over time, migrations split that language into dialects, and some of the tribes moved across the North Sea into the British Isles. Fifteen centuries of separate development turned the speech of the British Isles into varieties of English, while the language of the mainlanders turned into varieties of German. So we have two languages, obviously different, but also so alike that they are clearly part of the same language family.

Language families, like families of people, can be connected into larger and larger groupings, spreading outward in territory and backward in time, as our relatives do on a genealogy chart.

The Germanic family that English, German, and several other languages belong to has a cousin, the Romance family, which includes not only French, Spanish, Portuguese, Italian, and Romanian, but also several other languages that have Latin as their common ancestor; and there are other cousins as well.

Now let us look back a step further in time. The Germanic and Romance language families share a common ancestor called Proto-Indo-European. It was spoken by tribes living some 6,000–7,000 years ago, probably in the steppes north and east of the Black Sea. From there, the tribes spread westward across Europe and eastward and southward into Iran and northern India. As they spread and lost contact with each other, their language changed into Germanic, Romance, Celtic, Greek, Armenian, Albanian, Baltic, Slavic, Indic languages, Iranian languages, and several extinct languages. Taken together, they make up the Indo-European language family, the most widely spoken group of languages in the world today.

As different as the Indo-European languages were from one another, they all preserved bits of ancient vocabulary and grammar. Linguists have used these bits to figure out relationships and actually reconstruct the older languages. Sir William Jones opened the way at the end of the eighteenth century through a remarkable analysis of the classical Indic language Sanskrit, showing that Sanskrit was related to languages in Europe such as Latin and Greek. And now, even though no one has seen or spoken the original Indo-European parent language for thousands of years, we have a fairly good idea of what it may have sounded like. Moreover, by cracking the code of Indo-European, we have taken a big step toward answering the question, Can all languages be linked in a super family tree that begins with a single ancestral language?

To find out, linguists have increasingly studied and compared *non*-Indo-European languages, asking: What families do they belong to? How far back can those families be traced? Clearly, many non-Indo-European languages can be grouped together. For example, Finnish, Estonian, and Hungarian, which are surrounded by Indo-European in the heartland of Europe, are not in the Indo-European language family. But they do group together with several other languages to form a non-Indo-European language family called Uralic. Similarly, there is a family called Turkic, which takes in Turkish, Azerbaijani, Uzbek, Uighur, Kazakh, and several other languages in Central Asia. In East Asia, the Sino-Tibetan family includes over 250 languages, the largest of which is Mandarin Chinese. Linguists think that at least 200 language families exist; the obvious next question is, Are any of these families related to each other?

There are theorists who believe that we can lump all of the languages of the world—including even language isolates like Basque, which seems to fit nowhere—into a handful of giant families, called 'macrofamilies,' such as Nostratic, Dene-Caucasian, Amerind, and the like.

But maybe we cannot go that far. The fact that the word for 'dog' in an Australian native language called Mbabaram is 'dog' does not mean that Mbabaram is related to English; it is just a random resemblance. The fact that Chinese calls coffee *kāfēi* does not mean that Chinese is related to English, either; the origin is a Turkish word that happens to have been borrowed by both Chinese and English. Furthermore, we know that languages change continuously; new words join the vocabulary, while older words, including cognates, disappear, and the same has happened to grammar. After tens of thousands of years of change, can we reliably find a common ancestor? Do all languages come from the same source? The answer is: Maybe ... and maybe not. It is too soon to know.

About the author

Allan R. Bomhard is a linguist living in Florence, South Carolina. His main areas of interest are distant linguistic relationship and Indo-European comparative linguistics. He has published over eighty articles and thirteen books.

Suggestions for further reading

In this book

Chapters on the history and origins of language include 22 (earliest language), 24 (the language of Adam and Eve), 29 (language change), 30 (pidgins and creoles), and 27 (origins of English). Chapters focusing on language families include 44 (languages of India) and 50 (Native American languages).

Elsewhere

Baldi, Philip. *An Introduction to the Indo-European Languages* (Southern Illinois University Press, 1983). This book presents an excellent overview of the Indo-European language family. Both beginners and knowledge-able readers will find much of interest here.

Bomhard, Allan R. *Reconstructing Proto-Nostratic: Comparative Phonology, Morphology, and Vocabulary* (E. J. Brill, 2008). Though fairly technical, this book is the most comprehensive treatment of the subject that has been published to date. Revised, corrected, greatly expanded, and renamed *A Comprehensive Introduction to Nostratic Comparative Linguistics, with special reference to Indo-European* (published online under a Creative Commons License, 3rd edition 2018).

Comrie, Bernard, ed. *The World's Major Languages* (Oxford University Press, 2nd edition 2009). This book is a comprehensive survey of the major languages spoken in the world today.

Everett, Daniel. *How Language Began: The Story of Humanity's Greatest Invention* (Liveright Publishing Corporation, 2017). Everett theorizes that the origins of human language can be traced all the way back to Homo erectus. From those early beginnings, Everett details the critical changes over time that led to the development of modern languages.

Fortson, Benjamin W., IV. *Indo-European Language and Culture: An Introduction* (Wiley-Blackwell, 2nd edition 2010). This book is an exhaustive, up-to-date, and accessible overview of Indo-European comparative-historical linguistics. Beginners should start by reading Baldi's book listed above before tackling this work.

Pedersen, Holger, translated by John Webster Spargo. *The Discovery of Language: Linguistic Science in the Nineteenth Century* (Indiana

University Press, 1931). Though dated and lacking information about more recent scholarship, this book remains the most comprehensive introduction to the history of the study of languages.

Ruhlen, Merritt. *A Guide to the World's Languages, Vol. 1: Classification* (Stanford University Press, 1991). Though this work is a comprehensive and reliable guide to the classification of nearly all known languages, some of the proposals regarding larger groupings remain controversial.

24

What language did Adam and Eve speak?

E. M. Rickerson

Does the language of Adam still exist? What language did God speak in the Garden of Eden? Did Adam and Eve speak Indo-European?

In the Old Testament story of the Garden of Eden, Adam was created as a fully formed modern being, with all the faculties of *Homo sapiens*, including the ability to speak. We can only guess what Adam might have said to Eve in their early chats, but we do know that both of them could talk. Eve had a fateful conversation with a persuasive snake, and one of Adam's first tasks on earth was linguistic: '... *and Adam gave names to all cattle, and to the fowl of the air, and to every beast of the field*' (Genesis 2:19). But what language did Adam use? Presumably it was the same one in which the serpent's words were couched and which the first couple heard when they were sternly evicted from Paradise.

It certainly wasn't English, which is a relatively young language, nor was it any of the world's languages that you might think of as 'old,' such as Chinese or Greek. Leaving aside the question of how the first language-using people came into being, it is now fairly well accepted that humans were physiologically *able* to speak—that the vocal apparatus was ready to produce more than the calls or growls of our fellow mammals—as early as 50,000 years ago, or earlier. Because we can trace languages only as far as their early written records, and because writing itself emerged only around 5,000 years ago, we are left with a gap of thousands of years. And throughout those millennia, the language of the first human beings was undergoing constant and profound change. Therefore, whatever else we may say about the original language, it is clear that *none* of the languages currently spoken on the planet bears any resemblance to what may have been spoken in the legendary Garden of Eden.

That is the modern view, based on what we have learned about language since religious explanations gave way to the patient collection of linguistic data. But before the eighteenth century—from the earliest days of Christianity through the Middle Ages and Reformation—it was taken for granted that Adam spoke the first language, and that the *Lingua Adamica*, the language he used, still existed. For most of that time, the leading candidate for the honor was Hebrew, if only because it was the language in which the Old Testament was handed down. In the fourth century St. Jerome asserted that only the family of Eber had not been so foolish as to help build the Tower of Babel. As a result, when God destroyed the tower and scattered its builders, Eber's people—the Eberites, or Hebrews—were not punished, and continued to speak the original tongue. St. Augustine and other Christian church fathers accepted without question that Hebrew was the *Lingua Adamica* and, for the next thousand years or so, almost everyone agreed. I find it ironic that the scholarly discussion of this topic took place in Latin, which was as close to a universal language as there was in Europe during that time—yet no one suggested that Latin could have been the original tongue. The idea of Hebrew as the Adamic language had a firm hold on the imagination throughout the Renaissance, and even beyond.

The nature of Adam's language was an especially hot topic in the sixteenth and seventeenth centuries, when it was thought to be a divine or 'perfect' language, in which words coincided so harmoniously with the things they identified that people understood them without having to be taught their meanings. But not everyone accepted that this perfect language was, or had been, Hebrew.

With the Renaissance came a sense of nationhood in Europe, and the *Lingua Adamica* idea served as a way to build national pride. In Germany, people rallied to the language of Luther's Bible and asserted that German was closest to the language of Adam; some even claimed that Hebrew was derived from German. Linguistic nationalism also prompted a claim for Dutch or Flemish. The theory ran that citizens of Antwerp were descendants of Noah's son Japeth, who had settled in northern Europe after the Flood and *before* the Tower of Babel, so that Dutch preserved the purity of the Adamic tongue. Improbable arguments were also made for the divine status of Celtic, Basque, Hungarian, Polish, and many other languages. This was the time when Sweden was making itself felt as a world power, so it is not surprising that Swedish too was proposed as the original language, again based on the story of Japeth. And that leads us to my favorite theory: the suggestion that God spoke Swedish in Paradise, Adam Danish, and the snake ... French.

After the Age of Reason loosened the grip of religion on philosophical thinking, the divine origins of language became a lesser concern. In the eighteenth and nineteenth centuries it was gradually understood that words and the things they stand for are not magically connected, and that languages are not divinely given. They are created by human communities, not a heavenly force. It became clear that language was a matter of agreement that certain combinations of sounds would be used to mean whatever a community decided they should mean. Instead of theological debates, scholars in Europe used scientific criteria to compare known languages, and to figure out how they are related and how they developed over time. It is telling that when they discovered Indo-European, they made no claim that it was the original language. The discovery only made us realize that we cannot penetrate the linguistic past to its absolute beginnings. At that point the idea of an Adamic language became the stuff of poetry.

About the author

E. M. ('Rick') Rickerson served as the general editor of the first and second editions of this book. He is professor emeritus of German, director emeritus of the award-winning language program at the College of Charleston (South Carolina), a former deputy director of the U.S. government's Center for the Advancement of Language Learning, and an associate of the National Museum of Language. In 2005 he created the radio series on languages (*Talkin' about Talk*) from which *The Five-Minute Linguist* was adapted. He is currently retired in the mountains of North Carolina.

Suggestions for further reading

In this book

The origins and history of languages are also discussed in Chapters 22 (earliest languages), 23 (language relationships), 27 (origins of English), 29 (language change), and 30 (pidgins and creoles).

Elsewhere

Eco, Umberto. *The Search for the Perfect Language* (Blackwell, 1995). A comprehensive and very readable history of the ways in which the idea of an original or perfect language occupied European thinkers for close to 2,000 years.

Olender, Maurice, *The Languages of Paradise: Race, Religion and Philology in the Nineteenth Century* (Harvard University Press, 1992). A scholarly discussion of ideas that underlay the comparative study of languages in the nineteenth century. Chapter 1 touches briefly on the *Lingua Adamica*.

Rickerson, Earl. *The Lingua Adamica and its Role in German Baroque Literature* (unpublished Ph.D. dissertation, 1969; available at UMI Dissertation Services: www.umi.com/products_umi/dissertations). Chapters 1–3 provide an overview of how the Adamic language was viewed before the Age of Reason.

25
Where does grammar come from?

Joan Bybee

What aspects of language make up the grammar? Is it okay for grammar to change? How does change take place?

All languages have grammar, by which we mean those little function words (*the, a, will, some*) or prefixes and endings that signal meanings such as past, present and future. Grammar also includes the way we arrange words so effortlessly yet consistently in our native language; for instance, the fact that we say 'the dog is sleeping on the couch' rather than 'is dog ingsleep couch the on.' Although most of us are aware of words changing, we tend to think of grammar as more stable. But in fact, grammar is also constantly in flux.

The Language Police always deplore the loss of grammar—for instance, that we don't know when to use *whom* any more—but it's barely noticed that languages also develop *new* grammar. And yet they do! All the time.

For example, English has some old ways to indicate future tense by using *will* and *shall*. But these days American English speakers and younger Britons hardly use the word *shall* at all. A new way to mark future has evolved in the last few centuries from the expression *be going to* plus a verb. So when we say 'it's going to rain,' we mean it purely as a prediction about a future event—it doesn't mean that something or someone is going anywhere at all.

In Shakespeare's time, on the other hand, if you used *going to*, it always meant literally that someone was going from one place to another for some purpose.

How did this change happen? It is a process that linguists call 'grammaticalization,' through which a word or sequence of words like *be going to* may acquire a change of meaning and take on a grammatical function. Such changes happen very gradually, over long periods of time, and several things usually happen at once.

The change of meaning often starts when inferences get associated with certain phrases. For instance, if I say 'I'm going to visit my sister' I am telling you both where I am going and what my intentions are. After a while, the intention meaning becomes even more important than the movement meaning. From the intention meaning in turn you can make an inference about what will happen in the future. So eventually, we can use *be going to* to indicate future.

Humans are very interested in other people's intentions, so expressions of intent are a more important piece of information than expressions about movement in space. So when *be going to* began to be used for intention it was used more often. When phrases are used a lot they begin to lose some of their impact, and the original meaning seems to get bleached away. They also tend to be said faster, and pronunciation erodes: so when *going to* came into constant use as a main way to express the future, it started to turn into 'gonna'—a new bit of grammar. Not everybody has yet recognized 'gonna' as a future tense marker, but that is clearly the function it is serving, especially in spoken language. In another hundred years it will no doubt be firmly entrenched in our grammar books—until another way to express future develops.

Grammaticalization happens over and over, and in all languages. In fact, many languages use a phrase with a verb such as 'go' to signal the future. You can see it in Spanish, French, the African languages Margi, Krongo, Mano, and Bari, the Native American languages Cocama and Zuni, the Pacific language Atchin, and many more. One of the reasons languages are similar is that they develop over time in very similar ways.

And it is not just markers of future time that develop this way, but all kinds of grammatical markers. For instance, it is common for the indefinite article *a/an* (as in 'a dog') to develop from the word for 'one.' In English, you can still hear the 'n' of 'one' in the 'an' of 'an apple.' Also, in Spanish, French, German, and other European languages, the relation between the word for 'one' and the indefinite article 'a' or 'an' is quite clear. Spanish *un/una*, French *un/une* and German *ein/eine* all mean both 'one' and 'a/an.'

Or think about prepositions, those little words like *at*, *over*, *with*, *above*, or *through* that link up with a noun to talk about when, where or how something was accomplished ('at ten o'clock,' 'over the bridge,' 'with daring speed'). They too are what we think of as part of 'grammar' and have undergone changes in their meaning and use. Our words *before* and *behind*, for example, are composed of an old preposition *be-* and the noun *fore* meaning 'front' and *hind* meaning 'the back part of a body.' While these prepositions started out with meanings having to do with space ('before the castle,' 'behind the ramparts'), they are now also used for time ('before noon,' 'I'm running behind schedule').

There are many features of grammar whose origins we don't know, but because the process of grammaticalization is so common, it's safe to assume that all words and parts of words that have a grammatical function came from other words.

And that helps us explain how the very first language got grammar. The earliest language was no doubt fairly 'telegraphic' in nature, a collection of individual words, supplemented with gestures to convey meaning. But soon after human beings could use words as symbols and join two words together, they surely used some combinations very frequently. With the making of inferences and inevitable changes in pronunciation, the development of grammar was put in motion. And that was a great thing, because—despite its bad reputation among those who struggled with it in school—it is the existence of grammar that makes fluent, connected speech possible.

About the author

Joan Bybee (Ph.D., UCLA) is distinguished emerita professor of linguistics at the University of New Mexico. At the University of New Mexico she has served as associate dean and department chair. In 2004 she served as president of the Linguistic Society of America. Professor Bybee is considered a leader in the study of the way language use impacts language structure. She has authored books and articles on phonology, morphology, language typology and language change. Her book *The Evolution of Grammar* (1994) uses a database of seventy-six languages to study the way in which languages spontaneously develop new grammatical structures.

Suggestions for further reading

In this book

Other chapters discussing grammar include 4 (universal grammar), 12 (animal communication), 13 (language deprivation), and 50 (Native American languages). Chapters 29 (language change) and 30 (pidgins and creoles) discuss how grammar changes over time.

Elsewhere

Deutscher, Guy. *The Unfolding of Language* (Henry Holt and Company, 2005). A lively popular introduction to linguistics from the point of view of language change.

Heine, Bernd, and Tania Kuteva. *World Lexicon of Grammaticalization*. (Cambridge University Press, 2002). A reference work listing the words that take on grammatical functions across a large number of languages.

Hopper, Paul, and Elizabeth Traugott. *Grammaticalization* (Cambridge University Press, 2003). A textbook for linguistics students about grammaticalization.

26

Where did writing come from?

Peter T. Daniels

When did writing begin? How did it start? Was it invented more than once?

Dozens of writing systems have been used over the ages around the world, in a bewildering variety. They're written from left to right or right to left or top to bottom or even from bottom to top. Their symbols come in many shapes and sizes. The origins of spoken language, tens of thousands of years before writing, are cloudy; but we have a very good idea of how and when writing began. Fragments of some of the earliest writing still exist, carved on rocks, so we can trace its evolution through time.

The invention of writing was almost inevitable when a society grew complex enough to need it. As long as people are in small groups, everyone knows who did what for whom. But when people settle in towns, commerce becomes more complicated. A potter makes pots, a weaver makes cloth, an administration collects taxes. At some point, there's a need to keep track of everyone's contributions. Records might be kept with knots in string, or with notched sticks. And everywhere, people draw pictures to represent things. In Stone Age caverns, we drew pictures of prey animals. In modern times, we make pictures of things we want people to *buy*.

A second condition for inventing writing is a certain *kind* of language, a kind in which words are likely to consist of only one syllable. The reason seems to be that if you don't already know how to read with an alphabet, you aren't able to break down a syllable into its individual consonants and vowels. And if the words of your language are mostly just one syllable, then the picture you make to represent one of them is both a picture of its meaning and a record of its sound. That picture is useful when you need to write a different word, one that sounds similar but has a meaning not so easy to picture.

These conditions gave rise to writing at least three times that we know of, and probably more that have left no trace. Writing appeared over 5,000 years ago in ancient Mesopotamia (now southern Iraq), representing a now-dead language known as Sumerian. A completely different writing system was created in China close to 4,000 years ago for an ancestor of modern Chinese. And in Central America around the fourth century CE yet another system was developed out of earlier, little-known sign systems to write down the Mayan languages. That system died a few centuries later with the Mayan empire. So all the writing systems in the world today can be traced back to just two places: China and ancient Iraq.

Writing turns out to be a pretty useful thing to have. And once one group invents it, nearby peoples tend to adopt it. Japan adopted Chinese characters and started writing Japanese words with them. On the other side of the Asian continent, Sumerian writing was adopted for many languages between about 2500 and 1000 BCE, early in its history changing in form from pictures to easier-to-write abstractions. Sumerian inspired the Egyptian hieroglyphs we know from temples and tombs. And hieroglyphs became the raw material for the Phoenician abjad that gave the world its alphabets and abugidas. (See Chapter 16 for explanations of these terms.)

There are hundreds of such scripts in use today (now counting each variety of Roman alphabet, say, separately). Besides Europe and the Western Hemisphere, they're used across south and southeast Asia and on into Oceania. Most of them use twenty to thirty symbols. But they range in size from the alphabet used for a language of the Solomon Islands, with eleven letters, to the Khmer abugida of Cambodia, with seventy-four. They look as different as English, Russian, or Hebrew, but it's fairly easy to show that *every* abjad, alphabet, and abugida—those named above and many more—has a common origin: ancient Phoenicia on the eastern shores of the Mediterranean.

The Phoenicians brought their abjad to the Greeks, who (accidentally!) turned it into an alphabet and passed it via the Etruscans to the Romans, who gave our letters the shapes they have to this day. Greek was also the model for alphabets in eastern Europe, such as the Cyrillic alphabet of Russian and other tongues. Another descendant of Phoenician was the Aramaic abjad, from which came writing as different-looking as Hebrew and Arabic—and all the writings of India and beyond.

Writing originated from some pretty basic characteristics of human beings and human society. And yet it is not found everywhere. Despite writing's obvious uses, fewer than half of the world's languages even have a writing system! Most languages are only spoken. But that's changing as missionaries and linguists actively spread writing—mostly the Roman alphabet—to developing nations around the globe.

Where would we be without writing? It's a remarkable part of language—and of human history. Imagine all the things we might have never known about were it not for writing.

About the author
Peter T. Daniels is one of the few linguists in the world specializing in the study of writing systems. He has published articles in a variety of journals and edited volumes, and contributed to several encyclopedias. He co-edited *The World's Writing Systems* (1996) with William Bright and was section editor for Writing Systems for the *Encyclopedia of Language and Linguistics* (2006). His book *An Exploration of Writing* was published by Equinox in 2018.

Suggestions for further reading

In this book
Other chapters that talk about written language include 16 (scripts), 29 (language change), and 39 (Chinese), as well as 53 (social media) and 56 (text messaging).

Elsewhere
Daniels, Peter T. *An Exploration of Writing* (Equinox, 2018). Sets forth the author's ideas about the nature and history of writing systems, addressed to the general reader.

Daniels, Peter T., and William Bright, eds. *The World's Writing Systems* (Oxford University Press, 1996). A standard reference for facts about writing systems, past and present.

DeFrancis, John. *Visible Speech: The Diverse Oneness of Writing Systems* (University of Hawaii Press, 1989). Stresses that all writing is based on the *sounds* of languages.

Diringer, David. *The Alphabet* (Funk & Wagnalls, third edition 1968). Jensen, Hans. *Sign, Symbol and Script* (George Allen & Unwin, 1969). These two books may take some effort to find, but each offers a very full history of writing. Diringer is more readable, Jensen more reliable and scholarly.

Gnanadesikan, Amalia. *The Writing Revolution: From Cuneiform to the Internet* (Wiley-Blackwell, 2009). A well-written, compact summary of the important writing systems of the world.

Nakanishi, Akira. *Writing Systems of the World* (Tuttle, 1980). One-page descriptions of 29 current scripts, illustrated with newspaper front pages, and over 100 illustrations of other scripts, ancient and modern.

Rogers, Henry. *Writing Systems: A Linguistic Approach* (Blackwell, 2005). Preferable among the small number of textbooks on writing.

27

Where did English come from?

John Algeo

Was English originally a German dialect? If so, how did it get to be English? How did the Vikings and the French get involved? What can dictionaries tell us about the history of English?

English did come from the same ancestor as German, but there's a lot more to the story. In the fifth century, Celts lived in the British Isles. But warfare among them got so fierce that one local king asked for help from Germanic tribes living in southern Denmark and northern Germany. He got more than he bargained for: the tribes came as allies, but they liked the island so much they decided to take it over.

Two of the main tribes in this group came from regions called Angeln and Saxony, which is why we call the language they brought to Britain 'Anglo-Saxon.' The speech of the tribes who stayed on the European Continent eventually became modern German, Dutch, and Scandinavian languages; and Anglo-Saxon, also known as 'Old English,' grew into the English we speak today.

On their new turf, these Germanic Anglo-Saxons started to talk in new ways. The tribes they drove to the fringes of Britain left them some Celtic place names. But more important, the new-comers were converted to Christianity, so a good deal of Latin crept into their language. Another influence showed up in the ninth and tenth centuries, when Britain—which by then was called Angleland, or England—was invaded again, this time by Scandinavian cousins of the Anglo-Saxons: Viking raiders, who ruled all of England for a couple of decades. Their contact with the Anglo-Saxons was so close that they've given us some of our everyday words—like *sister*, *sky*, *law*, *take*, *window*, and the pronouns *they*, *them*, and *their*.

The greatest additions to English resulted from another invasion we all know about: '1066 and all that.' In that year, England was conquered by descendants of a different group of Vikings—the 'Normans,' men of the North, who had settled in the tenth century along the coast of France and there learned French. The region of France they ruled still bears their name—Normandy. When they took over England, they made French the government language. So England became a trilingual country: officials used Norman French, the church used Latin, and the common people spoke a version of English we call 'Middle English.'

The common people were by far the majority, and by the late fourteenth century their English reasserted itself over French as the language of Britain. But it was a different English from the Anglo-Saxon spoken before the Conquest. Over the years it had absorbed an enormous number of French words for legal, governmental, military, and cultural matters—words like *judge*, *royal*, *soldier*, and a host of food terms like *fruit* and *beef*. And its grammar had changed dramatically, losing many of its inflectional endings.

At the end of the fifteenth century, printing was introduced in England, which helped standardize the language. And in the sixteenth century, Englishmen began to explore the globe. They encountered new things that needed to be talked about with new words. They settled in North America, the Caribbean, Africa, South Asia, Australia, and the South Seas.

As it became a global language, English influenced other languages—and was influenced by them. Most of our core vocabulary comes directly from Old English: words like *mother*, *earth*, *love*, *hate*, *cow*, *man*, and *glad*. But we have borrowed words from many other languages: Greek (*pathos*), Welsh (*penguin*), Irish

Gaelic (*galore*), Scots Gaelic (*slogan*), Icelandic (*geyser*), Swedish (*ombudsman*), Norwegian (*ski*), Danish (*skoal*), Spanish (*ranch*), Portuguese (*molasses*), Italian (*balcony*), Dutch (*boss*), German (*semester*), Yiddish (*bagel*), Arabic (*harem*), Hebrew (*shibboleth*), Persian (*bazaar*), Sanskrit (*yoga*), Hindi (*shampoo*), Romany or Gypsy (*pal*), Tamil (*curry*), Chinese (*gung-ho*), Japanese (*karaoke*), Malay (*gingham*), Tahitian (*tattoo*), Tongan (*taboo*), Hawaiian (*ukulele*), Australian Dharuk (*boomerang*), Australian Guugu Yimidhirr (*kangaroo*), Bantu (*goober*), Wolof (*jigger* or *chigger*), Russian (*mammoth*), Hungarian (*paprika*), Turkish (*jackal*), Algonquian (*possum*), Dakota (*tepee*), and Navajo (*hogan*). Most of the words in a large dictionary—perhaps as many as 85 or 90 percent—either are loanwords from other languages or have been invented in English using elements borrowed from other languages.

By now the language has expanded far beyond its tribal beginnings. It's a first language in countries settled by the English. It's a second language in countries like India and the Philippines, which were part of the British Empire or under American influence. And it's a foreign language used around the globe for business, science, technology, and commerce. A Scandinavian pilot landing his plane in Greece talks with the air controller in English. It's also the main language of the worldwide internet.

So did English come from German? No—it's closely related to German, but what began as the tongue of a small Germanic tribe in northwestern Europe morphed over time into something very different—a blend of dozens of languages that came to be spoken in virtually every country in the world.

About the author

John Algeo is professor emeritus at the University of Georgia. He is the author of *British or American English? A Handbook of Word and Grammar Patterns* (2006) and *The Origins and Development of the English Language* (sixth edition 2010), and editor of *The Cambridge History of the English Language: Volume 6, English in North America* (2002) and

Fifty Years Among the New Words (1993). He was past president of the Dictionary Society of North America, the American Dialect Society, and the American Name Society. He and his wife, Adele, wrote 'Among the New Words' in the journal *American Speech* for ten years.

Suggestions for further reading

In this book

Other chapters on the origins and history of languages include 22 (earliest languages), 23 (language relationships), 30 (pidgins and creoles), and 31 (sign language). Chapters that discuss various aspects of how languages evolve include 29 (language change), 25 (grammar), 49 (U.S. dialect change), and 28 (Latin), as well as 53 (social media) and 56 (text messaging).

Elsewhere

Algeo, John. *British or American English? A Handbook of Word and Grammar Patterns* (Cambridge University Press, 2006). A guide to the many grammatical differences, often unnoticed, between the two principal national varieties of the language.

Algeo, John. *The Origins and Development of the English Language* (Wadsworth, sixth edition 2010). A detailed history of the English language from prehistoric Indo-European to present-day developments in vocabulary and usage.

Hogg, Richard M., ed. *The Cambridge History of the English Language* (Cambridge University Press, 1992–2001). A six-volume history of English written by some of the leading scholars in the subject, dealing with all aspects of the subject and including extensive bibliographies.

Leech, Geoffrey, and Jan Svartvik. *English: One Tongue, Many Voices* (Palgrave Macmillan, 2006). A masterful and up-to-date survey of the English language: its global spread, international and local varieties, history from obscurity to primacy, usage and uses, standards and creoles, style and change in progress, politics and controversy.

28

Is Latin really dead?

Frank Morris

Didn't people stop speaking Latin after the 'barbarians' sacked Rome? Why should anybody but a scholar care about a dead language?

Dead? Well, surely we can agree that Latin is vital for scholars, but doesn't that prove all the more that for the rest of us Latin is really dead and gone? Surely not! In fact, it is very much at work in today's world, and there is a long and varied list of evidence to show how alive it is.

To begin, Latin *vocabulary* has never fallen out of use. About 80 percent of words in Italian, Spanish, French, and Portuguese are inherited from Latin, their parent language. Even languages not so closely related to Latin can have an amazingly high percentage of words. For example, roughly 60 percent of all English words—and 90 percent of its multisyllabic words—are borrowed or derived from Latin. Words like 'labor,' 'animal,' 'deficit,' 'insomnia,' 'stimulus,' and 'vigil,' to name just a few.

Nor has Latin ever ceased being used to communicate ideas among human beings in the real world. In 2005 the world witnessed the Latin funeral mass for John Paul II; heard the announcement, *Habemus Papam* ('we have a Pope'), to mark the election of his successor; and listened to the Latin speech the elevated Benedict XVI delivered to the College of Cardinals. All that was on live international TV. And then, to announce a topic he would address at the next World Day of Social Communications, Pope Francis tweeted about *nuntii fallaces* ('fake news'). Beyond the Vatican, we can hear Latin at ceremonial occasions, such as Harvard University graduations, which for over 350 years have featured a graduate delivering a Latin oration. We can visit in person or online with enthusiasts who regularly meet for conversation in Latin. We can tune in to radio broadcasts or read the news online in Latin. We can also research topics on *Vicipaedia*.

Actually, Latin is ubiquitous. We find it at work in the courtroom: *habeas corpus* ('you should have a body'); *nolo contendere* ('I do not want to contest'); *subpoena* ('under penalty' to compel compliance); *alibi* ('somewhere else'). Every day we abbreviate our way with Latin: e.g., *exempli gratia* ('for the sake of an example'); i.e., *id est* ('that is'); etc., *et cetera* ('and others'); NB, *nota bene* ('note well'). We choose Latin mottos to inspire and guide us: *semper fidelis* ('always faithful') for the Marines; *e pluribus unum* ('one out of many') for all Americans. We turn to Latin for branding and advertising: Lava (Latin for 'wash') soap; Magnavox ('great voice') radio. We utilize and understand Latin words in medicine: *bacterium, coma, nausea, rigor mortis*; in biology: *phylum, species, larva, nucleus*; in anatomy: *biceps, cranium, sinus*; in astronomy: *Mars, Ursa Major, nova*; in mathematics: *calculus, parabola, isosceles, minus*; in schools: *campus, curriculum, alumnus*; in sports: *gymnasium, stadium, discus*; and in everyday speech: *ad hoc, alma mater, de facto, ex officio, ex libris, non sequitur, per capita, quid pro quo, status quo, vice versa*.

Latin, furthermore, has always had its place in popular culture. In the Harry Potter books, for example, we delight in the Latin phrases for curses, charms and spells: *avis* ('bird') creates a flock of birds; *impedimenta* ('hindrances, things on the foot') creates an obstacle; *obscuro* ('I conceal, I cover') hides something. In the Monty Python film *Life of Brian*, a Roman centurion gives the title character a gruff Latin grammar lesson by making him write *Romani exite domum* ('Romans go home') on the town wall 100 times.

Finally, headlines in various media over the years are delivering positive messages: 'Latin makes a comeback' (*Education World*, 2001), 'A dead language that's very much alive' (*New York*

Times, 2008), 'Pope Francis: It's good for young people to study Latin' (Catholic News Agency website, 2017). Indeed, enrollments in Latin in U.S. schools generally have been trending upward, and Latin remains the fourth most commonly studied language in U.S. schools.

What explains such positive interest in Latin? One driving force has been the so-called 'Back to Basics' movement. Administrators, teachers, and parents believe that studying Latin disciplines the mind, provides insight into Western civilization and its values, expands English vocabulary, gives an understanding of grammar that results in better use of English, and provides a basis for the study of other languages. They cite data that associates the study of Latin with the achievement of higher scores on standardized tests. For example, college bound seniors who have taken Latin consistently outscore students of all other languages and subjects on the SATs, and undergraduates in classical languages consistently rank first among all students in verbal scores on the Graduate Record Exam (GRE).

There is more to this story than just returning to the basics and increasing scores on achievement tests. New audiences and wider curricular applications have been developed. Innovative materials and teaching methodologies are making Latin and Classics accessible to all students, not just to the traditional elite. Teachers can capitalize on the vast cultural legacy of Greece and Rome to make interdisciplinary connections between Latin and subjects such as language arts, mathematics, science, social studies, literature, art, music, and mythology. The ultimate reason for Latin's vitality is that, with new, more interactive ways to learn it, students are finding the study of Latin and the Romans to be fun. There are even reports of grade school students who beg teachers to skip recess … so they don't have to stop their Latin lesson.

So is Latin really dead? Surely not. It is in play all around us. We can find it at the Vatican, on the radio, on the internet, in contemporary books and films, at ceremonies like graduations, in elementary school classrooms, and in conversations among a growing number of enthusiasts around the world. Speakers of English and many other tongues draw on Latin for their everyday words and expressions and for terminology needed in their techni-cal and professional lives. Although there were times, not so long ago, when Latin was less frequently taught in schools and perhaps was thought of as dull or out of fashion and near death, those days are obviously over. Latin is indeed alive and well!

About the author

Frank Morris earned a Ph.D. in classics from the University of Cincinnati and taught Latin and Greek at the College of Charleston in Charleston, SC from 1978 until his retirement in 2010. He continues to serve as director of the Charleston Latin Program, and has been training teachers to teach Latin in elementary schools since the mid-1980s.

Suggestions for further reading

In this book

Latin is a vivid case study in the endangered-language issues that are the subjects of Chapters 5 (languages of the world), 34 (language death), and 64 (language rescue), and 47 (languages of the U.S.). Its long history exemplifies the ways of language evolution discussed in Chapters 25 (grammar), 27 (origins of English), 29 (language change), 30 (pidgins and creoles), and 49 (U.S. dialect change), as well as 53 (social media) and 56 (text messaging).

Elsewhere

LaFleur, Richard A., ed. *Latin for the Twenty-First Century: From Concept to Classroom* (Foresman, 1998). A survey of trends in the teaching of Latin.

Ostler, Nicholas, *Ad Infinitum: A Biography of Latin* (Walker Books, 2007). A history of the Latin language.

Pearcy, Lee T. *The Grammar of Our Civility* (Baylor University Press, 2005). An examination of the history and purposes of the teaching of classics in the U.S.

www.promotelatin.org/ Website of the National Committee for Latin and Greek offering many informative links.

www.radiobremen.de/bremenzwei/rubriken/latein/latein114.html. A source for news broadcasts in Latin.

Language variation
and change

29
Do languages have to change?

John McWhorter

Why is our English different from Shakespeare's? What can English spelling tell us about language change? What kinds of changes do languages undergo? Can we stop English from changing?

Have you ever left a Shakespeare performance feeling worn out from trying to understand what the characters were saying? It wasn't just because Shakespeare's English is poetic, but because the English that Shakespeare knew was, in many ways, a different language from ours. When Juliet asked 'Wherefore art thou Romeo?' she wasn't asking where Romeo was—after all, he's right there under the balcony! *Wherefore* meant *why*. But we no longer have that word because languages shed words all the time. And they also take on new ones, like *blog*.

Languages are always changing. It's as inevitable for them to change as it is for cloud patterns in the sky to take on new forms. If we see a camel in the clouds today and walk outside and see the same camel tomorrow, then something's very wrong. It's the same way with languages—every language is in the process of changing into a new one.

In English, you can see this easily because our spelling often preserves the way the language was pronounced 700 years ago. The word *name*, for instance, used to be pronounced 'NAH-muh.' But we stopped saying the final *e* and the AH sound (NAHme) drifted into an AY sound (NAYm).

Pronunciation is not the only area of impermanence: grammar changes, too. English used to be a language where verbs at the end of the sentence came. That is, a thousand or so years ago that's how you would have said that last sentence, with 'came' at the end. We also used to have more pronouns. *You* was only used to mean 'y'all'; the singular form you used, for talking to an individual person, was *thou*. And then for the 'generic' *you*—as in a sentence like 'You only live once'—the pronoun was *man*. Now we just use *you* for all those meanings.

This kind of change is why we face the task of learning foreign languages. If language didn't change, we'd still all speak the first language that popped up in Africa when humans first started to talk. But once the original band of people split off into separate groups, the language took on new forms in each new place—different sounds, different word order, different endings. The result was that Chinese has tones; some Australian languages have only three verbs; some African languages have click sounds; many Native American languages pack a huge amount of information into single words; and English uses the same word *you* whether one or two or many people are involved.

The only thing that makes it look as if a language stays the same forever is print, because print does stay the same way forever. We think of Latin as a dead language, because it was written, we can see it on the page, and we know that the particular language captured on that page is not spoken by anybody any more. But technically, the Latin we struggle with in classrooms was just one stage in a language that never died. It just drifted into several new versions of itself, like French, Spanish, and Italian. We don't think of the language of the opera *Don Giovanni* as 'street Latin'—it's a new language altogether. There was never a day when people in Italy woke up and proclaimed 'We were speaking Latin last night but today we're speaking Italian!' Latin just morphed along like cloud formations, which might look like a camel one day and like a weasel the next.

But within our lifespans, it's hard not to think of changes in our language as mistakes. There was a time, fifteen or twenty centuries ago, when Latin was the official language of the territory we now call France. The bureaucrats and scholars who lived there and spoke it heard the beginnings of French around them, but to them it sounded like just grade-F Latin, not like a new language in its own right. Gray zones are always tricky. So, when young people say things like 'She's all "don't talk to me like that" and I was like "you shoulda known anyway,"' they're pushing the language on its way to new frontiers. It was through the exact same kinds of changes that English got from *Beowulf* to Tom Wolfe.

About the author

John McWhorter, a contributing editor at *The Atlantic* who also teaches linguistics at Columbia, earned his Ph.D. in linguistics from Stanford University in 1993 and became Associate Professor of Linguistics at the University of California, Berkeley, after teaching at Cornell. His academic specialty is language change and language contact. He is the author of *Our Magnificent Bastard Tongue: The Untold Story of English* (2008), *The Power of Babel: A Natural History of Language* (2003), *Words on the Move* (2016), *The Language Hoax* (2015), and *Doing Our Own Thing: The Degradation of Language and Music in America and Why We Should, Like, Care* (2003). He has written books on Black English such as *Talking Back, Talking Black* (2016) and on creoles such as *The Creole Debate* (2018). Dr. McWhorter has appeared on radio and television programs such as *The Colbert Report, Late Night with Don Lemon, AM Joy with Joy Reid, The Jim Lehrer NewsHour,* and *All Things Considered,* and he hosts *Slate*'s linguistics podcast, Lexicon Valley.

Suggestions for further reading

In this book

The origins and history of languages are also discussed in Chapters 22 (earliest languages), 23 (language relationships), 24 (the language of Adam and Eve), 27 (origins of English), 30 (pidgins and creoles), and 51 (African American English). Chapters specifically focusing on language change include 8 (prescriptivism), 25 (grammar), 27 (origins of English), 28 (Latin), 30 (pidgins and creoles), and 49 (U.S. dialect change), as well as 53 (social media) and 56 (text messaging).

Elsewhere

Bryson, Bill. *Mother Tongue* (Morrow, 1990). A great way to get a handle on how English became what it is after starting as a close relative of German (now a foreign tongue to English speakers); witty and goes down easy.

McWhorter, John. *The Power of Babel* (Perennial, 2003). A book-length survey of how one original language became 5,000, with discussion of what dialects and creoles are and why writing slows down language change.

Ostler, Nicholas. *Empires of the Word* (HarperCollins, 2005). A chronicle of the birth, spread and sometimes decline of languages of empire like English, Arabic and Sanskrit, lending a nice sense of how language change is natural and eternal.

30
Aren't pidgins and creoles just bad English?

John M. Lipski

What is a pidgin language? Is creole more than just food? Are pidgins and creoles the same thing? Are they real languages?

How una dé? Uskain nius? These two greetings, the first from Nigeria and the second from Cameroon, both mean roughly 'Hi, what's happening?' Both use words from English (like 'how', 'there', and 'news'), but combine them in new ways. They're the kind of language we're using when we greet someone by saying 'long time no see', or when we invite a friend to come have a 'look-see', or use 'no can do' when something's not possible. When we do that, what we're speaking is no longer English—it's a new language, based on English words but with simpler grammar and vocabulary. 'Look-see' and 'no can do' come from a language once called China Coast Pidgin English, which was used by sailors and merchants throughout the Pacific. But what kind of bird is this 'pidgin'?

Imagine for a moment that everyone reading this article spoke a different native language, and that the only English any of us knew was the result of a year or two of limited exposure somewhere earlier in our lives. If we all got stranded on the proverbial desert island, we might well find that the only way we could communicate would be to use our bits of English with one another. As the years went by, with no grammar books and no native speakers to correct us or teach us new words, we'd all develop survival skills in this way of talking, and we'd invent combinations that a true native speaker of English would barely recognize.

A language formed like this—among people who share no native language and are forced to communicate using elements of one that none of them speaks well—is what linguists call a pidgin. The word probably comes from South Sea traders' attempt to pronounce the word *business*. Most pidgins don't form on desert islands; they're created when speakers of different languages have to communicate with each other using bits and pieces of a language imposed on them—for example as slaves on plantations in the Americas, as contract laborers on South Pacific islands, or as itinerant vendors in urban marketplaces in Africa.

Pidgins start out as bits-and-pieces languages, but something happens when children are born to pidgin-speaking parents. Like children everywhere, as they grow they absorb the language they hear around them and make it their own. Unlike other children, though, as they learn their parents' language they expand and transform it from a makeshift jargon into a full-fledged new language. These new languages, spoken natively by the next generation in the family, are called *creole* languages by linguists (although sometimes the name 'pidgin' continues to be used in non-specialist contexts). There are dozens of creole languages scattered around the world, derived from European languages such as English, French, and Portuguese, but also from Arabic, Swahili, and other non-European tongues. English-based creoles are used in the South Pacific from Papua New Guinea to the Solomon Islands and northern Australia. Gullah in South Carolina and Georgia and Hawaiian Pidgin are creole languages native to the U.S., while Cape Verde Portuguese Creole in Massachusetts and Haitian Creole in Miami and New York are among the U.S.'s more recent immigrant languages.

Creoles and pidgins often include words and expressions that speakers of languages like English or French would recognize, but with very different meanings. For example, *beef* in west African Pidgin English refers to any animal whose meat can be eaten. So a pig could be a 'beef'. In Papua New Guinea the word *meri* (from the English name 'Mary') is a word for woman, any woman. The grammatical structures of creole languages are often simpler than the corresponding patterns in the source languages, but creoles can also express nuances not found in the sources. They're by no means simply 'light' or 'broken' versions of 'real' languages—they've earned their status as legitimate languages in their own right.

Creole languages have millions of speakers. They have grammar books, dictionaries, and written literatures. They're taught in schools and used in radio, television, and the press. They have their own names, such as Tok Pisin in Papua-New Guinea and Bislama in Vanuatu, and are increasingly serving as official or quasi-official languages in the Philippines, the Caribbean, South America, and elsewhere. The language used at the beginning of this article is spoken in much of west Africa. It's the language of African popular music and literature, including novels by the Nobel laureate Wole Soyinka.

Speakers of languages with long literary traditions sometimes laugh at creole languages, thinking of them—and their speakers—as inferior. But such views are not justified. Creoles are new languages, at most a few hundred years old, but they emerged through struggles similar to those that gave birth to many of the world's new nations, and they deserve the same respect.

Article 1 of the Universal Declaration of Human Rights, translated into Nigerian Pidgin English, begins: *Everi human being, naim dem born free and dem de equal for dignity and di rights wey we get, as human being.* Speaking a creole language with pride and dignity is one of those basic human rights.

About the author

John M. Lipski is Edwin Erle Sparks Professor of Spanish Linguistics in the Department of Spanish, Italian, and Portuguese and director of the Program in Linguistics at Pennsylvania State University. He received his Ph.D. from the University of Alberta, Canada. His research interests include Spanish phonology, Spanish and Portuguese dialectology and language variation, the linguistic aspects of bilingualism, and the African contribution to Spanish and Portuguese. He is the author of twelve books and more than 250 articles on all aspects of linguistics. He has served as editor of the journal *Hispanic Linguistics* and as associate editor of *Hispania*, and is currently acquisitions editor for the Spanish linguistics monograph series at Georgetown University Press. He has done fieldwork in Spain (including the Canary Islands), Africa, Brazil and all Spanish-speaking countries in Latin America, the Philippines, Guam, and many Spanish-speaking communities within the United States.

Suggestions for further reading

In this book
The ways languages begin and develop are also discussed in Chapters 22 (earliest languages), 23 (language relationships), 25 (grammar), 27 (origins of English), 28 (Latin), 29 (language change), 49 (U.S. dialect change), 51 (African American English), and 62 (dictionaries). Chapter 31 (sign languages) discusses the importance of children in transforming an invented language into a natural one.

Elsewhere
Holm, John. *An Introduction to Pidgins and Creoles* (Cambridge University Press, 2000).

Michaels, Susanne Maria, et al., eds. *The Atlas of Pidgin and Creole Language Structures (APiCS) Online*, http://apics-online.info. This website provides information on 130 grammatical and lexical features of 76 pidgin and creole languages from around the world, including interactive map of languages and features.

Mufwene, Salikoko. *The Ecology of Language Evolution* (Cambridge University Press, 2001). This book places creole language formation in a broader context of language in society.

Romaine, Suzanne. *Pidgin and Creole Languages* (Longman, 1988). Either of these books would be a good place for readers to pursue the topic of this chapter in greater detail. Holm is more accessible, Romaine more comprehensive.

Todd, Loreto. *Pidgins and Creoles* (Routledge and Kegan Paul, 1974). A very basic book, still not outdated in terms of the general concepts.

31

Do Deaf people everywhere use the same sign language?

Leila Monaghan

Is sign language really a language? Can you use it no matter what country you go to?

There are two widespread myths about sign languages. One is that they aren't languages at all. The second is that signing is a *universal* language—that any signer can understand all signers anywhere in the world. Both of these beliefs are false.

It's easy to understand why you might doubt sign languages are really languages; they're so different from what we often call 'tongues.' They have to be seen rather than heard. And some signs look like what they represent, making them easy to dismiss as mere gestures. But that view was refuted in 1960, when William Stokoe published the first scientific description of American Sign Language (ASL). Stokoe was an English professor at Gallaudet University (the world's only liberal arts university for Deaf people) and found the language being used around him as systematic and as grammatical as any other language. He showed that (except for sound) sign languages have all the linguistic features that spoken languages have.

A word in spoken language, of course, is composed of sounds, made with your mouth and tongue. In ASL, the components of a word can include how you shape your hand, where you place it, and how you move it. For example, the signs for APPLE and CANDY are made at the same place, by the side of the mouth, but their handshapes are different: APPLE is made with a crooked index finger while CANDY is made with a straight index finger.

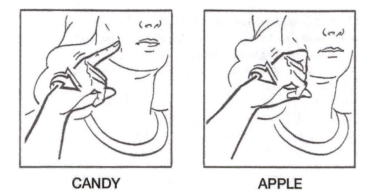

CANDY   **APPLE**

Sign languages have complex grammars, so that words can be strung together into sentences, and sentences into discourse, just like any language. With signs you can discuss any topic, from concrete to abstract, from street slang to physics. And if you have any doubt, think about public events you've seen recently. After watching a signer interpret a political speech or a play, could anyone still believe it's not a language?

As for the second myth, people often don't realize that sign languages vary, just as spoken languages do. Whenever groups of people are separated by time and space, separate languages, or at least separate dialects, develop. This is as true for sign as it is for spoken languages: there are, for example, differing dialects of ASL. Like spoken American English, it varies both geographically and across social and ethnic groups. For example, regional varieties of ASL exist and there is one variety of ASL that is primarily associated with Black Deaf communities.

The variations in sign language are even more evident internationally. The signs used in Italy aren't readily understood by a signer using ASL, and vice versa. Even languages that you might think are connected may or may not actually be. British Sign Language and American Sign Language, for example, are unrelated to each other, despite the fact that countries share English as their spoken language: the histories of the British and American Deaf communities are separate. American Sign Language is actually related to French Sign Language because a Deaf Frenchman helped start many of the earliest schools for deaf children in the United States. Although some signs in all sign languages are iconic (they look like the object they are representing), even iconic signs can differ. In ASL, the sign TREE is made by holding up a single hand with fingers spread. The Danish version is done by tracing the outline of a tree with both palms. Both signs are based on the same image, a classic leafy tree, but they look quite different.

American Sign Language   Danish Sign Language

Whenever people can see each other but are somehow prevented from communicating with speech or writing, they turn to signing of some kind. Think about monks who have taken vows of silence but need to cooperate on monastery business, or widows from certain Australian Aboriginal groups, who are expected not to speak during a long period of mourning. In cases like these, the sign languages developed reflect the grammar of the languages the monks or widows knew and could speak if they chose. But those are exceptions. Most sign languages are *not* based on the spoken language in the culture around them.

There are millions of sign language users around the world. For example, there are at least a half-million users of ASL in the U.S., and possibly as many as two million. It's routinely taught in schools across the country, and all 50 states recognize it in some way. At the last count, there were 218 colleges and universities whose language requirement could be satisfied by the study of ASL. In Britain, there are estimated to be over 150,000 people who use British Sign Language (BSL) as a home language, and on March 18, 2003, the U.K. government officially recognized BSL as an official British Language.

Sign language is remarkable for its ability to express everything spoken language does, using completely different human capabilities. According to Hearing people who have learned it, communicating in sign opens a window to a different culture and can give you a totally different perspective—especially an understanding of how Deaf people perceive the world. So the next time you think about learning a new language, think about learning how to sign.

About the author

Leila Monaghan teaches anthropology at Northern Arizona University. She received her Ph.D. in linguistic anthropology at the University of California, Los Angeles and her dissertation work was with the New Zealand Deaf community. She also has a recent M.A. in history from the University of Wyoming. Her publications include a co-edited book *Many Ways to be Deaf* (Gallaudet University Press, 2003), a 2002 *Annual Review of Anthropology* article on Deaf communities with Richard Senghas, *HIV/AIDS and Deafness* (co-edited with Constanze Schmaling, Forest Books, 2006), and 'Women at Little Bighorn' in *Montana Magazine of Western History* (2017).

Suggestions for further reading

In this book

Languages designed by their users are discussed in Chapters 11 (artificial languages in general) and 17 (Esperanto). Other chapters discussing language acquisition by children include 30 (pidgins and creoles), 35 (babies and language), 18 (language and the brain), 13 (language deprivation), and 59 (children and second languages).

Elsewhere

Gertz, Genie, and Patrick Boudreault. *The Sage Deaf Studies Encyclopedia* (Sage Publications, 2016). Up-to-date encyclopedia with over 300 reference articles written by a range of international scholars. Topics include diversity, health, history, and education.

Klima, Edward, and Ursula Bellugi. *Signs of Language* (Harvard University Press, 1979). Classic and very readable introduction to sign language linguistics.

LeMaster, Barbara, and Leila Monaghan. 'Variation in sign languages', in Alessandro Duranti, ed., *A Companion to Linguistic Anthropology* (Blackwell, 2004), pp. 141–165. Introduction to the study of sign languages and Deaf communities in linguistic anthropology and sociolinguistics. Both disciplines look at the interaction between language and culture rather than just at languages themselves.

Mathur, Gaurav, and Donna Jo Napoli. *Deaf around the World* (Oxford University Press, 2011). Review of sign language linguistics and Deaf civil rights issues from an international group of Deaf and hearing scholars and activists.

Monaghan, Leila, et al., eds. *Many Ways to be Deaf* (Gallaudet University Press, 2004). A collection of fifteen articles from fourteen countries on the history, culture and language of local Deaf communities. Includes a brief overview of 500 years of Deaf history.

Padden, Carol, and Tom Humphries. *Inside Deaf Culture* (Harvard University Press, 2006). Two of the United States' foremost experts on Deaf culture. Interesting and accessible.

Interesting websites

http://library.gallaudet.edu

www.aslpro.com/cgi-bin/aslpro/aslpro.cgi

www.sematos.eu/index.html

www.signcommunity.org.uk

www.sign-lang.uni-hamburg.de/dgs-korpus/index.php/welcome.html

32

Do men and women talk differently?

Deborah Cameron

Is the way you talk affected by your sex? What are the real differences between men and women? How should we explain them?

How many of the following statements have you heard before? And how many do you think are true?

1 Women talk more than men.
2 Women have more advanced verbal skills than men.
3 Women use more emotionally expressive language than men.
4 Men's speech style is competitive and self-assertive; women's is co-operative and supportive.

These are all common beliefs in contemporary Western societies. But does the linguistic evidence support them?

In the case of the first statement, 'women talk more than men,' the answer is clearly 'no.' Research shows that if there's a difference, it is usually men who talk more than women.

The second statement, 'women have more advanced verbal skills,' is supported by evidence from experimental studies. But what's rarely pointed out is that the differences are tiny. Our cultural obsession with differences between men and women prevents us from recognizing how much overlap there is.

The third and fourth statements are misleading, because they fail to acknowledge that the way we talk is most strongly influenced by the context—who we're talking to, what about, in what setting, and for what purpose. Many things that get described as gender differences have more to do with these contextual factors than with gender as such: we confuse the two because of the tendency for activities and roles, and the ways of speaking that go with them, to be associated with either women or men. However, research suggests that it's a speaker's *role* rather than their *gender* which has most effect on the way they speak. Male nurses talking to patients adopt the same emotionally expressive style as their female counterparts; women police officers adopt the same unemotional style as their male colleagues.

There's another problem with all the statements I've listed. They imply that there are two groups, 'men' and 'women', whose members all share certain ways of behaving. But in reality men and women come in many different varieties. What it means to talk like a man or a woman is affected by other aspects of identity and experience: age, race, ethnicity, social class, education, national origin, (dis)ability ... the list could go on and on. A lot of common-sense beliefs about language and gender are based on an idea of masculinity or femininity which is specifically young, white, educated and monolingual (usually in English): this does not reflect the real-world diversity of men's and women's linguistic behavior.

Contemporary Westerners are not alone in having beliefs about the way men and women talk. Most societies have beliefs on that subject, but what they are can vary considerably. In some traditional non-Western societies, it's men who are thought to be more verbally skilled than women. (A hundred years ago that was also what Western scientists thought: they assumed men were more intelligent, and that their linguistic behavior reflected that.) In some places, such as the village of Gapun in Papua New Guinea, it's generally agreed that men are co-operative and polite, whereas women are impolite and often downright aggressive. In every culture, the way men and women are said to talk reflects more general ideas about what men and women are like. Or sometimes, what people think they *should* be like. Statements like 'women don't swear,' or 'men don't talk about their feelings' are not so much descriptions of reality as prescriptions for properly feminine or masculine behavior.

So, am I saying that really there are *no* differences? Not at all: if you take any group of people and examine the linguistic behavior of its male and female members, you will usually find some differences (the same applies if you compare group members who differ on some other dimension, like age or education). Many studies of local dialects have found men and women favoring slightly different pronunciations of the same sound. Some researchers analyzing large data samples have found that men use words like 'the' and 'of' more frequently than women, while women use words like 'you' and 'and' more frequently than men. It has also been observed that men are more likely to fill a pause with 'uh,' whereas women are more likely to fill it with 'um.' If these cases are less familiar, it's probably because they resist the popular explanation of gendered linguistic behavior as a direct reflection of what men and women are like. What they illustrate is the way we use small linguistic details to mark identities and social distinctions—a bit like men's and women's shirts buttoning in opposite directions.

Do men and women talk differently? The short answer is 'yes,' but a better one might be 'it depends.' It depends on which men and women you're comparing; it depends on the context they're talking in. And it also depends on what you mean by 'differently': overall, men and women are far more similar than different.

About the author

Deborah Cameron is professor of language and communication at Oxford University in England, where she teaches linguistics and women's studies. Her main research interest is the relationship between language and gender: her books include *The Myth of Mars and Venus: Do Men and Women Really Speak Different Languages?* (2007), and most recently, with Sylvia Shaw, *Gender, Power and Political Speech* (2016). She broadcasts regularly on BBC radio, and occasionally on U.S. National Public Radio. Her blog, Language: a Feminist Guide, aims to make language and gender research accessible to readers around the world.

Suggestions for further reading

In this book

Other chapters that address gender include Chapters 10 (grammatical gender) and 46 (gendered language). Chapters that discuss themes of language and identity include Chapters 31 (Deaf culture), 33 (gay speech), 51 (African American English), and 56 (text messaging).

Elsewhere

Cameron, Deborah. *The Myth of Mars and Venus: Do Men and Women Really Speak Different Languages?* (Oxford University Press, 2007). This book sets out to counter popular myths with evidence from linguistic research.

Coates, Jennifer, and Pia Pichler, eds. *Language and Gender: A Reader* (Wiley-Blackwell, second edition 2011). This collection of articles covers a wide range of topics, from lesbian bar talk to the use of exclamation points in online discussion groups.

Eckert, Penelope, and Sally McConnell-Ginet. *Language and Gender* (Cambridge University Press, second edition 2013). This textbook, written by two of the field's leading scholars, is an excellent guide for anyone seriously interested in the subject.

33

Can somebody 'sound gay'?

Rusty Barrett

Is there a 'gay voice'? Can you tell if someone is gay by the way they talk? Do gay men talk like women?

A voice can sound gay to any listener who has some stereotyped idea of how gay people ought to sound. That doesn't really mean much, though. Somebody can sound like a cantaloupe to a listener who believes they know how cantaloupes talk. Unlike cantaloupes, however, it seems that many people *do* tend to have stereotypes about what gay people (particularly gay men) sound like. This raises two related—and more interesting—questions: *What are the features associated with 'sounding gay'?* and *Can you tell if someone is gay by the way they talk?*

One might assume that a man who sounds gay somehow talks like a woman, but studies have found that the features associated with the perception of femininity and masculinity are not equivalent to those involved in the perception of sexual orientation. A man may sound gay and masculine at the same time. While stereotypes would suggest that gay men might have higher pitched voices or use a wider range of intonation, such patterns do not seem be perceived as marking sexual orientation (e.g., gay or straight), although they do tend to convey gender identity (e.g., masculine or feminine). So, for men to sound gay is *not* the same as sounding effeminate or sounding 'like a woman.'

The features that are perceived as gay-sounding may vary considerably across dialects, languages, and social contexts. Studies of speakers of American English have found that significant patterns involving both vowels and consonants are utilized in projecting gender identity. Particularly with regard to vowels, these patterns tend to involve sounds that are undergoing change, such as the vowel in the word 'sock', which is changing to sound more like *sack* in parts of the northern U.S. (like in *Wis-CAN-son*). In general, the patterns among gay men and lesbians are not particularly different from the features that *all* people use to convey aspects of their social identities.

With respect to the perception of sexual orientation in the speech of men, the most widely studied feature seems to be the production of sibilants (hissing sounds, like *s*, *z* and *sh*)—especially the pronunciation of the *s* sound. Although the stereotype of a 'gay lisp' relates to the pronunciation of *s*, the use of the term 'lisp' to refer to this feature is highly inaccurate. Differences in the positioning of the tongue are a regular part of variation in dialects of English, and obviously not the result of some epidemic speech disorder afflicting men who happen to be gay.

While there are clearly details of pronunciation that listeners associate with sexual orientation, there is no direct relationship between *sounding* gay and actually *being* gay. There are gay men who do not fit the stereotype and straight men who happen to sound gay. Like other forms of 'gaydar' (colloquial term meaning 'gay radar'), using voice quality to try to determine whether people are gay is not going to be 100 percent accurate.

Of course, some gay men may adapt stereotypes of gay speech as way to convey their identities as gay men. However, the social meanings associated with the features of a stereotypically 'gay' voice may be subtler than simply meaning 'I'm gay'. For example, the pronunciation of consonants in ways that are stereotypically perceived as 'emphatic' or 'overproduced' (like the *s* sound), may also mark being articulate, educated, well-spoken or middle class. So, speakers may 'sound gay' simply because they are trying to present themselves as possessing these types of personal attributes (which tend to be positively viewed in gay communities).

It is certainly the case that someone can 'sound gay,' but a person's voice cannot be used to determine if that person is actually gay. So, unless the voice is literally saying, 'I'm (not) gay,' it isn't telling you the person's sexual orientation. You might as well listen to a cantaloupe.

About the author

Rusty Barrett is an associate professor in the Linguistics Department at the University of Kentucky. His research focuses on language and gender, language and sexuality, Mayan languages and language revitalization. He is the author of *From Drag Queens to Leathermen: Language, Gender, and Gay Male Subcultures* (Oxford University Press) and (with Kira Hall) is a co-editor of the (forthcoming) *Oxford Handbook of Language and Sexuality*.

Suggestions for further reading (and viewing)

In this book

For more information about pronunciation, see Chapter 7 (sounds of language). Chapters that discuss themes of identity include Chapters 31 (Deaf culture), 32 (men's and women's speech), 51 (African American English), and 56 (text messaging).

Elsewhere

Munson, Benjamin, and Molly Babel. 'Loose lips and silver tongues, or projecting sexual orientation through speech,' *Language and Linguistics Compass* vol. 1 (2007), pp. 416–449. A general overview of research on the perception of sexual orientation in speech.

Podesva, Robert J., and Penelope Eckert, eds. *Sociophonetics and Sexuality*, special issue of *American Speech* vol. 86 (2011). A collection of articles concerning phonetic studies of sexual orientation.

Thorpe, David, director. *Do I Sound Gay?* (Sundance Selects Distributors, 2014). A documentary about stereotypes regarding people 'sounding gay.'

34
Why do languages die?

Christopher Moseley

What do we mean when we speak of a language 'dying'? How does it happen? Can it be predicted? Can it be prevented?

This is not a happy subject. For those of us who love languages, it's tragic to see that they're dying at a very rapid rate. About half the world's languages have fewer than 10,000 speakers—about enough to fill a small-town football stadium—and some are down to only a handful. When those last speakers die, the language dies too. Some experts think that nearly 90 percent of the languages spoken in the world today, including even some that still have millions of speakers, may be lost by the end of this century.

Why do languages disappear? The short answer is that they are no longer passed on to younger speakers, and eventually only the elderly speakers are left to die out. But what would make a community no longer want to pass on its spoken heritage to the younger generation? Circumstances vary from place to place. Let's look at some examples. In the mountains of India we can find—if we hurry—the Sulung people, now down to only a few thousand, who've been driven to a remote area by constant warfare with neighboring tribes. If they're wiped out by their enemies, their language will vanish. Wars destroy more than people.

You might ask, can there be any new languages to discover? Surprisingly, yes. A few have recently come to light when previously uncontacted peoples were found in isolated places. In 1991, for instance, a previously uncontacted language known as

Gongduk was discovered in the Himalayas. For linguists, this was like finding the fabled lost valley of Shangri-La. And in the deep Brazilian interior there are still languages being discovered, some of them apparently unrelated to any other known tongue. But stories like that are rare. The overwhelming trend is in the direction of extinction.

For the most part, geographical barriers—high mountains, steep valleys, lack of infrastructure or roads—afford little protection, not even in the far corners of the earth. Think about the speakers of Rapanui, on Easter Island in the Pacific. After a millennium and a half of separation from the world, in the nineteenth century they were taken from their island as slaves to collect guano from the coast of South America. Very few came back; today there are just a few thousand people who have kept Rapanui alive in the face of Spanish, imported from Chile.

Thirty years ago in Brazil, ranchers and illegal timber cutters drove the Jiahui people out of their traditional lands into the hands of hostile neighbors. The few that were le joined a less hostile group or drifted to the cities. Now the Jiahui have reclaimed some of their lands, but how many of them are left? Just fifty.

Or what about the Rikbatsá people in Brazil's Mato Grosso state? They were great warriors, but they couldn't fight epidemics of influenza and smallpox that were brought by Jesuit missionaries. Diseases imported from Europe decimated them and dozens of other native peoples of the Americas—and with them their native tongues.

And if human invasions aren't bad enough, nature itself can swallow up languages. In 1998 a terrible tsunami struck the north coast of Papua New Guinea, killing nearly all the speakers of the Warapu and Sissano languages. Just a few who weren't home at the time are the only ones le to keep the languages alive.

Finally, so-called 'killer languages'—like English or Spanish—are so dominant that people may *voluntarily* give up their mother tongue—for convenience or economic reasons. Indigenous peoples sometimes abandon their language to overcome discrimination, or fit into a majority culture. As children stop learning them, the languages slowly wither away.

Why should we care? Because with the loss of a language comes the loss of inherited knowledge, an entire thought-world. I've often heard it compared to losing a natural resource or an animal species. Yes, linguists have ways of reconstructing an extinct language from surviving evidence, but what that leaves us with is not much more than words on paper. We can't bring back from the dead a society that spoke the language, or the heritage and culture behind it. Once a language is gone, it's gone forever. The best cure for endangerment is to put self-confidence back into the minds of the speakers—by encouraging education and literacy from an early age.

It's only in the past couple of decades that the urgency of the question of language extermination worldwide has been realized. Organizations have been set up to do what they can to preserve language diversity. There are the U.S.-based Terralingua and the U.K.-based Foundation for Endangered Languages, both dedicated to encouraging and supporting research into threatened languages and their maintenance; there is the UNESCO Endangered Languages Project; and a department for Endangered Languages at the School of Oriental and African Studies, University of London. UNESCO itself has published an Atlas of the World's Languages in Danger of Disappearing, using a color-coded system of pointers indicating a scale from Vulnerable through Severely Endangered to (recently) Extinct. It paints a grim, but not hopeless, picture.

About the author

Christopher Moseley is a university lecturer, writer and freelance translator, editor of the *Encyclopedia of the World's Endangered Languages* (2006), and co-editor of the *Atlas of the World's Languages* (1993). In 2009 he edited the third edition of the UNESCO *Atlas of the World's Languages in Danger.* He has a special interest in artificial languages (and has created one himself).

Suggestions for further reading

In this book
The topic of how languages become extinct (or escape extinction) is discussed in Chapters 5 (languages of the world), 28 (Latin), 49 (U.S. dialect change), and 64 (language rescue).

Elsewhere
Abley, Mark. *Spoken Here: Travels among Threatened Languages* (Heinemann, 2004). A personal travelogue of the author's visits to some of the world's smallest language communities to see how they are faring in the modern globalized community.

Crystal, David. *Language Death* (Cambridge University Press, 2000). An impassioned plea on behalf of the world's smaller languages, full of interesting anecdotal information about the treasures we are losing.

Evans, Nicholas. *Dying Words: Endangered Languages and What They Have to Tell Us* (Wiley-Blackwell, 2010). A fascinating tour through some of the world's more obscure language communities, living, dead and half-dead, explaining what exactly is lost from human expression in each language that dies.

Nettle, Daniel, and Suzanne Romaine. *Vanishing Voices* (Oxford University Press, 2000). A serious and thoughtful study of the problems, causes and effects of language endangerment all over the world, relating the issue to biological diversity.

Ostler, Nicholas. *Empires of the Word* (HarperCollins, 2005). Takes a sweeping overview of the world's recorded history from the point of view of the big victorious languages—the other end of the telescope—and shows how successive empires have spread their 'international languages' all over the known world. English is just the latest in a long line of conquerors.

Language learning

35
How do babies learn their mother tongue?

Lauren J. Stites, Roberta Michnick Golinkoff and
Kathryn Hirsh-Pasek

*When do babies start learning to talk? How do they do it? Can babies
learn any language they are exposed to?*

'Goo goo gaa gaa' is often thought to be the beginning of how
babies learn to talk, but language learning starts well before babies
utter their first words or babbles. There's no question that babies
in the womb *jump* in response to noises, such as fireworks. Even
before they're born, from 5 months on, they eavesdrop on every
conversation their mother has. At birth, they can show us that they
recognize their mother's voice as well as stories and songs they've
heard in the womb. At first, language is just like a melody, but
babies enter the world prepared to learn any of the world's more
than 6,000 languages, and prefer to hear language above other
environmental noises.

The first linguistic challenge babies face is finding the *units*
in the speech they hear. Where does one word end and the next
begin? By 4.5 months of age, babies are well on the way to finding words in the stream of speech that washes over them. They
start by recognizing their own name. The first clue is its stress
pattern ('IRVing' is clearly different from 'AnnETTE'); in very
little time, they can distinguish their name even from other names
with the same stress pattern. Having noted the sound pattern of

their names, babies begin to recognize other frequently occurring words—like 'mama'—that can serve as anchors in the mass of sounds coming at them. By six months of age babies can recognize a word they hear when it comes *after* their own name, such as 'Annette's bottle.' And if their mother pronounces the words, they will begin to recognize others like 'banana' and 'foot' and 'baby,' even if these words are not preceded by their name. By 8 months, babies can use the *probability* that one syllable follows another to pick likely words out of a speech stream. Consider the phrase 'pretty baby.' Babies notice that the syllables 'pre' and 'tty' are often heard together but the last syllable of pretty ('tty') and the first syllable of baby ('ba') are not heard together that often. This allows babies to discover that 'pretty' and 'baby' are words but that 'tty-ba' is not.

Next, babies need to figure out what words *mean*; recognizing sound patterns is but a first step. Naturally enough, some of the first words babies understand are 'mama' and 'daddy.' But as their internal vocabularies expand, learning what words mean can be complicated. Imagine yourself in a foreign country where you know very little of the language. A rabbit hops by, and a native says 'zotil!' What might 'zotil' mean? 'Rabbit' is a pretty obvious guess. However, she could be saying 'look,' or 'hopping,' or 'ears.' Picking up the new language this way will take time for you to sort out the possibilities. Babies are in the same situation. By twelve months, they prefer to use words like 'rabbit' to refer to whole objects (like rabbits) as opposed to parts (like ears) or actions (like hopping). As babies get a little bit older, they begin to use gesture to guide their learning. When a baby points to something, we often give that object a name. So just as the baby is attending to the object, the caregiver names it. In fact, items that the baby points to enter their spoken vocabulary within three months!

After babies find words and know some meanings comes the step that marks true language acquisition: they recognize that words link together to make sentences. What they know about their language far exceeds what they can say. While their first *spoken* words appear at around twelve months, they may already understand hundreds of words. By 18 months, they can understand five- and six-word sentences when they may be saying only one or two words themselves.

But how could we know what babies understand of language? Picture an oversized TV screen, split between two moving images: On the left side, Cookie Monster is feeding Big Bird; on the right, Big Bird is feeding Cookie Monster. Babies watch these events with rapt attention. When they hear 'Where's Big Bird feeding Cookie Monster?' they look more at the right side of the screen than at the left. This means that babies, amazingly enough, are already using *grammar* (the order of the words in English) to figure out who's doing what to whom—even if they aren't *saying* much at all.

While the TV method may be a great way to get babies to show us *what* they've learned, it may not be the best way to *teach* them language. Babies learn most of their language in conversational duets with adults. In fact, babies have a hard time learning language from media such as tablets. No computer can yet provide them with the back-and-forth interaction they have with real life caregivers. Tablet and phone screens may actually interfere with the baby's language development, as they miss those rich, teachable moments from the people around them.

Here's a paradox: Babies can't tie their shoes or be left alone for more than 30 seconds, and yet they are excellent when it comes to learning languages. They're paying attention to language—even when they can't yet talk—and constantly working on cracking the code!

About the authors

Lauren J. Stites is an instructor at Georgia State University, where she obtained her Ph.D. and was a graduate fellow in the Challenges in the Acquisition of Language and Literacy Institute. She was a postdoctoral researcher at the Temple Infant and Child Lab (TICL). Her background focused on research methodology, specifically looking at parental interactions with their children. Her research has concentrated on language acquisition as well as the role of gesture in children's later language.

Roberta Michnick Golinkoff holds the Unidel H. Rodney Sharp Chair in the School of Education at the University of Delaware and is also a member of the Departments of Psychological and Brain Sciences and Linguistics and Cognitive Science. She directs the Child's Play, Learning and Development Laboratory, whose goal it is to understand how children tackle the amazing feat of learning language. Having obtained her Ph.D. at Cornell University, she has written 16 books—some for lay readers like *How Babies Talk*, and dozens of research articles, many with her long-standing collaborator, Kathy Hirsh-Pasek. The recipient of a prestigious John Simon Guggenheim Fellowship and a James McKeen Cattell Sabbatical award, Golinkoff blogs for the *Huffington Post* and is frequently quoted in newspapers and magazines.

Kathy Hirsh-Pasek is the Stanley and Debra Lefkowitz Professor in the Department of Psychology at Temple University, Pennsylvania, where she serves as Director of the Temple Infant and Child Lab (TICL). She is also a senior fellow at the Brookings Institute. Her joint research projects with Golinkoff in the areas of early language development and infant cognition have been funded by the National Science Foundation, the National Institutes of Health and Human Development, the Institute of Education Sciences, and the Bezos Foundation. Her work has resulted in 14 books and numerous journal publications. She has appeared on *Today*, *20/20*, and other national television programs and is often quoted in newspapers and magazines.

Suggestions for further reading

In this book
Other chapters discussing language acquisition by children include 13 (language deprivation), 18 (language and the brain), 30 (pidgins and creoles), 31 (sign languages), and 59 (children and second languages).

Elsewhere
Golinkoff, Roberta Michnick, and Kathryn Hirsh-Pasek. *How Babies Talk: The Magic and Mystery of Language in the First Three Years of Life* (Dutton/Penguin, 1999). This is a fun read that reviews the latest research in language acquisition and offers tips to parents.

Golinkoff, Roberta Michnick, and Kathryn Hirsh-Pasek. *Becoming Brilliant: What Science Tells Us About Raising Successful Children* (APA, 2016). Among the skills that children need for success is communication—speaking, writing, and listening.

Hirsh-Pasek, Kathryn, and Roberta Michnick Golinkoff. *Einstein Never Used Flash Cards: How Our Children Really Learn and Why They Need to Play More and Memorize Less* (Rodale, 2003). This award-winning book shows how important language is for reading, expressing emotion, and succeeding at school.

Hoff, Erika. *Language Development* (Cengage Learning, fifth edition 2009).

36

How many languages can a person learn?

Richard Hudson

What is the most languages anybody has ever mastered? Do you have to be abnormal to learn so many?

Most of us are impressed by people who know a lot of languages, but how many is 'a lot'? A typical American or Brit knows precisely one language, maybe with smatterings of one or two others; so we're impressed if someone knows three or four well. But if you lived in some parts of India or the Australian outback you'd probably know six languages as a matter of course; three would be rather a limited repertoire.

What, then, is the human capacity for language learning? Rather surprisingly, nobody really knows. Linguists and psychologists have done enormous amounts of research on people with linguistic handicaps, but almost nobody has looked at those who are superbly good at languages. We don't even know how many languages such people know, let alone how they do it. Most of what I say below is based on the excellent book by Michael Erard that I cite in my suggested reading.

'Human capacity' is rather vague, so let's be more precise and ask about 'normal capacity' (how many languages could any average one of us learn?) and 'extreme capacity' (what's the world record for language learning?). As we'll see, although we don't have solid answers, we do know enough to guess.

First, then, what language-learning capacity comes with a normal collection of human genes? The gene pool is pretty much the same across the whole world—after all, we know that any human baby, regardless of genetic origin, can learn the language or languages of any community in which they happen to be raised. So to determine what capacity is normal, we should study communities where most or all members are multilingual. Ideally these would be places where a lot of languages meet on fairly equal terms, like India or the Australian outback (but unlike, say, London, where hundreds of immigrant languages meet on very unequal terms with English).

This kind of research has not yet been done systematically, but impressions based on partial studies seem to converge on about five or six as the upper limit for what we can call 'community multilingualism.' The communities concerned have so many languages in circulation that ordinary people grow up naturally speaking five or six, without any formal instruction at school.

A quibble: are the languages of these communities similar enough that it's not so hard to learn five or six of them? In a word, no. We're talking about languages at least as different as (say) English and German, and in some cases as different as English and Chinese. Not surprisingly, perhaps, when a particular combination of languages is shared by a community for a long time—hundreds of years—their grammars tend to converge. They stay resolutely different in vocabulary, though. This is because each language belongs to a different sub-community (such as a tribe or a caste), and may be the most important evidence of membership in that community. So long as the sub-communities keep separate, they need their languages to stay distinct as well.

We could also quibble about how well these people speak their various languages. Are they totally fluent and 'native-like' in every language? Once again, we simply don't know, but we can be sure that they know them well enough to get by in everyday conversation. Maybe they know more words and constructions in some languages than in others (and doubtless there are some concepts, linked to group cultures, that they can talk about more easily in just one of the languages). And almost certainly they won't be able to read and write all of them—indeed, they may not be able to read and write any of them. But their knowledge of all the languages goes well beyond what we'd call a smattering, and also beyond the stumbling and limited ability reached in most of our schools. Maybe the best way to describe their ability is as 'a good working knowledge.' Moreover, so long as interaction is regular and frequent, these languages are all ready for immediate use—they don't get 'rusty.'

So you and I have inherited brains that could, in principle, hold a good working knowledge of at least five or six completely different languages. The only thing that prevented me from achieving this feat is my social history—the fact that the people round me have always spoken only one language, so I never needed to learn more. Your social life may, of course, have been different from mine—and that may be why you're reading this chapter. If so, rejoice! But the main point is that learning five or six languages is completely within the normal range, and requires no skills other than those we use when we learn our first language in childhood. We are all born as potential polyglots.

What about the world champions, the great and exceptional language learners (for whom I've coined the term 'hyperpolyglot')? This is where Erard is the expert. Most famous among the hyperpolyglots of history was Cardinal Giuseppe Mezzofanti (1774–1849), who claimed to speak 50 languages and to understand 20 more, as well as reading 114. Another nineteenth-century figure, Sir John Bowring, was said to have spoken 100 languages and to have read an additional 100. These people were famous in their day, so we have plenty of independent reports from people such as Lord Byron, who visited Mezzofanti and confirmed his ability in some languages; but it is impossible now to check the extraordinary numbers.

There are real hyperpolyglots walking the earth today, and Erard has succeeded in tracking some of them down. Their language numbers may seem modest—the 20–30 range is typical—but unlike Mezzofanti's, they have been verified by reasonably objective tests (such as U.S. government scales of language proficiencies). None of these prodigies can speak all their languages equally easily; typically, some languages are always available, some need to be brushed up, and others need the help of a dictionary. But even so, some really do deserve the name 'hyperpolyglot'; for example, an Englishman called Derick Herning told Erard that he knows 30 languages, of which 12 are always available. (In 1990, 22 of these languages were independently certified.)

How do hyperpolyglots do it? Certainly not by leaving it to 'natural' language learning. These are scholars who learn from books and follow strict schedules for learning and practicing their languages. They just love learning languages. Do they have a special aptitude? Nobody knows for sure, but I leave you with a fascinating fact: they are nearly all men.

About the author

Richard Hudson is professor emeritus of linguistics in the Department of Phonetics and Linguistics at University College, London, where he worked from 1964 through 2004. He has a B.A. in modern and medieval languages from Cambridge and a Ph.D. from the School of Oriental and African Studies, London, with a thesis on the grammar of the Cushitic language of the Beja (or Bedawie) people in the northeast of the Sudan.

Suggestions for further reading

In this book

Multilingual societies are discussed in Chapters 43 (lingua francas), 44 (official languages of India), and 45 (language conflict). The development of multilingual individuals is discussed in Chapters 20 (language and the brain), 35 (babies and language), 38 (bilinguality), 40 (adult language learning), and 59 (children and second languages).

Elsewhere

Erard, Michael. *Babel No More: The Search for Extraordinary Language Learners* (Free Press, 2012). A highly readable book that surveys the research, or lack of it.

Parkvall, Mikael. *Limits of Language* (Battlebridge, 2006). See pages 117–120 for a discussion of polyglots.

http://dickhudson.com/hyperpolyglots/ This page provides a collection of information about the extremes of multilingualism, both individual and societal.

37

What causes foreign accents?

Steven H. Weinberger

Where do foreign accents come from? What makes one foreign accent different from another? Can you learn to speak a foreign language without an accent?

Foreign accents have been around for as long as humans have had language. The Hebrew Bible tells a story about how the Gileadites destroyed the infiltrating army of their enemy, the Ephraimites: They set up roadblocks and made each man who approached them say the Gileadite word *shibboleth*. The Ephraimites couldn't pronounce the 'sh' sound, so when they said the word it came out *sibboleth*—and the Gileadites killed them on the spot.

The consequences aren't often that dramatic, but we're all experts at detecting things about people from the way they talk. Not only do we often make immediate biased judgments about a person simply based upon their accent, but even on the phone we can accurately guess a person's sex, approximate age—even whether he or she is smiling. And like the Gileadites, we usually know right away whether the person is a native speaker of our own language.

For example, if you heard a recording of someone saying a sentence including the words *zeeze seengs*, you might be able to recognize that the speaker meant 'these things,' but you'd certainly know that she was a foreigner. You'd draw a similar conclusion if you heard a different voice say *deeza tings*.

What is it about the speech of these two people that would let you immediately recognize them as non-native English speakers? And why would their accents be different from one another? While many factors influence foreign accents, much of the answer lies in something linguists call *cross-linguistic influence*. When you first learn a new language, you'd like to sound like a native, but you unavoidably carry over (or transfer) some of the characteristics of your own language to it.

The *'zeeze seengs'* speaker, for example, wants to say 'these things,' but her native language (which in this case happens to be French) doesn't have the 'th' sounds of English, so she uses the closest approximations to them that she can find in her inventory of French sounds: a 'z' for the voiced 'th' of *these* and an 's' for the unvoiced 'th' of *things*. Another English sound missing from the French inventory is the short 'i' vowel of *things*, so native French speakers will tend to replace it with the nearest handy sound, the long 'ee': *zeeze seengs*.

The *'deeza tings'* speaker has similar issues, but he's attempting the English phrase under the influence of his own native language (which happens to be Italian). He doesn't have the problem the French speaker has with the short 'i' vowel of English, but he, too, lacks our voiced and unvoiced 'th' sounds; he substitutes a 'd' and 't' for them instead of the 'z' and 's' the French speaker used. He also seems to avoid ending a word with a consonant—English has lots of final 'p,' 't,' 'k,' 'b,' 'd,' 'g,' 'f,' 's,' 'v,' 'z' sounds, but Italian does not not—so he tends to tack a little neutral vowel after some English final consonants: *deeza tings*. Linguists find these speech behaviors to be a legitimate area of study. Indeed, foreign-accented speech provides a window from which to view a second language speaker's native language grammar.

It's the ability to recognize and reproduce these features of cross-linguistic transfer that enable professional actors to portray foreign speakers of English convincingly, and sometimes for comic effect. Think of Chico Marx (of the Marx Brothers) portraying an Italian aviator, or Peter Sellers transforming himself into the incomparable Inspector Clouseau. Each of them filters his

English through a foreign sound inventory, exaggerates a bit, and the results are humorous.

Does this mean that when foreigners speak English—and when we try to speak foreign languages—we're doomed to sound like comic caricatures forever? Of course not. While we may initially start out a little like that, language learners can, with a bit of practice, pronounce a second language well enough to be understood without comic effect.

Can we ever sound just like native speakers? Well, almost. Most professional linguists believe that people who start learning a new language after childhood can never completely get rid of traces of their original tongue—most listeners can spot these characteristics, and certainly sensitive instruments in a linguistics lab can detect them. This inability to completely learn a second language sound system is due to our human biology—something called the *critical period*. But even if we are biologically constrained to speak a language with an accent, there's nothing wrong with that so long as we can make ourselves understood. In any case, accents certainly add to the interesting diversity and recognizability of human speech.

About the author

Steven H. Weinberger is associate professor and director of the linguistics program at George Mason University in Virginia. He teaches courses in phonetics, phonology, and second language acquisition. His principal research deals with language sound systems and foreign accents. He is co-editor of *Interlanguage Phonology: The Acquisition of a Second Language Sound System* (1987), and he is the founder and curator of the Speech Accent Archive (http://accent.gmu.edu), a web database of thousands of different accents in English.

Suggestions for further reading

In this book
Chapters relevant to language learning by adults include 20 (language and the brain), 40 (adult advantages in language learning), 41 (history of

language teaching methods), 54 (language-teaching technology), and 60 (study abroad). Chapter 7 (phonetics) discusses the sounds of language. Frictions between language-defined groups are addressed in Chapters 43 (lingua francas), 30 (pidgins and creoles), 44 (official languages of India), 45 (language conflict), and 51 (African American English).

Elsewhere

Blumenfeld, Robert. *Accents: A Manual for Actors* (Proscenium, 2000). A guide to producing more than eighty different speech accents for English speakers. It is designed for actors, but it contains insights into speech production and comparative linguistics.

Lippi-Green, Rosina. *English with an Accent* (Routledge, 2012). A thorough analysis of American attitudes towards English accents. It focuses on language variation linked to geography and social identity, and looks at how institutions promote linguistic stereotyping.

Swan, Michael and Bernard Smith. *Learner English* (Cambridge University Press, 2001). A practical reference text that presents and compares relevant linguistic features of English with about twenty-two other languages. It utilizes linguistic transfer to predict learners' errors, and is a valuable resource for ESL teachers.

Weinberger, Steven. Speech Accent Archive, http://accent.gmu.edu. A web-based phonetic analysis of native and non-native speakers of English who read the same paragraph that is carefully transcribed. The archive is used by people who wish to compare and analyze the accents of different English speakers.

38

What does it mean to be bilingual?

Agnes Bolonyai

Who is bilingual? What is code-switching and why do bilinguals do it? What are the benefits of being bilingual? Does bilingualism make you smart?

Bilinguals are all around us. The truth is they have been for some time. And in today's increasingly mobile and globalizing world, more people become bilingual every day. Bilingualism has become so prevalent that you have passed it walking down the aisles of your local grocery store; you have passed it on as you hand over a bag of *biscotti*; you have enjoyed it while catching up on *Modern Family* and again during the commercial break when Target's new bilingual commercial comes on. Your YouTube history is probably filled with it: from K-pop band BTS rapping in English, Korean and Japanese to Justin Bieber's complicitous appearance on Puerto Rican artists Luis Fonsi's and Daddy Yankee's number 1 hit, 'Despacito.' The growing presence of bilingualism and bilinguals in all spheres of our daily life can be easy to miss, but impossible to ignore. Now that we are aware that bilingualism is here to stay (in pop music and beyond!), let's try to understand this phenomenon better.

It is estimated that well over half of the world's population is bilingual. The majority lives in Asia and Africa—continents with long history of societal multilingualism, due in part to Western colonialism. Today, as a result of globalization, widespread

migration and mobility, we are seeing the rise of bilingual popu-
lace in many of the traditionally monolingual countries in Europe
and North America.

Linguists define bilingualism as the regular use of two or
more languages—separately, consecutively or mixed together—in
social interactions in everyday life. Bilingualism has captured the
imagination of researchers who see it as a unique window onto the
human language and its use in society.

One of the hallmarks of bilinguals is the seamless fluidness with
which they are able to move back and forth between languages, a
phenomenon called *code-switching* or code-mixing. While it is
not uncommon for people to dismiss the use of two languages
together as 'bad' and refer to it pejoratively as Tex-Mex, Chinglish,
or Franglais, bilingual code-switching is actually a pretty remarkable cognitive feat. Linguists would tell you that far from being a
random mishmash and a sign of confusion or laziness, language
alternation is a skillful, creative and context-sensitive deployment
of linguistic prowess. In fact, code-switching has its own grammatical rules that bilinguals follow without ever being taught how.

According to conventional wisdom, a 'true' bilingual is someone who possesses equal and native-level fluency in both languages. But linguists suggest that this a pretty narrow and outdated
view, a product of ingrained linguistic purism and modernist
language ideologies. Research overwhelmingly suggests that *bilinguals are not the sum of two monolinguals in one body*—a metaphor
coined by François Grosjean. The fact is, most bilinguals neither
acquire nor (need to) use both of their languages under identical
circumstances. While speaking with a foreign accent might sound
funny to a monolingual, it is simply a badge of bilingualism.

In reality, being bilingual is as much a matter of juggling
languages as identities. Choosing what language to speak, with
whom, where and when is a fundamentally social phenomenon. Bilinguals navigate their social world, connect with others,
handle conflict, joke around, and make sense of who they are by
masterfully switching between languages and playfully mixing
them together. It is quite common for bilinguals to use different

languages in different situations (e.g., Spanish at home vs. English at school), with different people (e.g., English with co-workers vs. Spanish/English with bilingual siblings), on different topics (e.g., Spanish when it comes to grandma's recipe vs. English when talking politics), and for different communicative purposes (e.g., 'cool' English slang vs. affectionate Spanish nicknames). It is because of these unique use cases and contexts that the majority of bilinguals are not equally fluent and yet functionally competent in both languages.

Living in a bilingual environment has beneficial effects on cognitive functioning in people of all ages. Bilingual children are typically better than monolinguals at cognitively demanding activities that rely on the so-called 'executive function' of the brain such as attentional control, switching tasks, mental flexibility, and divergent thinking. These enhanced cognitive muscles are thought to develop from the mental workout that constant monitoring and juggling of languages provide the bilingual mind. Indeed, the more you code-switch with your fellow bilinguals the better, because that is when the magic of cognitive muscle building happens.

The cognitive benefits of bilingualism do not end at childhood but extend throughout the lifespan. Those who maintain the use of multiple languages throughout their lives benefit from better memory and efficient cognitive functioning even in old age. Elderly bilinguals may also experience age-related mental decline such as dementia and Alzheimer's disease by about five years later than their monolingual counterparts.

So, there you have it: listen to 'Despacito' with abandon, learn all the words, dust off your foreign language textbooks, and join the movement. Your brain will thank you.

About the author

Agnes Bolonyai is associate professor of linguistics at North Carolina State University. Her current research interests include issues of language, identity, mobility, and migration, in particular code-switching and other language contact phenomena, bi-/multilingual discourse, and identity practices and linguistic landscapes in sociolinguistic contexts of globalization and transnational migration. Her empirical work has mostly focused on Hungarian–English bilingualism. She is also interested in right-wing populist political discourse. Her work has appeared in *Bilingualism: Language and Cognition*, the International Journal of Bilingualism, The Cambridge Handbook of Code-Switching, Journal of Sociolinguistics, Language in Society, and *Journal of Language Aggression and Conflict*.

Suggestions for further reading

In this book

Persons with skills in multiple languages are discussed in Chapter 36 (hyperpolyglots), and the cognitive aspects of learning/knowing multiple languages are discussed in Chapter 20 (the brain and multiple languages). Opportunities and requirements for professional use of language abilities are discussed in Chapters 2 (what linguists do), 48 (America's language crisis), 62 (dictionaries), and 63 (interpreting and translating). To learn more about bilingualism in schools, see Chapter 61 (bilingual education).

Elsewhere

Bialystok, Ellen. *Bilingualism in Development: Language, Literacy, and Cognition* (Cambridge, 2001). A classic by a leading cognitive scientist in bilingualism, this book is an authoritative discussion of cognitive and language development in bilingual children.

Bullock, Barbara E., and Almeida Jacqueline Toribio, eds. *The Cambridge Handbook of Linguistic Code-switching* (Cambridge, 2009). This collection of essays by prominent sociolinguists, psycholinguists, and neuro-linguists explores every aspect of the phenomenon of code-switching.

Grosjean, François. *Bilingual: Life and Reality* (Harvard University Press, 2010). Written in non-technical language by a renowned psycholinguist and leading authority in bilingualism, this book clarifies common misconceptions about bilingualism and makes it easy to understand the ins and outs of living with two languages.

Shin, Sarah J. *Bilingualism in Schools and Society: Language, Identity, and Policy* (Routledge, 2013). In a highly readable book, Shin provides an excellent introduction to bilingualism and bilingual education. Suitable for those new to the field, while an invaluable resource for students, educators and researchers alike.

39

What makes some languages harder to learn than others?

Barry Hilton

Are some languages harder to learn than others? Is Chinese the most difficult language in the world? What makes Chinese so tough to learn?

If you ask professional linguists questions like these, most will probably say that every language is complex in some ways and simple in others, and that they average out to around the same level of complexity. But that's probably not the kind of answer you're looking for. If we rephrase the question, though, and ask which major language is *hardest for native English speakers to learn*, well, yes, a pretty good case can be made for Chinese. (Background note: the name 'Chinese' refers to at least half a dozen regional languages that are closely related but as different from each other as French, Spanish and Italian. What I have to say applies to all of them, especially to the one most widely spoken, called 'Mandarin' by foreigners. It is the official language of both mainland China and Taiwan.) Let's look at some of the reasons.

One difficulty is that Chinese is unrelated to English. When you study a cousin of English in the Indo-European language family, like Spanish, Russian or Hindi, you find plenty of cognates—related words, similar in sound and meaning—to use as stepping stones. To learn Chinese you have to acquire a vocabulary that is totally new, except for a few borrowings like 'typhoon,' 'gung ho,' 'coolie,' and 'kowtow.'

As a second obstacle, Chinese has a phonetic feature that can be difficult for English-speaking learners to hear and reproduce. Like English words, Chinese words are made up of consonant and vowel sounds, but each Chinese syllable also has an *intonation* pattern that's *not optional*. Mandarin syllables come in five patterns: (1) high level (think of a cartoon opera singer warming up: 'mi-mi-mi'); (2) rising (like answering a knock at the door: 'Yes?'; (3) dipping-and-rising (like a drawn-out, pensive 'we-e-ll'); (4) sharply falling ('Stop!'); and (5) toneless or unaccented (like the second syllable of 'cattle'). The Chinese word *lyou⁴* (falling tone) means 'six'; *lyou²* (same consonant and vowels but rising tone) means 'remain.' *Ying²mu⁴* means 'tent'; *ying¹mu³* means 'acre'; *jya⁴jr⁵* means 'value'; *jya³jr¹* means 'artificial limb.' Learners of Chinese who get tones wrong can sound as odd—or incomprehensible—to native ears as learners of English sound to us when they mix up the vowel sounds in words like 'fit' and 'feet,' or 'hall' and 'hull.'

Now, many other languages—like Hungarian and Arabic and Indonesian—have no cognates for English-speaking students to rely on. And some, like Vietnamese, Thai and various African languages, are also tonal. But there's another obstacle that puts the difficulty of Chinese on an entirely different level: its writing system.

If you've ever done volunteer work in a literacy program, you know what a frustrating handicap illiteracy is, and how empowered an adult learner feels as he or she masters the 'code' that links familiar sounds with the few dozen squiggles that represent them on paper. People learning Chinese have a very complicated 'code' to master, which impedes not just their ability to read but their ability to broaden their vocabulary and develop other linguistic skills.

The squiggles the Chinese writing system uses—usually called 'characters'—don't represent simple consonant and vowel sounds, the way English letters do. Each one stands for a whole one-syllable word or word element, combining sound *and meaning*. For example, if a Chinese-like system were used to write English, the word 'unbearable' might be written with three squiggles, one for 'un,' one for 'bear,' and one for 'able.' And *that* 'bear' squiggle would be different from the squiggles representing the same sound in 'polar bear,' 'childbearing' and 'the right to bear arms'—to say nothing of 'barefoot' or 'Bering Strait.' That adds up to a *lot* of squiggles for learners to memorize—several thousand characters instead of a couple of dozen alphabet letters. Not surprisingly, illiteracy is a major problem in China.

And when you meet a new character (or one whose sound and meaning you've learned and forgotten), how do you look it up? There are hundreds of Chinese dictionaries, and almost as many different systems for arranging characters. Without alphabetical order, tracking down an unknown character is much more labor-intensive than flipping pages while silently mouthing the ABC song. Even when you find the character, you won't necessarily know—without still more dictionary research—whether it's a stand-alone word or part of a compound like 'unbearable.'

I hope these comments serve less to discourage than to challenge people interested in learning Chinese. Learners can take heart from the fact that the *sound* system of Chinese is pretty simple except for the tones; and Chinese grammar—unlike, for example, Navajo grammar—poses no real difficulties for English speakers. Even the writing system, devilish as it may seem, has fascinated foreigners for centuries, and offers a key to understanding the classical literature and modern economic vitality of one of the great civilizations of the world.

About the author

Barry Hilton served as the associate editor of the first and second editions of this book and was a member of the review board of the radio series from which it was adapted. He is a freelance writer/editor and independent scholar living in Maine. He is an honors graduate of Harvard College who, after graduate studies at Cornell, Yale, and George Washington

Universities, and the Foreign Service Institute, has travelled extensively and lived in both Europe and Asia. In a variety of U.S. government assignments, he has made professional use of Vietnamese, Chinese, Japanese, French, and German. He describes himself as an 'armchair philologist and recovering polyglot.'

Suggestions for further reading

In this book
Other chapters about specific languages include 28 (Latin), 44 (languages of India), 50 (Native American languages), and 52 (Spanish). Writing systems are also discussed in Chapters 16 (scripts) and 26 (history of writing).

Elsewhere
DeFrancis, John. *The Chinese Language: Fact and Fantasy* (University of Hawai'i Press, 1984). The grand old man of Chinese instruction in the U.S. (1911–2009) authoritatively debunks a number of myths about Chinese—particularly about the writing system—in a highly entertaining style.

Dong, Hongyuan. *A History of the Chinese Language* (Routledge, 2014). For those interesting in the history of the language, this introductory— and fascinating—book offers a detailed overview of what the Chinese language was like hundreds of years ago, and chronicles its development into its current state.

Moser, David. 'Why Chinese Is So Damn Hard,' http://pinyin.info/readings/texts/moser.html. An accurate and amusing detailed account of the difficulties of Chinese, which almost in spite of itself serves as an invitation to potential learners: 'The more you learn about Chinese characters, the more intriguing and addicting they become.'

Yin, John Jing-hua. *Fundamentals of Chinese Characters* (Yale University Press, 2006). This book focuses on connections between the shapes and meanings of Chinese characters, and provides interactive exercises and rhymes for all of the (thousands of) characters covered in the book, as well as illustrations for all the basic characters.

40

Can monolingualism be cured?

Katherine Sprang

Is it possible to learn a new language as an adult? Isn't it a lot harder than it is for children? Are there any tricks to learning?

When was the last time you studied a foreign language? Some of us think about that experience with pleasure; others think of it as one we wouldn't *ever* want to repeat. If you're over sixteen and trying to learn a new language—or thinking about learning one (and I hope you are)—remember that adults and children learn languages in very different ways.

When we ask ourselves why it takes so long to learn a foreign language, it is easy for us, as adult language learners, to envy children. They learn language as part of learning about the world; their minds absorb the words, phrases, and sentences they hear while they are playing or exploring—and with no apparent effort. Language learning is the child's exciting full-time job for the first few years of life: no studying necessary, and no homework!

But don't forget that even with that sponge-like ability to absorb linguistic information, children have to hear and use their mother tongue for thousands of hours in order to master it; it typically takes them over ten years before they're fully capable of non-childish everyday language use. Adults usually don't have that much time to spare, but that doesn't mean that we can't learn languages and learn them very well. In some ways adults have an *advantage* over children. First, some elements of language can be categorized, analyzed, and explained, and these can be learned by adults more rapidly than by children learning their first language. Second, because we already have a language, adults can use what we know of our first language to organize our learning of the sounds, words, and grammar of the new one. We don't start from scratch when we learn another language.

For example, even if a language has some sounds that English doesn't (maybe a trilled *r* as in 'burro'—or an *ng* sound at the beginning of a word, like 'nga'), chances are that *most* of its sounds will be familiar. Adults can take advantage of this to prioritize their pronunciation effort where it is most needed.

Or the new language may use word orders like 'The boy brave with his rifle the tiger fierce shot.' That sounds unnatural to an English speaker, but foreign grammatical patterns are not so different from English that they can't be figured out and mastered, like a puzzle—again, a skill that improves with age.

Learning foreign vocabulary inescapably requires many exposures to the words in different contexts, but even here adults are well equipped to spot words related to words they already know and use them as stepping stones into the new language. They can recognize prefixes and suffixes, and understand the roles that those parts of words play in the new language. Adult language students—especially when aided by good teachers, textbooks, and technical aids, have the knowledge, experience, and analytic ability to recognize what's already understandable in a new language and what's different from our first language. By *focusing attention on the differences*, we as adults can jump-start our learning.

By contrast, other elements of language need to be absorbed through continual and repeated exposure. When the mind is relaxed and not seeking explanations or patterns, it's capable of categorizing and sorting information about some elements of language without conscious effort. The aspects of language taken in best through this unconscious process—called implicit learning—tend not to be captured in textbooks, and they're seldom explained well by teachers. In fact, in some ways it can be more effective simply to watch TV or listen to the radio in the language you're trying to learn, rather than poring over rules and patterns and vocabulary lists.

The better we are at combining both approaches—explicit learning and implicit learning—the more effectively and quickly we can build our knowledge of a new language. And it's not enough just to acquire knowledge. To a great extent, speaking, writing, and understanding a foreign language are a matter of developing skills—like learning to play the piano—that you can't master without practice, practice, *practice*. Here again, children have it easier, if only because they're uninhibited. Practicing a foreign language means you have to get past the very adult fear of embarrassment, the discomfort of doing something you are not expert at. Are you willing to walk up to strangers from another country—say, a group of tourists—and try to talk with them in their language? To the extent that you are willing to try out your budding language skills, to practice them (even if your performance is not perfect), and to learn from making mistakes, your ability in the foreign language will continue to grow.

Until around the middle of the twentieth century, language learning in school was pretty dull. It was all about memorizing vocabulary, talking about grammar—in English—and translating as many paragraphs as you could stand. We've learned a lot about teaching languages since then. Since the 1970s, the new discipline of Second Language Acquisition, an interdisciplinary field combining cognitive science and applied linguistics, has also emerged. Through it we are gradually discovering which elements of a language are best taught through explicit instruction and which are best absorbed through sustained exposure to the language. As answers to these questions are uncovered through research, language instruction continues to improve, and adults are learning languages better than ever. So, if you're a monolingual adult, there's no reason to continue in that sad condition. Monolingualism *can* be cured.

About the author

Katherine Sprang holds a Ph.D. from the German Department at Georgetown University, with primary specialization in second language acquisition (SLA). She is particularly interested in how excellence in teaching can help language students achieve superior foreign language skills. She works currently at the Foreign Service Institute, U.S. Department of State, as coordinator of FSI Regional Programs and Training.

Suggestions for further reading

In this book

Language learning by adults is also discussed in Chapters 20 (language and the brain), 37 (foreign accents), 41 (history of language teaching methods), 54 (language-teaching technology), and 60 (study abroad).

Elsewhere

Byrnes, Heidi, and Hiram Maxim. *Advanced Foreign Language Learning: A Challenge to College Programs* (Heinle, 2003).

Larsen-Freeman, Diane. *Teaching Language: From Grammar to Grammaring* (Heinle, 2003).

Roberts, Richard, and Roger Kreuz. *Becoming Fluent: How Cognitive Science Can Help Adults Learn a Foreign Language* (MIT Press, 2015).

41

How have our ideas about language learning changed through the years?

June K. Phillips

What is the history of foreign language teaching? Have there been a lot of different methods? How different are they? Are today's methods best?

The first language taught to European settlers in what is now the United States was, of all things, Algonquian. Seventeenth-century arrivals from England learned to communicate in First Nation languages as a matter of survival. But later settlers, as European priorities changed, built schools that taught languages for academic purposes, which meant learning to read and write—not speak—Ancient Greek or Latin or both.

When U.S. students began learning modern languages—only western European languages at first—they approached them the same way they did the classical languages, to read rather than speak. This method held true for institutions of higher education as well. In 1825, with the establishment of his new University of Virginia, Thomas Jefferson wrote, 'We generally learn languages for the benefit of reading the books written in them.'

For the next century and beyond, Americans continued to study languages, not to converse with native speakers but to learn to read—and not to read newspapers or pamphlets of the day but to read literature. Even just a hundred years ago, language classes were still all about reading, translating, and analyzing grammar—not just in Latin and Greek but in modern languages too. So if you studied a language in the first half of the twentieth century, you probably didn't learn to speak it, because no one intended that you should. Speaking wasn't the goal.

And then came World War II. Suddenly the U.S. urgently needed to mass-produce *speakers* of foreign languages—soldiers and civilians—who could not just conjugate French verbs or read *Don Quixote* but actually talk with people in all parts of the world. And what was needed included a dazzling *variety* of languages—everything from Dutch to Burmese.

The linguistic profession was pressed into war service and the teaching of languages changed dramatically. This time period was the heyday of behaviorism as an explanation for learning in all fields. Foreign language teachers were trained to use stimulus and response to imprint language patterns in student minds. Students learned by memorizing dialogues and producing rapid-fire responses in all kinds of oral drills, rarely by producing messages of their own, as parodied by a book by Sesyle Joslin and Irene Haas called *There is a Dragon in My Bed = Il y a un dragon dans mon lit, and other Useful Phrases in French and English for Young Ladies and Gentlemen Going Abroad or Staying at Home* (published in 1961).

The 'audio-lingual' method worked, to an extent. More people learned more languages faster and more fluently (if you define fluency as rapid repetition and recitation) than could ever have been trained through the reading-oriented grammar-and-translation method. U.S. government needs for foreign language specialists—Russian in particular—remained high as World War II gave way to the Cold War. Ancient Greek fell off the charts. Latin experienced ups and downs in popularity and was successfully promoted as a way of building vocabulary competency in English.

However, the audio-lingual paradigm still clung to the concept of mastery of form: students practiced and practiced until they could handle building-block materials perfectly and pronounce well. This was not unlike Henry Higgins's lament in *My Fair Lady* that 'the French never care what they do as long as they pronounce it properly.' But the world was changing rapidly; students were going abroad to travel, to study—and yes, they wanted to 'do' things with the language. What piano student would be content just doing five-finger drills and never reaching the point of playing a piece or creating a tune?

By the mid-1970s, second-language acquisition grew as a field and began to highlight flaws in the audio-lingual method. Stimulus-response was inadequate as a model for learning something as complex as languages. Researchers focused on how language is acquired and came to see the process as developmental and socially constructed rather than as something one could accomplish mechanically, through daily exercises. Language teaching changed again to reflect those insights.

The new paradigm recognizes that novice learners can and do communicate; they get their message across even if all they can produce is a series of words without grammatical structure. In a bistro, the equivalent of 'Me want beer' gets you one! If you're a more advanced speaker, your request can be more nuanced: 'What do you have on draft?' The U.S. language teaching community has adopted a communication-first, content-rich paradigm as the cornerstone of *Standards for Foreign Language Learning in the 21st Century*, a document that lays out goals for improving language programs in the twenty-first century.

And none too soon. Students today have unprecedented access to resources that enable them to take on real-world tasks and actually use the languages they study. If Jefferson were brought back now, he'd mourn the diminished status of Greek and Latin and literary studies in Western European languages. But he'd no doubt be fascinated to visit a typical classroom. He'd see computers and video clips and games and smart phone apps in the target language, students working in pairs, moving around the room, chattering in short sentences, using imperfect but understandable grammar, and filling in meanings with gestures when necessary. They are reading and watching current events and soap operas online, with and without subtitles. Their learning is enhanced by their ability to learn *from* and learn *with* authentic materials in chosen fields or interests. They Skype and FaceTime with peers in other countries. They are immersed in real world language contexts both oral and written. Above all, they are communicating. I suspect the learning, if not the technology, looked a lot like that when their ancestors were learning Algonquian.

About the author

June K. Phillips is professor and dean of arts and humanities emeritus from Weber State University in Utah. She has taught French (at the junior high school through college levels) and methods of foreign language teaching. She served as president of the American Council on the Teaching of Foreign Languages (ACTFL) in 2001. She was ACTFL's project director for the National Standards for Foreign Language Education and was co-director of a project looking at their influence after a decade or more; she also co-chaired the development of Program Standards for the Preparation of Foreign Language Teachers, jointly promulgated by ACTFL and the National Council for Accreditation of Teacher Education. She served as a consultant to the National Assessment of Educational Progress evaluation of Spanish teaching in the U.S. and to the WGBH/Annenberg Video Library for Foreign Languages, a nonprofit educational resource. She has published and edited extensively on pedagogical topics.

Suggestions for further reading

In this book

Adult language learning is also discussed in Chapters 20 (language and the brain), 37 (foreign accents), 40 (adult advantages in language learning), 54 (language teaching technology), and 60 (study abroad).

Elsewhere

American Council on the Teaching of Foreign Languages (ACTFL). *Standards for Foreign Language Learning in the 21st Century* (National Standards in Education Project, 2006).
ACTFL. *The World-Readiness Standards for Learning Languages* (NSEP, 2014).

These two ACTFL books provide background information on the widely adopted U.S. National Standards, a broader set of goals than were aimed at in past language learning. They are commonly called the 'Five Cs': communication, cultures, connections, comparisons and communities.

Hall, Joan Kelly. *Methods for Teaching Foreign Languages: Creating a Community of Learners in the Classroom* (Merrill Prentice Hall, 2001). This book grounds methods of teaching and learning in the sociocultural context created in the language classroom. Hall's notion of 'constructed classroom conversation' emphasizes planned but active acquisition of communicative competencies.

Shrum, Judith L. and Eileen W. Glisan. *Teacher's Handbook: Contextualized Language Instruction* (Cengage Learning, fifth edition 2016). Chapter 2 provides a chart that summarizes historical theories and methods associated with each (fig. 2.1, p. 45).

Language and society

42

What is the connection between language and society?

Jon Forrest

How does our social background affect our speech? Why do we think certain accents sound better than others? Do our ideas about race, class, or gender affect our views of language?

Language is more than a code for transmission of information. Language carries a great deal of social information along with content. Imagine someone speaking these three sentences out loud:

'I like totally hate that movie.'

'I shall take a look at it promptly.'

'He be working hard every day.'

Now, think about the way your imagined speaker looked and sounded for each sentence. What was the race or ethnicity of the speaker? Where were they from? What was their gender? How old might they be? Did they sound educated? Annoying? Relatable? Chances are, you have a clear answer to most (if not all) of these questions. But how do we glean all of these details from a single sentence? It turns out that language tells us far more than just the meaning of words; it can give us critical social information, too.

Part of the reason we can infer information about a speaker from their language is that our social context partly determines how we talk. That's the basic premise behind regional accents—you sound like you're from the South, New England or California because that's where you grew up. We learn language and pick up our accents from our peers during adolescence, meaning that the people you spent time with during this period shape your speech for the rest of your life. That doesn't mean that how you talk remains completely static, but changing the fundamental rules of how you talk—what linguists call your 'grammar'—becomes much more difficult as you grow older. Because of this persistent effect of our adolescence, our speech always bears the trace of where we spend our formative years.

Speech is shaped by many other factors of our social background beyond region. For example, Latinx residents of Miami often have different accents than African American residents, and white Miamians often sound distinct from both groups—despite all being natives of Miami. If they all live in the same city, how do they learn different ways of speaking? The answer is that social factors like race, ethnicity, gender, and social class affect the structures and experiences of our lives, including how we learn language.

These social factors have a profound influence on our cultural tastes and social circles. Take sports, for example. Who plays basketball? What about lacrosse? Or golf? Though they may seem like simple preferences, activities like sports have strong connotations of race or class. Less voluntary aspects of our lives like neighborhoods and housing also play a crucial role in determining our friends and acquaintances. Persistent segregation in housing and schooling in the United States, especially along racial lines, means that race can determine the people you see in your neighborhood or in your classroom, shaping the peers you have during adolescence. Since our adult speech owes a great deal to our adolescent interactions, the makeup of neighborhoods and schools have lasting effects, creating substantial dialect differences even within the same city.

We also change how we talk because we want to *fit in* better with who we're talking to. Politicians are prime examples of how people change their speaking style in different contexts. If you watch a politician, especially one travelling the United States to give speeches, note how different they might sound in different parts of the country. For politicians who are from the South (and even sometimes for those who aren't!), you might hear some features you associate with a Southern twang appear when they make stops in the Southern United States. Language can show that you're part of a community, and—consciously or unconsciously—people may adopt features of a dialect to show that they belong. Shifting your speech this way can be risky if you aren't actually from the community, however, as news stories about politicians' 'inauthentic accents' often demonstrate.

The final way language is connected to society is through our ideology, or the way that we think about the social value of language. Remember reading those sentences earlier and thinking about the people speaking them? You probably had feelings about the personality characteristics of the speaker like their friendliness or intelligence in addition to their social background. These perceptions of accents or dialects aren't innate to how they sound; they're ideas that we have to learn. Linguists emphasize that dialects aren't *wrong* ways of speaking a language, just *different* ways of speaking a language—yet negative perceptions of certain dialects persist.

Unfortunately, how we feel about certain kinds of speech stems from the social inequalities present in our society. The dialects that we tend to view as 'ugly,' 'uneducated,' or 'annoying' tend to be those that are spoken by the socially disadvantaged. Even as languages and dialects change, the speech of people of color or the working class tend to garner only negative attention, often being viewed as a problem that needs to be fixed. (Think about it; African American, Latinx, and Caribbean dialects are often labeled '*broken English*,' and the speech of the working class is often referred to as '*slang*').

Because of these connections, language is often used as a proxy to talk about the people speaking it, attaching negative stereotypes to social groups. It's no coincidence, for instance, that people who view women as weak, demure, and emotional tend to believe that women's speech is (or at least *should be*) weak, demure, and emotional. It's also no coincidence that the gender group with less power in society—women—is also the gender group whose speech is policed and corrected more often. Just think about the policing of women's language on social media (or even news media) related to vocal fry, uptalk, etc. Or think about the assumptions you made about the speaker of this chapter's first quote ('I like totally hate that movie').

These negative feelings about certain dialects or speakers have broader consequences that can affect our society and its structure. Discrimination in housing based on the dialect of a prospective home buyer or rental applicant is a persistent problem in the United States, despite being illegal. Studies have shown that rental applicants who speak African American English are less likely to get callbacks from landlords, and more likely to be charged higher fees. Similar discrimination in hiring or assessment of job candidates also occurs based purely on dialect or speech. Studies of the corporate workplace have shown, for instance, that employees often prefer managers with masculine speaking styles over feminine speaking styles. These and other issues serve to disadvantage these groups, meaning that our assessments of linguistic differences play a role in creating some of the social problems that we face.

In short, the connection between language and society is complex, and it goes much deeper than you might expect. Language reflects who we are in the social world, and it also works as a tool to reveal how our society works. The next time you hear someone's accent and have a reflexive negative reaction, take a minute and ask yourself, 'How did they grow up differently than I did?' Or, 'Why do I feel that way about how they talk?' Or maybe, 'I wonder what they would think about me?'

About the author

Jon Forrest is assistant professor of linguistics at the University of Georgia, and he received his Ph.D. in sociology from North Carolina State University. His research examines the social reasons for language variation and change, especially in urban centers of the U.S. South. His most recent work investigates differences in dialect production within the workplace, as well as the ways in which dialects and accents can affect workplace experiences for employees.

Suggestions for further reading

In this book

Further discussion of racial and ethnic inequality is included in Chapters 51 (African American English), 57 (linguistics for teachers), and 61 (bilingual education). Chapters addressing gender inequality include 10 (grammatical gender), 32 (women's and men's language), and 46 (gendered language). Other chapters discussing language and identity include 31 (Deaf culture), 33 (gay speech), 45 (language conflict), and 49 (U.S. dialects).

Elsewhere

Alim, H. Samy, and Geneva Smitherman. *Articulate While Black: Barack Obama, Language, and Race in the U.S.* (Oxford University Press, 2012).

Finegan, Edward, and John Rickford, eds. *Language in the USA: Themes for the Twenty-first Century* (Cambridge University Press, 2004).

Fought, Carmen. *Language and Ethnicity* (Cambridge University Press, 2006).

Mooney, Annabelle, and Betsy Evans. *Language, Society and Power: An Introduction* (Routledge, fourth edition 2015).

Wolfram, Walt, and Natalie Schilling. *American English: Dialects and Variation* (Wiley, third edition 2016).

43

What are lingua francas?

Nicholas Ostler

Why are lingua francas needed? What are some examples? How does a language become a lingua franca? How does it stop being one?

Each of us has a mother tongue, which we speak within our own language community. But what happens when two communities that don't speak each other's language come into contact and need to talk? Sometimes they can learn enough of each other's language to get by, but sometimes that's not feasible—for example, what if there are three communities in contact, or five or more? In many cases they resort to a lingua franca, a kind of 'bridge' language that is distinct from the mother tongues of each group. An example from recent history is French, which was used from the seventeenth century until after World War I as the language of diplomacy in Europe. Written Classical Chinese served for an even longer period as a diplomatic lingua franca in countries bordering on China. Today's best example of a lingua franca is undoubtedly English, which supports international communication in fields ranging from aviation to business to rock music.

So how do lingua francas come about?

About 10,000 years ago, as agriculture and stock-breeding increasingly replaced hunting and gathering, human groups became larger and more hierarchical, and had more occasion to interact with neighboring groups that had different mother tongues. In some cases, perhaps, the groups were brought into contact by some dominant power—such as a regional strongman, or an early empire. In others the contact may have arisen spontaneously, as networks of markets came into existence. Later on—since maybe 5,000 years ago—another motive for intergroup contacts emerged: enthusiastic religious believers conceived it as their duty to pass on valuable knowledge of spiritual life to strangers. So imperialists, merchants, and missionaries have all been motivated to establish communication beyond their mother-tongue groups. A lingua franca is a technical fix that helps overcome language barriers across a set of groups that is too large—or too recently united—to have a common language. Performing that fix is the job of a new kind of specialist who must have begun to appear around this time: interpreters, who learned the regional lingua franca in addition to their mother tongue and used it to communicate with interpreters in other groups.

Sometimes a lingua franca replaces the mother tongues it bridges. Latin, for example, spread far and wide through the settlement of soldiers within the Roman Empire. It gradually became a mother tongue throughout western Europe (replacing languages like Etruscan and Oscan in Italy, Gaulish and Ligurian in France, and Tartessian and Celtiberian in Spain). But for Latin to remain a common language over so large an area, the groups that spoke it as a mother tongue would have had to remain in contact. This didn't happen. Germanic conquests after the fifth century broke the Roman Empire into distinct regions that had little to do with one another, and Latin eventually broke up into distinct dialects and languages, like French, Provençal, Tuscan, Corsican, Spanish, Catalan, and Galician.

A lingua franca may be a language like Latin or Sanskrit, taught according to strict rules, and capable of surviving for many centuries with little change. On the other hand, it need not be a full-fledged language at all. An important subcategory of lingua francas is pidgins, which result when people who lack a common tongue make up a new one out of pieces of the languages they already know. The first language to be known specifically as 'Lingua Franca' was a medium of this kind. It was a kind of simplified and highly mixed Italian, used by traders and others in the eastern Mediterranean around the year 1000. Such a loosely structured language may change unpredictably; communication depends more on cooperative imagination and mutual good will than on a clearly shared grammar and vocabulary.

Goodwill can't be taken for granted. Although lingua francas may be envisaged as neutral 'bridges' between the potentially competing groups they serve, they are a human phenomenon and subject to being drawn into the conflicts they mediate. They are typically used only by a skilled minority, whom other groups can perceive and resent as an unfairly privileged elite, out for its own interests. This was true of Greek speakers in the eastern Mediterranean and west Asia at the end of the first millennium BCE, and true of Latin speakers, the educated elite in medieval Europe. It remains true for English speakers today. The recent bloody civil war between the Sinhala-speaking majority in Sri Lanka and the Tamil-speaking minority grew out of legislation that suppressed Tamil language and culture. The same legislation also replaced English with Sinhala as the country's official language, because the Tamils were seen as being more skilled in English and drawing too many benefits as a result.

By definition, a lingua franca is not the mother tongue of most of the people it serves. People learn it deliberately, in order to achieve some purpose. This means that its fate in the long term is vulnerable to changes in the balance of wealth and power. It may survive as the mother tongue of the ethnic group that originally spoke it, but the purpose that has made people want to learn it as a lingua franca may disappear. Empires may be dissolved or conquered by other empires: hence Persian, which had been the official lingua franca in medieval India for almost a millennium, faded when the territory was taken over by English-speaking Britons. Trade networks may cease to operate for reasons of politics or economics, and their medium of communication may be forgotten: Sogdian, for example, for centuries the lingua franca for trade from Iran to China, ceased to be current after the decline of the Silk Road. Religions have been known to die out, and with them the need for a common language; for example, the use of

Aramaic was largely lost in Asia in the first millennium AD, with the decline of Nestorian Christianity. Which brings us to the question: if storied languages such as Latin, Persian, Sogdian and Aramaic ceased to be lingua francas after hundreds or thousands of years, how long will English survive in that role? Changes can come very fast in the modern connected world, as patterns of influence surge and fade away.

About the author

Nicholas Ostler holds degrees in Greek, Latin, philosophy and economics from Balliol College, Oxford, and a Ph.D. in linguistics and Sanskrit from the Massachusetts Institute of Technology, where he studied under Noam Chomsky. He is the author of *Empires of the Word: A Language History of the World* (2005), *Ad Infinitum: A Biography of Latin* (2007), *The Last Lingua Franca: English until the Return of Babel* (2010), and *Passwords to Paradise: How Languages have Re-invented World Religions* (2016). In addition to these four books, he has published, as author or editor, some five dozen scholarly articles, book chapters, book reviews, and general magazine articles on topics ranging from language history to language technology to general linguistics. He is currently the chairman of the Foundation for Endangered Languages, and lives in Hungerford, England.

Suggestions for further reading

In this book

Other chapters discussing languages that have bridged gaps between communities include 17 (Esperanto), 27 (history of English), 28 (Latin), 30 (pidgins and creoles), 42 (language and society), 44 (languages of India), and 45 (language conflict).

Elsewhere

Collitz, Hermann. 'World Languages,' *Language* vol. 2, no. 1 (1926), pp. 1–13. A classic article about international languages in history, by a German-born scholar who became the first president of the Linguistic Society of America.

Crystal, David. *English as a Global Language* (Cambridge University Press, 2003). A historical exploration of the processes that have converged to expand the influence of English throughout the world.

Ostler, Nicholas. *The Last Lingua Franca: English until the Return of Babel* (Penguin, 2010). A wide-ranging account of lingua francas and their role in history, with particular attention to the unprecedentedly powerful current position of English.

44

How can a country function with more than one official language?

Vijay Gambhir

Does every country have an official language? Why do some countries have more than one official language? How does a country like India juggle multiple official languages? What are the functions of India's multiple official languages?

Some countries, such as the United States and Mexico, don't have any officially recognized language; but most countries have one or more. Germany has one official language (German); Canada has two (English and French); Belgium has three (French, Dutch, and German); Singapore has four (English, Tamil, Malay, and Standard Mandarin); South Africa has eleven; and Bolivia has thirty-seven! In order to gain an insight into how a country functions with multiple official languages, we briefly examine India's situation where the Central Government has two official languages, and each of India's 29 states and union territories have their own and additional official language(s).

According to the People's Linguistic Survey of India in 2012, there are 780 living languages in India! In fact, the 2001 census recorded 1,635 distinct speech communities, 234 of which had 10,000 or more speakers. The Constitution of India officially recognizes 22 major Indian languages that belong to four different language families. Hindi, the most widely spoken language in the country, belongs to the Indo-European language family, like English. Other languages of India come from the Dravidian family, the Sino-Tibetan family, and the Austro-Asiatic family, as well as Indo-European.

How can India function with so much language diversity? Most Indian states are organized on linguistic basis and languages are a central part of people's regional and political identities. Indian states and union territories specify their primary and 'second' official language(s) based on their regional administrative and socio-political milieu. Most of them have two or more official languages: Tamilnadu has two (Tamil and English); Delhi has four (Hindi, English, Urdu, and Punjabi); Puducherry has five (Tamil, English, Malayalam, Telugu, and French); and West Bengal has twelve (Bengali, English, Nepali, Urdu, Odia, Santhali, Punjabi, Hindi, Kamtapuri, Rajbanshi, Kurmali, Kurukh).

So which languages get used where, when, and by whom? The rules for official language(s) use are stated in the Official Languages Act of each of the state and union territory. According to the Delhi Language Act 2000, all four official languages of Delhi are used to receive and reply applications & petitions in the government offices, publish government rules and regulations, and record and issue the proceedings of legislative assembly. Also, signboards of official buildings, government offices, and roads are written in all the official languages in their scripts.

While Indian states and union territories have more than two dozen official languages, the Central Government of India has only two, Hindi and English. Hindi is the primary official language spoken by about 54 percent of people as the first or second language. Initially, after the independence in 1947, English was chosen as a co-official language for fifteen years only until the colonial laws and administrative rules could be replaced and rewritten in Hindi. However, there was opposition to Hindi in some Indian states. After serious linguistic riots in the southern state of Tamilnadu against Hindi in the mid-1960s, the government passed a legislation to continue English as an official language for an indefinite period.

Although freedom fighters like Mahatma Gandhi shunned English during India's struggle for freedom from the British Empire, English has continued to be an important language because of rivalry among the many regional languages of India and the global status of English. In India, English is the language of higher education and elites, and it provides increased access to higher paying jobs at home and abroad. Children learn English in school under the 'three-language formula,' which recommends that students learn Hindi, English, and a regional or another modern Indian language. Today, many parents prefer to send their children to private English-medium schools as opposed to Hindi-medium public schools, known as 'government schools' in India. English coaching centers are in high demand because college graduates seek to improve their speaking skills to secure jobs in multinational companies. India's Call Centers train their employees for a variety of English accents in order to work for American, British, and Australian companies.

What is the status of Hindi? Hindi is continuously promoted by the Department of Official Language of India for official purposes. It provides incentives to the central government employees for learning and using Hindi at work. The Central Hindi Directorate and Central Hindi Institute are engaged in the propagation of Hindi in non-Hindi-speaking states. Hindi is spreading rapidly as a lingua franca in the urban centers of India because of internal migration for jobs and increased business opportunities. Hindi media is also growing, and it is creating new employment opportunities. The Indian film industry, popularly known as Bollywood, has also popularized Hindi throughout the country. The linguistic profile of cosmopolitan cities like Mumbai (Bombay), Kolkata (Calcutta), and Bengaluru (Bangalore, the 'Silicon Valley' of India) has changed significantly in recent times. The dominant regional languages of those cities are Marathi, Bengali, and Kannada, respectively, but Hindi is widely spoken on their streets.

As for the functions of the official languages of the Central Government, members of Lok Sabha (Lower House of parliament) and Rajya Sabha (Upper House of parliament) can choose to conduct parliamentary business in either English or Hindi. Although parliamentary proceedings are primarily in Hindi, parliamentary enactments are always recorded in English. Written communication between the offices of the Central Government can be in Hindi or English, but a translation is always provided in the other language. For communication between the Central Government and the states or union territories, the center has established three regions. It communicates with 'Region A' (Bihar, Haryana, Himachal Pradesh, Madhya Pradesh, Rajasthan, Uttar Pradesh, Jharkhand, Uttrakhand, Chhattisgarh, Delhi, and Andaman & Nicobar Islands) in Hindi; with 'Region B' (Gujarat, Maharashtra, Punjab, Chandigarh, Daman & Diu, and Dadar & Nagar Haveli) in Hindi or English (if in English, it is accompanied by its Hindi translation); and with 'Region C' (states and union territories not included in categories 'A' and 'B') in English.

All administrative documents for the public are available in Hindi as well as in English. There is a Central Translation Bureau that translates all non-statutory procedural literature of the central government from Hindi to English and vice-versa. Regarding the language of the courts, all proceedings, judgments, decrees, and orders of the Supreme Court and High Courts are in English. However, Hindi or another Indian language can be used in a High Court with the permission of the Governor of the State.

Working with multiple official languages can be challenging! But there is no other choice for a multilingual country like India. Overall, India is functioning quite smoothly with its numerous official languages, with the exception of occasional linguistic tensions due to regional politics and strong linguistic identities.

About the author

Dr. Vijay Gambhir is a retired professor of South Asian languages and linguistics from the University of Pennsylvania. She received her M.A. in linguistics from Delhi University and Ph.D. in linguistics from the University of Pennsylvania. Her areas of interest include syntax, second language acquisition, assessment, and heritage language learning. She has published articles in scholarly journals and books. She is the editor of the book *Teaching and Acquisition of South Asian Languages* published by the University of Pennsylvania Press. She is also guest editor of *Teaching and Learning South Asian Heritage Languages*, the first volume of the online journal *South Asia Language Pedagogy and Technology*.

Suggestions for further reading

In this book
Other chapters discussing multilingual societies include 43 (lingua francas) and 45 (language conflict). The importance of Hindi is a theme of Chapter 48 (America's language crisis), and a Hindi grammatical example is cited in Chapter 19 (language and thought). The relationships among languages are discussed in Chapters 3 (dialects) and 23 (language families).

Elsewhere
Kachru, Braj, Yamuna Kachru, and S, N. Sridhar, eds. *Language in South Asia* (Cambridge University Press, 2008). The introduction discusses the linguistic impact of Sanskrit, Persian, and English on South Asian languages. Part 2 of the book discusses the status of South Asia's major, minor and tribal languages.

Paranjape, Makarand, R, and G. J. V. Prasad, eds. *Indian English and 'Vernacular' India* (Published by Pearson, 2010). It examines the uneasy relationship between English with Indian languages in the age of globalization.

Schmid, Carol, L. *The Politics of Language: Conflict, Identity, and Cultural Pluralism in Comparative Perspective* (Oxford University Press, 2001). It analyzes history and important aspects of language politics in the United States, Canada, and Switzerland.

www.rajbhasha.gov.in/en. This website describes official language rules of the Indian union in detail.

www.mapsofindia.com/maps/india/indianlanguages.htm. This web page shows India's political map with their primary languages.

45

Why do people fight over language?

Paul B. Garrett

Are language differences important enough to fight about? How do conflicts over language get started? What are the underlying causes?

The idea of fighting over language might seem strange, but it's all too common. Why do people sometimes feel so strongly about their language that they take up weapons against speakers of another? What is it about language that can give rise to tensions that last for generations? The answers to these questions lie in the close relationship between language and identity, particularly cultural and ethnic identity.

Many of us who speak only English tend to think of monolingualism as the normal state of affairs. We may also tend to think that there is a one-to-one correspondence between language and nation: in France they speak French, in Japan they speak Japanese, and so on. Worldwide, though, there are more than 6,000 languages—and only about 200 nations. This means that there are many multilingual nations. And languages tend to correspond with ethnic groups, which means that there are many multi-ethnic nations as well. Of course, some are far more multilingual and multi-ethnic than others. At one extreme are countries like Japan, where the vast majority of people are ethnically Japanese and speak Japanese. At the other extreme are countries like India and Nigeria, each of which has about 400 languages and ethnicities within its borders.

During the course of an ordinary day, an ordinary Nigerian might use three, four, or more languages, depending on where she goes, what she does, and whom she meets along the way. But she considers only one of those languages to be *her* language, the language of her own group. In most situations, her *ethnic* identity—whether it's Yoruba or Igbo or Efik or Igala—is more relevant and meaningful than her *national* identity as a Nigerian. Similarly, although she may speak multiple languages, only one of them—her home language, her language of ethnic identity—is linked to strong feelings about who she is and how she fits into the complex larger society in which she lives.

She's certainly not alone. No matter where we live, and no matter what language or languages we speak, we experience the language of our own group—even the particular way in which we speak it—as an essential part of who we are.

In a great many parts of the world, people of different language backgrounds interact on a daily basis. For the most part, things go smoothly enough. But sometimes, tensions arise; and sometimes these tensions reach a breaking point, giving way to open hostility and outright conflict. This is especially likely to happen when speakers of one language feel threatened or oppressed by speakers of another. When that's the case, language differences become highly salient markers of social, cultural, and political differences. Wherever you find conflicts over language, you're sure to find struggles over other issues as well, such as territory, religion, and political power.

The weapons used in these conflicts may be more than harsh words. Language-based conflicts can escalate into riots, insurrections, wars, even genocide. A case in point: conflicts over language played a major part in the separation of Bangladesh from Pakistan in 1971. What began as a Bengali language movement escalated into a nine-month war for independence in which more than three million people died and another ten million people were displaced.

About a decade later, in Sri Lanka, the Tamil Tigers, a separatist group whose members were speakers of the Tamil language, took up arms against a government dominated by the country's

Sinhala-speaking majority. Significantly, the government had passed a 'Sinhala-Only Act' in 1956, and in later years it had banned the importing of Tamil-language books, films, and other media. In response to these and other forms of exclusion and oppression, the Tamil Tigers set out to establish an independent Tamil nation in the north and east of Sri Lanka. Their armed rebellion evolved into the Sri Lankan Civil War, which lasted until the Sri Lankan military finally defeated the Tamil Tigers in May 2009. By that time, more than a quarter of a century of fighting had resulted in as many as 100,000 deaths, and several hundred thousand Tamil civilians had fled the country as refugees.

In various other parts of the world today, language is at the heart of ongoing conflicts characterized by constant social tensions and, in some cases, sporadic outbreaks of violence. In Spain between 1961 and 2011, the separatist group ETA used bombings, kidnappings, and other violent tactics in pursuit of its goal of an independent Basque homeland, where Basque would be the national language. (ETA is an acronym for *Euskadi Ta Askatasuna*, meaning 'Basque Homeland and Liberty' in the Basque language.) Belgium is deeply divided between the Dutch-speaking northern region (known as Flanders) and the French-speaking southern region (Wallonia). Thus far there has been no violence, nor is any expected; but many Belgians fully expect—indeed, some hope—that the country will ultimately break in two. Meanwhile, in the United States, the relationship between English and Spanish has been the focus of much debate and political action—some of it quite acrimonious and polarizing—as Spanish-speakers (many of whom also speak English) from a great diversity of backgrounds have become an increasingly large and influential part of the country's population.

Conflicts over language don't always lead to physical violence, but they can generate tensions that persist for many years, affecting the lives of millions on a daily basis. Take the case of Canada—generally a peaceful place, but one that has certainly had its share of conflict over language issues. Canada as a whole is officially bilingual, but most French-speaking Canadians live in the province of Quebec. Surrounded by English-speaking provinces, they often feel that their language and culture are under siege. They feel particularly threatened by the presence of English-speakers within Quebec itself, where, historically, English-speakers have been a disproportionately powerful minority whose political and economic dominance has been deeply resented.

In 1977, French-speakers in Quebec took action to protect their language by passing the controversial Bill 101. Ostensibly, Bill 101 was intended to safeguard the status of French in Quebec and, by extension, the cultural and socio-economic well-being of French-speakers. It was controversial because it did so largely by *restricting* the use of English. For example, it required any business with more than fifty employees to operate primarily in French, and it made it difficult for English-speaking parents to send their children to English-speaking schools. In these and other ways, Bill 101 affected the most mundane aspects of everyday life in Quebec: making a telephone call or ordering a cup of coffee now had the potential to become a politically charged event with legal implications.

One of the most controversial parts of Bill 101 was the requirement that all signs in public places had to be in French, and French alone. This meant that even signs for Eaton's, the venerable old Canadian department store, became illegal: use of the family name Eaton was perfectly permissible, but the apostrophe + s on the end of the name ('s) made the signs 'English,' and therefore violations of the new law. This signage element of Bill 101 quickly became a point of resentment among English-speakers, particularly small-business owners like Allan Singer. For years, Mr. Singer had run his modest shop beneath a simple hand-painted sign that read 'Allan Singer Limited—Printers and Stationers.' Under the new law, Mr. Singer's sign became illegal; he would have to replace it, at his own expense, with a sign in French.

Well, Mr. Singer refused to do that—and he took his case all the way to Canada's Supreme Court. The court's ruling was a compromise of sorts, but one that reflected the realities of Canadian society in a way that most Canadians found fair and just. The court decided that Mr. Singer did *not* have the right to keep his sign in English only. But the new law could *not* require him to replace it with a sign in French only, to the exclusion of English—or of Spanish, Chinese, Polish, Vietnamese, or any other language that he might wish to use in addition to French. So business owners in Quebec *could* be required to use French on their signs, but the law *could not* interfere with their freedom to post bilingual or multilingual signs—signs reflecting the linguistic diversity of Quebec, and of Canada as a whole.

Ultimately, this brouhaha over signs provided an opportunity for Canada to clarify its commitment to protecting the language rights of *all* of its citizens. But the underlying tensions didn't go away; on the contrary, the longstanding rivalry between francophone and anglophone Canadians persisted and continues to flare up periodically. A particularly dramatic incident was the 1995 referendum in which Quebec's citizens went to the polls to vote on whether their province should secede from Canada and become an independent French-speaking nation. It didn't happen—but the vote was extremely close, with a margin of less than one percent.

In these and virtually all other conflicts over language, much more than language is at stake. That's because the language that we speak is part of who we are. It gives us a powerful sense of belonging with those who speak like us, and an equally powerful sense of difference from those who don't. Little wonder, then, that when someone attacks our language—or even just our accent—we feel that *we* are being attacked. And we respond accordingly. Discriminate against a language, and you discriminate against its speakers; disrespect my language, and you disrespect me.

About the author
Paul B. Garrett, an associate professor of anthropology at Temple University, is a linguistic anthropologist whose research focuses on the creole languages and cultures of the Caribbean. His other interests include language contact, ideologies of language, and interspecies communication.

Suggestions for further reading

In this book

The topic of frictions and hostilities in multilingual environments is addressed in Chapters 30 (pidgins and creoles), 37 (accents), 43 (lingua francas), 44 (languages of India), and 52 (New World Spanish).

Elsewhere

Harris, Roxy, and Ben Rampton. *The Language, Ethnicity and Race Reader* (Routledge, 2003). This collection of classic and contemporary readings examines the relationships between language and such issues as identity, ethnic diversity, nationalism, colonialism and migration.

Joseph, Brian D., et al., eds., *When Languages Collide: Perspectives on Language Conflict, Language Competition, and Language Coexistence* (Ohio State University Press, 2003). Fifteen essays examine various cases of language contact worldwide (associated with trade, migration, war, etc.), considering the factors that give rise to both peaceful and conflictual outcomes.

Schmid, Carol L. *The Politics of Language: Conflict, Identity, and Cultural Pluralism in Comparative Perspective* (Oxford University Press, 2001). Focusing on the many languages spoken within the USA, this book examines both historical and contemporary conflicts and controversies.

46

What is gendered language?

Caroline Myrick

Does the English language reflect gender inequality? Are there alternatives to gendered language? What about in languages like Spanish and French, which have formal grammatical gender? Does the push for gender-inclusive language really matter, or are we just being overly critical?

Fill in the blank: 'Someone left ___ shoes in the car.' What did you put? His? Her? Their? Many English teachers, grammar books, and style guides of the past have instructed us to write 'his' (or 'he' or 'him') when we don't know the gender or a referent, or when we aren't talking about a specific person. This system of using a masculine default is often referred to as the 'generic masculine.' This is an example of gendered language, because it treats men (via the masculine form) as the default.

Generic masculines are especially prevalent in languages with formal grammatical gender. In Spanish, for example, *los gatos* can mean 'male cats' or simply 'cats'; an all-female group of cats would be *las gatas*. In fact, a group of 99 female cats and a single male cat would technically be called *los gatos*. The generic masculine doesn't just affect discussions of animals, though. In languages with formal gender, many jobs take the masculine form by default. Professor (*professeur* in French, *profesor* in Spanish) and musician (*musicien* in French, *músico* in Spanish) are masculine;

they require spelling changes or affixes to denote a female professor (*professeure, profesora*) or female musician (*musicienne,
música*).

Languages with formal grammatical gender aren't the only
languages with a gendered job problem! Think about English
terms like *firemen, chairmen,* and *congressmen,* which are often
used to mean 'men and women firefighters,' 'heads of organizations' and 'senators/representatives.' These words are gendered
because they assume maleness, using it as the default. But does this
pattern really matter?

Many argue that the generic masculine is purely grammatical,
or simply a reflection of privileging men in the past. Some say
that using words like *chair* in place of *chairman* or *congressperson*
instead of *congressman* is just an attempt at being 'politically correct'. Others disagree, arguing that it's really about being *correct*.
After all, women can now be the heads of organizations as well as
members of Congress; our language should reflect that!

Moreover, many claim that the 'generic masculine' can erase
women and non-binary folks, or at least place them as secondary—and there is research to back them up. Studies have shown
that terms like 'chairmen' and 'firemen' do influence the ways in
which children view job possibilities for their gender, just like
generic 'he' causes us to imagine a man or masculine figure, even
when it's being used in general terms.

In addition to generic masculines, English has other gendered
practices. One example is the implementation of suffixes to mark
something as female (e.g., 'host' becomes 'host<u>ess</u>,' 'actor' becomes
'act<u>ress</u>'). Other examples are most salient in the sports realm: a
high school men's lacrosse team is called the 'Tigers,' while the
women's lacrosse team may be called the 'Lady Tigers'; similarly,
the men's professional basketball league in the United States is
called the 'National Basketball League' (or NBA), while the wom-
en's league is called the 'Women's National Basketball League'
(or WNBA). All of these practices place men as the default and
women as a linguistic addition. Many argue that this reflects the
privileging of men over women in society.

But not all gendered language places men as the default. Some forms of gendered language place men as the addition. For example, terms like 'male nurse' reflect an assumption of nurses being women. These male + profession forms are likely a result of the markedness of a man being part of *feminized* (and often undervalued) care-centered work, such as nursing, teaching, counseling, and social work. Thus, terms like 'male nurse' are examples of gendered language as well.

So is it possible to ungender language?

Luckily, in English, inclusive language solutions are fairly easy, and they don't have to be awkward or clunky. Rather than attempting the mouthful 'congressperson' every time, you can just be more specific and say 'representatives' or 'senators.' Similarly, 'firefighters,' 'police officers', and 'mail carriers' can replace 'firemen,' 'policemen', and 'mailmen.' Folks to whom you announce that Greg is the new nurse in your department can figure out Greg's gender based on context clues, or upon meeting Greg, just as that person eavesdropping on your conversation about how Meryl Streep is your favorite *actor* will likely not be confused either. And all lacrosse players can be Tigers!

But what about when *someone leaves* _____ shoes? How can we possibly ungender personal pronouns? Fortunately, we have another easy solution there: singular *they*! In other words, you can say 'Someone left their shoes in the car.' Odds are, if you speak English, you already use singular *they* regularly, without notice; but it's possible that when you see singular *they* written, such as in the previous sentence, it makes you cringe. If that described your reaction, here are three points that should put you at ease: First, singular *they* is nothing new! Its usage has been documented by the *Oxford English Dictionary* as far back as the fourteenth century. Second, singular *they* has been used by authors such as Geoffrey Chaucer, Jane Austen, and Lewis Carroll. Third, singular *they* has been added to numerous 'official' style guides, including the AP Style Guide and Chicago Style Guide, and has been adopted by news outlets like the *Washington Post*. So even the biggest rule-sticklers can rest easy when it comes to singular *they*.

But what about languages with formal grammatical gender, like Spanish or French? Some inclusive language proponents have offered solutions in the form of the @ sign or *x* in Spanish. Words like *Latinos* can be written as '*Latin@s*' or '*Latinxs*.' Similarly, French speakers experimented with placing a middot (also called 'middle dot' or 'median-period') at the end of masculine nouns, followed by feminine endings. In French, male musicians are *musiciens*, and a female musicians are *musiciennes*. Traditionally, male and female musicians would be *musiciens* (the generic masculine). But the inclusive form, incorporating the midline dot, would be written as *musicien·ne·s*.

These alternatives have not been met without resistance. In addition to pronunciation and reading difficulties, some argue that the '-@' and '-*x*' suffixes in Spanish corrupt the language and its history; after all, the -*o* and -*a* suffixes been around since the reign of Queen Isabella in the fifteenth century! Others have pointed out that the term is used overwhelmingly in the continental United States within an English-language context, and accordingly call the use of these suffixes a form of linguistic imperialism. As for the French middle dot, while this new inclusive form was indeed creative, linguistic purists claimed that it threatened to corrupt the French language. The use of the middle dot was officially banned by the French prime minister in 2017.

What is the future of gendered language? Can it be eradicated from all languages? Should it be? While we can be certain that language users will continue to come up with new creative linguistic alternatives to elude gendered language, only time will tell what which forms will fade away as fads, and which ones will be adopted into standard forms.

About the author

Caroline Myrick, co-editor of this book, holds a Ph.D. from the Department of Sociology at North Carolina State University, where she specialized in sociolinguistics and social inequality. Her research has examined language and gender ideologies as well as language variation and change in the Caribbean. Her doctoral dissertation examined gender inequality as it relates to language ideologies in higher education. She frequently gives campus and community workshops related to dialect diversity, many of which have focused on gender-inclusive language.

Suggestions for further reading

In this book
Other chapters discussing issues of language and gender include Chapters 10 (grammatical gender), 32 (men's and women's speech), and 33 (gay speech). Chapters addressing issues of language evolution as a result of social processes include Chapters 9 (new words), 29 (language change), and 49 (American dialects), as well as 53 (social media) and 56 (text messaging).

Elsewhere
Hellinger, Marlis. 'Guidelines for non-discriminatory language use', in Ruth Wodack, Barbara Johnstone and Paul E. Kerswill, eds., *The Sage Handbook of Sociolinguistics* (Sage, 2011).

Sczesny, Sabine, et al. 'Can gender-fair language reduce gender stereotyping and discrimination?', *Frontiers in Psychology* vol. 7, no. 25 (2016).

'Gender-inclusive language.' The Writing Center, UNC Chapel Hill. Available at https://writingcenter.unc.edu/tips-and-tools/gender-inclusive-language.

'Why "Latinx" is succeeding while other gender-neutral terms fail to catch on.' *TIME* (Apr 2, 2018). Available at http://time.com/5191804/latinx-definition-meaning-latino-hispanic-gender-neutral

'The Push to make French gender-neutral.' *The Atlantic* (Nov 24, 2017). Available at www.theatlantic.com/international/archive/2017/11/inclusive-writing-france-feminism/545048

Language in
the United States

47

What is the language of the United States?

David Goldberg

Isn't the U.S. monolingual? What languages other than English are spoken there? How do you find out who speaks what languages where?

It seems peculiar when people say that the U.S. is an English-speaking country, and that Americans 'aren't good at languages.' In many towns and cities in the U.S., you certainly hear different languages all around you, and tens of millions of Americans speak languages other than English—a lot of other languages. Over 60 million people speak languages other than English at home in the U.S. (this was reported by the U.S. Census, the last time it did a full count, surveying the years 2009–2013); about 78 percent of these people also speak English well or very well. In Idaho alone, people currently speak over seventy languages, including about 800 who speak the Native American language, Shoshoni. In Cook County, Illinois, more than 140,000 people speak Polish, and almost half of New York City's residents don't speak English at home. In fact, only some less-populated or rural areas of the country are exclusively English-speaking: places like Appalachia, the deep South, and parts of the Midwest. In most of the country, and especially in the larger cities, multilingualism is the rule.

How do we know about how many Americans speak which languages and where? One way is to refer to an online Language

Map created by the Modern Language Association of America. Using data from the 2000, 2005, and 2010 U.S. Censuses and the American Community Survey, the MLA has created interactive maps and tables that show the linguistic composition of the entire U.S., state by state, county by county, city by city—down to the neighborhoods defined by postal delivery codes—at the touch of a button. The Language Map is regularly updated with new Census data.

You can use the map to see how languages are distributed across the country, and to zoom in on places that have speakers of a language you're interested in. You can call up tables that rank the fifty states according to numbers of speakers for each language. If, for instance, you want to know where Vietnamese is most spoken you'll see that California, Texas, and Washington are the top three states. If you look for Americans who speak Gujarathi, you'll find the biggest communities in New Jersey, California, and Illinois. And tables in the MLA Language Map's Data Center will show you how well speakers of other languages speak English, too.

If you look at Minnesota, which you may think of as full of Scandinavians, you'll find that Spanish, German, and the Southeast Asian language Hmong are the most spoken languages—in fact, there are three times as many speakers of Hmong as there are speakers of Swedish, Norwegian, and Danish combined. You could look up Androscoggin County in Maine and find that it has 13,951 speakers of French, but also 271 speakers of German—not to mention speakers of well over thirty other languages. The MLA Map also gives a breakdown of speakers by age, separating those under the age of 18, those between 18 and 64, and those 65 and over. You can compare the numbers and ages of Yiddish speakers in New York with the numbers and ages of Yiddish speakers in Miami. In Brooklyn, for instance, the map shows 24,000 Yiddish speakers under the age of eighteen; in Miami, there are none. Data like these may provide clues to a language community's future—or in the case of the languages of recent immigrants, clues to whether they have come by themselves to work and send money home, or have come with their families to stay.

The MLA Language Map also displays data from the current MLA survey, 'Enrollments in Languages other than English in United States Institutions of Higher Education.' By clicking a link labeled 'Show where this language is taught,' all U.S. college and university programs in the language displayed are pin-pointed on the map, so that the viewer can see where languages are studied in the context of where they are spoken. Language programs are displayed according to the size of their current enrollments. You can also drill down deeper into the enrollment data and compare the sizes and locations of U.S. language programs by institution since 1958.

There are dozens of ways planners, teachers, students, corporate researchers, librarians, or ordinary citizens can use the information presented in the online MLA Language Map. Marketers who want to reach speakers of Urdu or Korean can find the postal codes where a mass mailing might be most effective. Government agencies can use it for providing social services, or for disaster preparedness. The MLA Language Map can tell Justice Department officials which languages they need to use to inform new citizens of their rights and responsibilities; it can tell officials in the Office of Trade and Information how it might help a company with interests in China find Americans who know the language (extensive data relating to international trade is available at the Asia Society and Longview Foundation's map and data site, Mapping the Nation (https://asiasociety.org/mapping-nation). And the MLA Language Map can help language learners find a place in the U.S. where they can practice the languages they're studying without spending money to go abroad.

The U.S. has long been described as a cultural melting pot into which languages other than English disappear upon arrival. The MLA Language Map reveals that this is far from being the case. You can investigate for yourself by going to www.mla.org, clicking on 'Language Map,' and typing in the name of a language, or a county, town, or U.S. postal code (ZIP Code). You may be surprised.

About the author

David Goldberg retired in 2016 from the position of associate director of the Office of Foreign Language Programs and the Association of Departments of Foreign Languages (ADFL) at the Modern Language Association, where he was responsible for the development of the MLA Language Map. Goldberg holds a Ph.D. in Yiddish studies and has taught Yiddish language and literature in heritage language schools and at Columbia University and the University of Pennsylvania. He is the author of an intermediate-level Yiddish textbook published by Yale University Press.

Suggestions for further reading

In this book

The language landscape of the U.S. is discussed in Chapters 48 (America's language crisis), 50 (Native American languages), 52 (New World Spanish), and 64 (rescuing threatened Native American languages). Other linguistic uses of technology are the subjects of Chapters 54 (language teaching technology), 55 (machine translation), 65 (forensic linguistics), and 66 (the Museum of Languages).

Elsewhere

Ferguson, Charles A., and Shirley Brice Heath. *Language in the USA* (Cambridge University Press, 1981). Discusses language issues from the perspective of the year 1981 in communities of Native Americans, African Americans, Filipino Americans and American speakers of European languages, including Spanish, Italian, French, German, Yiddish, Russian, and Polish. Includes studies on language and law, language and education, and data from the 1970 Census.

McKay, Sandra Lee, and Sau-ling Cynthia Wong, eds. *New Immigrants in the United States: Background for Second Language Educators* (Cambridge University Press, 2000). Discusses language issues from the perspective of the year 2000 in communities of Americans from Mexico, Puerto Rico, Cuba, Vietnam, Southeast Asia, China, Korea, the Philippines, Russia, and India. Includes studies on language and law, as well as on language and education.

McKay, Sandra Lee, and Sau-ling Cynthia Wong, eds. *Language Diversity: Problem or Resource?* (Newbury House, 1988). Discusses language issues from the perspective of the year 1988 in communities of Americans from Mexico, Puerto Rico, Cuba, Vietnam, China, Korea, and the Philippines. Includes studies on language and law, language and education, and data from the 1980 Census.

Ryan, Camille. *Language Use in the United States: 2011* (American Community Survey Reports, 2013). Discusses the U.S. Census and the American Community Survey's research into language use, and provides important historical perspective on Census data.

www.mla.org

https://asiasociety.org/mapping-nation

48

Is there a language crisis in the United States?

Julie Tetel Andresen

What kind of foreign language capabilities does America need? Where are the gaps? What can be done?

The answer to the title question is an unequivocal 'yes.' In order to conduct affairs of national interest concerning defense, intelligence, diplomacy and international business, as well as to provide domestic public services, the U.S. needs a population of competent world citizens who can communicate effectively in a language other than English. At present, however, the U.S. has neither a sufficient number of multilingual citizens to fill the needs nor the educational apparatus in place to produce them.

The crisis is compounded by the fact that *critical languages*—languages considered critical to U.S. national security—are not widely studied at the university level. According to the 2018 Modern Language Association (MLA) study of foreign language enrollments, only four of the top 15 most commonly taught languages are critical languages. They are Chinese, Arabic, Russian, and Korean, and rank seventh, eighth, tenth and eleventh, respectively, on the top 15 list. While there are needs for speakers of other critical languages such Persian/Farsi, Somali, Hindi, Urdu, and Vietnamese, the three most studied foreign languages at the university level are Spanish, American Sign Language, and French.

The MLA study, furthermore, reports that from 2013 to 2016 enrollments in languages other than English fell overall by 9.2 percent. This decline continues the downward trend that began in 2009. Of the Top 15 most studied languages, only Japanese and Korean saw an increase in enrollments between 2013 and 2016, with Japanese posting a 3.1 percent increase and Korean 13.7 percent. Despite these recent increases, however, more students were enrolled in Japanese in 2009. Korean could be considered the great success story with enrollments nearly doubling nationwide between 2006 and 2016. This apparent success is tempered by the fact that only one in five students who take introductory Korean go on to an upper level class. The 5:1 ratio of introductory to advanced enrollments also applies to French, German, Japanese, and Spanish, as well, documenting the limited proficiency levels of those who study these languages

Study abroad trends do nothing to brighten the picture. Although the number of U.S. students studying abroad for credit during the 2015/2016 academic years grew 3.8 percent, the total number (namely 325,339 students) represents just over 1.6 percent of all U.S. students enrolled in colleges and universities. More than half of these students go to Europe, and most choose just five countries: the United Kingdom, Italy, Spain, France, and Germany. The next most visited region is Latin America, which attracts 16.3 percent of the study abroad population, and then Asia with 11.1 percent. Australia and New Zealand, both English-speaking countries, garner 4.2 percent of study abroad interest.

On the high school level, only 11 U.S. states have foreign language graduation requirements, while 16 have none. The other states have graduation requirements that may be fulfilled by a number of subjects, one of which is foreign language.

In this bleak picture, however, glimmer some rays of hope.

After a few decades of decline in foreign language education in grades K-8, the trend is reversing itself. According to the National K-12 Foreign Language Enrollment Survey Report (N K-12), Spanish remains the most frequently taught language, followed by French, Chinese, and then Latin.

High school foreign language learning has remained fairly steady across the years, which is good but could be better. The distribution of high school programs by language puts Spanish at the top with 46 percent, followed by French with 21 percent, then German with almost 9 percent. Although Mandarin has 6.5 percent, Japanese 2.5 percent and Arabic a mere 1 percent, these three languages were not taught *at all* only a few decades ago. It is to be hoped that students exposed to critical and lesser-taught languages in their pre-college years will put pressure on colleges and universities to offer courses in those languages.

A growing—and welcome—trend in high school language education is the increased reliance on resources and facilities of neighboring institutions, such as other high schools, community colleges, or university campuses. Thus, the lack of offerings in a particular high school does not necessarily preclude students from foreign language instruction through telecourses and online courses.

Additionally, the findings from the 2010 MLA foreign languages report have had an effect in higher education. The 2010 study found that the current crisis in language education could be overcome if foreign languages came out of their relative isolation, in which students take courses in the confines of national language departments. Instead, the study argued, language-learning needs to be connected with other fields in order to provide students with opportunities to meaningfully apply their existing language skills in courses outside of language departments. This kind of global initiative, sometimes called 'languages across the curriculum', has taken root in colleges and universities around the country. Notable examples can be found at SUNY Binghamton, the University of Connecticut, and Auburn University.

Finally, studies such as the ones undertaken by the MLA and N K-12 did not survey the many heritage, community-based, after-school and weekend-and summer school programs which provide significant amounts of training and cultural education for languages such as Arabic, Chinese (Mandarin and Cantonese), Korean, and Russian. Also not included in the MLA and N K-12 efforts are teacher-led school programs and exchanges or intensive language summer programs such as Concordia Summer Language Camp, National Security Language Initiative for Youth, and the STARTALK project, the third of which provides summer programs for students and teachers of ten critical languages in almost every state of the U.S. Thus, there is more robust foreign language learning occurring than what can be seen from education surveys.

So, what can be done?

The single most important factor fueling the crisis in foreign language education is ignorance on the part of decision-makers of the vital importance of the ability to communicate in languages other than English. Until there is widespread acknowledgment among legislators, administrators, and other education policy makers that *knowing a foreign language is as important as knowing science, mathematics, and history*, not much progress will be made. Thus, the single most important factor in solving the crisis is for linguists and other language professionals to become education policy activists. Foreign language learning must be part of a core curriculum!

About the author

Julie Tetel Andresen is Professor of English and Linguistics at Duke University. She holds an M.A. in French Language and Literature from the University of Illinois, Champaign-Urbana and a Ph.D. in Linguistics from the University of North Carolina, Chapel Hill. She is the author of *Linguistics in America 1769–1924: A Critical History* (Routledge, 1990), *Linguistics and Evolution. A Developmental Approach* (Cambridge, 2014), and *Languages in the World. How History, Culture and Politics Shape Language* with Phillip M. Carter (Wiley-Blackwell, 2016).

Suggestions for further reading

In this book

Opportunities and requirements for professional use of language abilities are discussed in Chapters 2 (what linguists do), 38 (bilingualism), 62 (dictionaries), 63 (interpreting and translating), and 65 (forensic linguistics). Another view of U.S. language capabilities is presented in Chapter 47 (U.S. language survey).

Elsewhere

Government Accountability Office. *Foreign Language Proficiency Has Improved, but Efforts to Reduce Gaps Needs Evaluation* (Department of State, 2017).

Levine, Glenn S. 'Stability, crisis, and other reasons for optimism: University foreign language education in the United States' in *Arts and Humanities in Higher Education* vol. 10, no. 2 (2011) pp. 131–140.

Looney, Dennis, and Natalia Lusin. *Enrollments in Languages Other Than English in United States Institutions of Higher Education, Summer 2016 and Fall 2016; Preliminary Report* (Modern Language Association of America, 2018).

The Language Flagship and American Councils. *The National K-12 Foreign Language Enrollment Survey Report* (American Councils for International Education, 2017).

49

Are American dialects dying?

Walt Wolfram

Is shared popular culture wiping out dialects in the United States and elsewhere? Can new dialects appear in today's world? Do you speak a dialect?

How do you say the word 'bought'? In the United States alone there are at least four distinct regional pronunciations of the vowel, from 'awe' to 'ah,' to a rural southern version that sounds almost like 'ow,' to the 'wo' used by comedians to lampoon dyed-in-the-wool New Yorkers (as in 'cwoffee twok').

Is the carbonated beverage you drink *pop*, *soda*, *tonic*, *co-cola*— or maybe even the older Appalachian mountain term *dope*? When you take the highway circling a city, do you drive on a *beltline*, a *beltway*, a *loop*, or a *perimeter*? And do you get cash at a *bank machine*, an *automated teller*, a *cash machine*, or an *ATM*?

Everyone notices dialects—we can't help it. But most of the time, we notice them in *other* people. 'We don't speak a dialect where we live, we speak normal English.' Speakers from Boston to Birmingham (Alabama and England) and from Medicine Hat to Melbourne (Florida and Australia) all echo the same sentiment. Of course, they do this while pronouncing the vowel in words like *bought* and *caught* in quite different ways. Or while using different names for the same sandwich—a *sub*, a *grinder*, a *hoagie*, or a *hero*.

Dialects are everywhere, not just in those regions—like Appalachia, Liverpool or the Outback—that seem to get the most dialect press. The fact of the matter is that it's impossible to speak the English language without speaking a dialect, some dialect. Everyone has an accent. When you pronounce the vowel in *bought* or *caught* (or was that *baht* and *caht*?) you've made a dialect commitment—you can't help it. We are all players in the dialect game, whether we like it or not.

But isn't this a different world? A global community where people move fluidly, travel frequently, and speak to each other by cell phone? Aren't dialects dying out, thanks to mobility and the media? Think again! Dialectologists counter the popular myth that dialects are dying by showing that major U.S. dialect areas like the North, Midland, and South remain very much alive—as they have been for a couple of centuries. But the dialect news is even more startling: research shows that Northern and Southern speech in the U.S. are actually diverging—not becoming more similar. Blame those shifty vowels, which in large Northern cities like Buffalo and Chicago are acquiring sounds different from those we hear in other regions. So *coffee* becomes *cahffee*, *lock* sounds almost like *lack*, and *bat* sounds more like *bet*. Have you noticed? Don't worry if you haven't. The change is pretty subtle, and a lot of it flies under the impressionistic radar. But it's very real—and it's gradually making the speech of Northern U.S. cities quite different from that of the South and West.

How can this be? In today's compressed world it seems illogical that dialects could continue developing and diverging the way they did when language communities were more isolated. But language is always changing, and sometimes behaves as though it has a mind of its own. Yes, we all watch the same TV programs; but most of us don't model our accents on TV newscasters—that's way too impersonal. We follow the lead of those we interact with in our daily lives—*they're* the ones who judge how well we fit in with the community.

And there remain plenty of regions where encroaching global culture is held at bay by a strong sense of community that includes local dialect. So working class Pittsburghers are proud to root for the Pittsburgh *Stillers*—instead of the *Steelers*; go *dahntahn*—instead of *downtown*; and put a *gum band* around their papers—instead of what other Americans would call a *rubber band* and Britons would call an *elastic band*. Part of being a Pittsburgher is speaking Pittsburghese.

But aren't *some* dialects dying, like the ones once spoken in isolated mountain and island communities now flooded by tourists? Some may be, but there are also rural communities that (like Pittsburgh on a smaller scale) keep their dialects alive as a way of fighting back, and ensuring that they won't be confused with what they call *furriners* (foreigners).

Perhaps the most surprising news of all is that some areas of increasing prosperity and cultural influence—like Seattle and northern California—are starting to express their new regional identity by developing dialect traits that didn't exist before.

So some traditional dialects may be disappearing, but they're being replaced by new dialects, in a process that can seem like the carnival game 'whack-a-mole.' The famous words of Mark Twain apply well to English dialects in America and elsewhere: rumors of their death are greatly exaggerated. Dialects remain alive and well—and an important part of the regional and sociocultural landscape.

About the author

Walt Wolfram, William C. Friday Distinguished Professor of English Linguistics at North Carolina State University, describes himself as a dialect nomad. He has studied dialects ranging from African American varieties in large metropolitan areas to the speech of small, isolated island and mountain communities. He has authored more than 20 books and 300 articles, in addition to producing a number of documentaries. More information on Dr. Wolfram's media productions is available at languageandlife.org and linguistics.chass.ncsu.edu.

Suggestions for further reading

In this book

Dialects are further discussed in Chapters 3 (dialects versus languages) and Chapter 51 (African American English). Language extinction is discussed in Chapters 5 (languages of the world), 28 (Latin), 34 (language death), and 64 (language rescue). Chapters talking more generally about how languages evolve include 4 (grammar), 27 (origins of English), 29 (language change), 30 (pidgins and creoles), and 53 and 56 (social media and texting).

Elsewhere

Labov, William, Sharon Ash and Charles Boberg. *The Atlas of North American English: Phonetics, Phonology and Sound Change* (Mouton de Gruyter, 2006). A major work on the dialects of North America, based on the pronunciation of various vowel sounds. It is mostly intended for the dedicated scholar. A more accessible overview of some of the results from this project can be found at the TELSUR (telephone survey) website: www.ling.upenn.edu/phonoatlas.

Wolfram, Walt, and Natalie Schilling. *American English: Dialects and Variation* (Wiley, third edition 2016). This textbook provides a readable, up-to-date description of language variation in American English, ranging from regional to ethnic to class-based variation. The book has a companion website, which includes audio and video enhancements, at www.americanenglishwiley.com/

Wolfram, Walt, and Ben Ward, eds. *American Voices: How Dialects Differ from Coast to Coast* (Blackwell, 2006). This collection contains brief, popular profiles of major and minor dialects in North America. Both dying dialects and new dialect traditions of American English are included in the presentations by major researchers, as well as descriptions of sociocultural varieties of English.

50

How many Native American languages are there?

Marianne Mithun

Do the Native American languages have any connection with languages in Europe or Asia or Africa? Are they all related to each other? Are they dying out? Is there any point in trying to save them?

A surprising number of people think there's just one language native to the U.S.: 'Indian.' Nothing could be further from the truth. In fact, we know of nearly 300 languages that were spoken north of Mexico before the arrival of Europeans. Many have disappeared, but around half are still known. Languages are often grouped into what are termed 'language families': groups of languages that are all descended from the same ancestral language. English, for example, is a member of the Indo-European family, along with such languages as German, French, Russian, Greek, Albanian, Hindi, Persian, and many more. The languages indigenous to North America constitute between 55 and 60 different language families of their own—groups of languages that have developed from completely different ancestors.

Some language families are quite large. The Athabaskan-Eyak-Tlingit family, for example, contains 39 different languages, spoken in communities scattered over an enormous area stretching from Alaska through western Canada into Oregon, California, and the southwestern U.S. This family includes Navajo, the most widely used indigenous language on the continent, with well over 100,000 speakers.

Another language family, called Algic, is best known for its largest branch, Algonquian, spoken along the Atlantic seaboard from Labrador to Virginia. It was Algonquian speakers who met the Pilgrims and Sir Walter Raleigh, and gave American English such words as *caribou*, *skunk*, *moccasin*, *hominy*, and *raccoon*. Algonquian languages are also spoken across most of Canada and down into the Plains in the U.S. Midwest: languages like Shawnee, Fox, Potawatomi, Cree, Cheyenne, and Blackfoot.

A third well-known group is the Siouan-Catawban family, which includes Lakota and Dakota, Winnebago, Crow, Hidatsa, Mandan, Omaha and Ponca, and others. At the time of first contacts with European languages, most speakers of these languages inhabited the prairies, from modern Alberta and Saskatchewan south into Montana, the Dakotas, Minnesota, and Wisconsin, through Nebraska, Iowa, Missouri, and Kansas, down into Arkansas and Mississippi. A few others were spoken in the Carolinas and Virginia. The name *Minnesota* is itself a Siouan word, literally 'clear water'. Another familiar Siouan word is *teepee* literally 'dwell-thing'.

The Iroquoian family is somewhat smaller, with eight modern languages, among them Mohawk—which is still spoken in Quebec, Ontario, and New York State—and Cherokee, which in the seventeenth century was spoken over a wide area in the southern Appalachians. Like several other indigenous peoples, most Cherokee were forced to march westward in 1838–1839 along what is called the 'Trail of Tears'. As a result, the largest Cherokee community is now in Oklahoma. Iroquoian languages gave us place names like *Canada*, *Schenectady*, *Ontario*, *Ohio*, and *Kentucky*. The term *Canada* comes from what was probably the first language recorded in North America, when Jacques Cartier sailed into the Bay of Gaspé and encountered a group now known as the Laurentians. It is *Kaná:ta* 'town'. The name *Schenectady* is from the Mohawk *Skahnéhtati* 'beyond the pines', originally the name for Albany, which was on the other side of the pine forest from where the Mohawk were. *Ontario* means 'large/beautiful lake', *Ohio* is 'large, beautiful river', and *Kentucky* is 'grassy place'.

North America even has language isolates, languages with no identifiable relatives at all. Zuni, spoken in what is now New Mexico, is an isolate.

Native American languages generally show no relation to languages anywhere else in the world. One hypothesis has emerged, however, a possible link between the Athabaskan-Eyak-Tlingit family and the Yeniseian family of Siberia.

The languages indigenous to North America differ tremendously among themselves. But none are simple or 'primitive.' In fact, their grammars can be very complex, in ways completely unlike those of the better-known languages of Europe or Asia. If you saw the 2002 film *Windtalkers*, for example, you know that the U.S. Marine Corps in World War II had speakers of Navajo use their language as a secret code to baffle the Japanese.

Many Native American languages use sounds unfamiliar to English speakers. Some have consonants called ejectives, sounds like *p*, *t*, or *k* but made with an extra popping sound. Some use distinctive tone, so that the same syllable spoken with different pitches can mean entirely different things. Navajo has both of these features.

Words in some languages can be very long, sometimes carrying as much meaning as a complete sentence in English. The Mohawk word *wa'tkenikahrà:ra'ne'*, for example, means 'they saw it.' This word consists of several parts. The first is the factual prefix *wa'-*, which indicates that the speaker feels that this is a fact, that the event actually happened. It is usually translated as the past tense in English. The second part is the prefix *t*, which indicates a change of position. The third is the pronominal prefix *keni-* ('they') but it is more specific than the English translation. It tells us that just two female persons were involved. The fourth part is an incorporated noun *-kahr-* ('eye'). The core of the word is actually the verb root *-hr-* 'be on.' Next is the suffix *-a'n-*, which means 'come to' or 'become.' Finally we have the suffix *-e*,' which tells us that the event happened all at once. The word thus means literally 'the girls came to be visually on it,' that is, 'their eyes fell upon it,' or 'they saw it.'

Each of the languages indigenous to the Americas shows us a unique way of looking at the world, of packaging experience into words, of expressing subtle and fundamental distinctions. If you speak an Eskimoan language, for example, and you want to say 'that caribou,' there is no single word equivalent to English 'that.' You first have to notice whether the caribou is standing or moving. If it is stationary, you have to specify whether it is visible or out of sight. If you can see it, you must specify whether it is near you, near the person you're talking to, far away, or whether it's above or below you. Or that it's approaching, or that it's the same caribou you were talking about earlier. Each of these ideas is packaged in just one word—translated simply as 'that' in English.

Unfortunately, the world is losing the melodies and unique perspectives of these aboriginal tongues. Languages are disappearing. Some are already gone because their speakers perished in warfare or epidemics; others have faded, because their speakers chose to use other languages instead. Our heritage as humans has been enriched by these languages, but it is likely that no more than a dozen of them will survive this century. And like an environmental disaster, this will be a great loss.

About the author

Marianne Mithun is professor of linguistics at the University of California, Santa Barbara. Her work covers such areas as morphology (word structure), relations between grammar and discourse, language typology, language contact, and language change, particularly the mechanisms by which grammatical structures evolve. She has worked with speakers of a number of North American languages, including Mohawk, Cayuga, Tuscarora, Seneca, Lakota, Central Alaskan Yup'ik, and Navajo, as well as several Austronesian languages. She has also worked with a number of communities on projects aimed at documenting their traditional languages and training speakers to teach them to younger generations.

Suggestions for further reading

In this book
Chapters on how groups of language are related include 23 (language families), 37 (origins of English), and 44 (languages of India). Languages of the U.S. are discussed in Chapters 47 (languages spoken in the U.S.), 48 (America's language crisis), 52 (New World Spanish), and 64 (rescuing threatened Native American languages),

Elsewhere
Grenoble, Lenore A., and Lindsay J. Whaley, eds. *Endangered Languages: Language Loss and Community Response* (Cambridge University Press, 1998). A collection of articles on various aspects of language loss around the world, including discussions of what is lost when languages disappear, the processes by which languages disappear, and community responses to the loss of heritage languages.

Kari, James, and Ben Potter, eds. *The Dene-Yeneiseian Connection* (Anthropological Papers of the University of Alaska, new series, vol 5:1–2, 2010). A collection of articles by linguists, archaeologists, physical anthropologists, and ethnologists examining the hypothesis of a genealogical connection between the Athabaskan-Eyak-Tlingit languages, centered in Alaska, and the Yeneiseian languages of Siberia.

Mithun, Marianne, *The Languages of Native North America* (Cambridge University Press, 1999/2001). An encyclopedic compendium describing the languages and language families indigenous to North America, along with the special structures and areas of complexity and elaboration found in these languages.

Silver, Shirley, and Wick R. Miller. *American Indian Languages: Cultural and Social Contexts* (University of Arizona, 1997). An introductory textbook on the languages of the Americas with special emphasis on the cultural and social contexts in which they have developed and are used.

51
What is African American English?

Nicole Holliday

Is African American speech different from other dialects of English? If so, why? How did it develop? Who speaks it?

When you ask Americans about language, they'll often point out that people from different regions have different 'accents,' and often tell you how they feel about them (e.g., 'people from NYC sound rough' or 'I like the way Californians talk'). Though many people have an idea that similar types of language differences exist for members of different ethnic groups, folks are often less willing to discuss this type of variation. Because of the racially loaded nature of American history, some may find it impolite to imply that there are a variety of ways of speaking sometimes associated with folks of different ethnic backgrounds, though there are sociopolitical and historical reasons for these differences. African American English (AAE)—or African American Language (AAL)—is the term that linguists use to refer to the variety (or varieties) of English spoken within predominately black communities across the U.S. While not all African Americans speak AAE, and some non-African Americans do speak it, linguists use the term AAE to refer to this variety because of its origins as well as widespread and predominant use in many African American communities.

AAE, like much of African American history, has deep connections to slavery, which was legally practiced in the U.S.

from the early seventeenth century to the late nineteenth century. When enslaved Africans were forcibly brought to the land that is the modern U.S., they were mostly isolated from their linguistic communities, and placed in a new land where they came into contact with a number of other African languages, as well as the different varieties of English spoken by slave masters and indentured and poor white folks. Over time, generations of enslaved Africans adapted to using English as their primary language, though their dialect was influenced by the myriad of African languages that their ancestors had brought from Africa, as well as the Englishes that they came into contact with once they were in the U.S. Following the formal end of slavery in 1863, most African Americans remained in the southern U.S., and worked as sharecroppers or in menial positions, which were largely the only jobs available to them. Jim Crow laws, which enforced segregation in almost all aspects of life, also served to maintain social as well as linguistic distance between blacks and whites. Even after the Great Migrations of the early twentieth century, in which millions of blacks moved from the South to Northern cities, blacks still faced discrimination and de facto segregation nationwide, which served to linguistically isolate them from the surrounding white communities. This social separation that took place in both the South and the North after the migration, along with growing sociopolitical movements for black liberation, also helped to preserve AAE. With the growth of the Civil Rights and Black Power movements of the mid-twentieth century, many activists and citizens also began to describe AAE as an important marker of black culture, history, and identity. Though AAE may sometimes be stigmatized as 'bad English' or 'poor grammar,' it is a rule-governed variety of English, which is primarily only stigmatized due to discriminatory language ideologies.

Many words and phrases that have become popular in the mainstream were originally in use in AAE, such as 'cool,' 'dope,' and 'woke.' But AAE is so much more than words. Like a number of other languages, such as Hebrew or Hawaiian, AAE sometimes allows sentences without the verb *is/are*. This means that in AAE, the rules allow for a sentence like 'That ish cray' as well as one with the verb, like 'That ish is cray.' In addition to these differences in words and sentences structure, speakers of AAE may also use a pronunciation system that is different from mainstream U.S. English, the variety that many think of as general American. For example, it is common for speakers of AAE to pronounce the word 'mouth' with a final *f* sound instead of the *th*, such that it sounds like *mouf*. AAE speakers also have a unique system of pitch and tone, which determines the ways in which their voices may go up and down throughout a sentence. Since AAE encompasses such a large, complex linguistic system, the reader is encouraged to consult the suggestions for a full description of the structure and use of AAE.

Despite its differences, AAE also bears many similarities to mainstream U.S. English. The meanings of words, structure of sentences and sounds that are used can also often be similar in both varieties. Because AAE is sometimes stigmatized, many speakers use both mainstream U.S. American English and AAE, and they choose their variety based on listener, topic, and social situation. This linguistic dexterity (often referred to as 'code-switching') is also a reflection of the ways in which many black Americans have accommodated to mainstream white society while also maintaining cultural and linguistic traditions that reflect their history and culture.

About the author

Nicole Holliday is an assistant professor of linguistics at Pomona College in Claremont, California, where she teaches courses on sociolinguistics, phonetics, and linguistic discrimination. She received her Ph.D. in linguistics from New York University in 2016. Her academic specialties are African American Language, linguistic profiling and discrimination, sociophonetics, and intonational phonology. She is especially interested in prosodic variation among individuals and communities with multiple and complex racial identities. Her work has appeared in venues such as *American Speech* and the *Journal of the International Phonetic*

Association, as well as popular venues such as NPR, Dictionary.com, and the Oxford Dictionaries blog.

Suggestions for further reading

In this book

Other language varieties of the U.S. are discussed in Chapters 47 (languages of the U.S.), 50 (Native American languages), 52 (New World Spanish), and 52 (Native American languages). Further discussion of dialects can be found in Chapters 3 (dialects vs. languages) and 49 (U.S. dialects). Language history and evolution are discussed in Chapters 22 (origins of language) and 27 (history of English). More about examples of language variation can be found in 9 (new words) and 29 (language change). Issues of language and identity are mentioned in Chapters 31 (sign language and Deaf culture), 32 (men's and women's speech), and 33 (gay speech). Connections between language and inequality are drawn in Chapters 30 (pidgins and creole), 45 (language conflict), and 46 (gendered language).

Elsewhere

Green, Lisa J. *African American English: A Linguistic Introduction* (Cambridge University Press, 2002).

Lippi-Green, Rosina. 'What we talk about when we talk about Ebonics: Why definitions matter,' *The Black Scholar* vol. 27, no. 2 (1997), pp. 7–11.

Rickford, John. *African American Vernacular English: Features, Evolution, Educational Implications* (Wiley-Blackwell, 1999).

Rickford, John R., and Russell J. Rickford. *Spoken Soul: The Story of Black English* (John Wiley & Sons, 2000)

Smitherman, Geneva. *Talkin that Talk: Language, Culture, and Education in African America* (Routledge, 2000).

52

What is the future of Spanish in the United States?

Maria Carreira

Is Spanish in the U.S. here to stay? Will it remain the same as Spanish in other countries?

> Apply yourself to the study of the Spanish language with all of the assiduity you can. It and the English covering nearly the whole of America, they should be well known to every inhabitant, who means to look beyond the limits of his farm.
>
> (Thomas Jefferson, Letter to Peter Carr, 1788)

More than two centuries since Jefferson wrote them, these words have proven remarkably prophetic. With forty million Spanish speakers, the U.S. is home to the second largest speaking population in the world, after Mexico. New York has as many Puerto Ricans as San Juan, the capital of Puerto Rico. Miami is the second-largest Cuban city, Los Angeles the second largest Mexican city.

But what about the future? During more than three centuries of immigration, dozens of languages have landed on American shores, only to fade away in a generation or two. Think of Italian, Dutch, or Polish. Judging purely from history, Spanish could be expected to follow the same path, gradually losing speakers and eventually disappearing. But will Spanish go the way of other immigrant languages—or will it find a way to survive?

As a general rule, immigrants to the U.S. strongly prefer their native language over English. This certainly applies to the millions of foreign-born Latinxs* here. However, with each successive generation of Latinxs, Spanish use declines sharply. By the third generation, few remain proficient in the language of their parents and grandparents. Attitudes and misinformation play a key role in the rapid language shift. Keenly aware of widespread negative stereotypes surrounding Spanish and its speakers, many young Latinxs abandon their home language to fit in. Some worry that Spanish will interfere with their ability to speak English and their prospects for making a good living, despite widespread evidence to the contrary. On the other hand, Latinx youth who do want to develop their skills find limited opportunities to study Spanish in school. So it's only a matter of time before Spanish fades away. Or is it?

The sheer number of speakers in the country gives Spanish the advantage of critical mass—far larger than any other immigration in history—which will give it staying power, at least in the short run. So far, the generational loss of speakers has been offset by a steady flow of new immigrants from Latin America—around half a million a year. But the numbers paint a worrying picture. Immigration from the Spanish-speaking world is on the decline: roughly a third of U.S. Latinxs today are foreign born, down from 40 percent in 2000. Also the number of bilingual Latinxs has dropped from 78 percent in 2006 to 73 percent today. This suggests that Spanish is following the path of other immigrant languages.

But Spanish is not like other immigrant language. With a continuous presence in the United States since 1513, it is the oldest European language spoken here, predating English. At their peak, in the late eighteenth century, the Spanish Borderlands (areas of Hispanic settlement) encompassed more than half of what is today the United States, extending along the southern rim of the country from Florida to California, and along the Pacific coast to Alaska. Today, Spanish is the most commonly spoken language

---

* The terms 'Latinx' and 'Latinxs' are used in this chapter to refer to Latin Americans of any gender (Latinos, Latinas, etc.).

other than English, in forty-five U.S. states. Most Latinxs live in the Southwest, particularly California and Texas, which together account for nearly half of the U.S. Latinx population. Florida, New York, and Illinois also have large populations. Recently, Spanish has made its presence felt in places as far away from the nation's southern contours as Washington State, Oregon, and Minnesota, as new waves of immigrants travel further into the country in search of a livelihood.

From the newly arrived to the native born, Latinxs in the U.S. are avid consumers of all things in Spanish. In Los Angeles and Miami, Spanish-language television and radio have a larger audience than their English-language counterparts. Everywhere Latinxs live, Spanish can be heard and seen in the public domain, from churches, to medical facilities, the legal arena, businesses, schools, etc. These endeavors provide a myriad of opportunities for Latinxs to use Spanish beyond the confines of the home, thereby contributing to keeping the language alive and possibly helping offset generational loss. Schooling is particularly important in this regard.

One out every four students in K-12 and 17 percent of students in higher education in the U.S. is Latinx. Not all these students speak Spanish, but many do. Spanish-language programs, including bilingual education programs and language classes separate and different from those for non-Latinx students, can help them become more proficient and can foster attitudes and behaviors that support language maintenance. These kinds of programs are on the rise throughout the nation, but many more are needed before all Latinx students have access to them.

Meanwhile, many non-Latinxs are seeking to tap into the vast social and economic opportunities that Spanish presents. From kindergarten to post-graduate programs, Spanish is the most widely studied language in the U.S. At the secondary level, it is the language of choice of an astounding 70 percent of learners, and in higher education it accounts for over half of all foreign language enrollments. And Spanish is now spoken by more non-Latinxs in the U.S. than any other foreign language.

However, the future of U.S. Spanish doesn't depend just on external factors like social pressures, economic incentives, educational opportunities, and demographics; it may also be affected by linguistic developments. Impressive as the numbers of speakers are, what's perhaps even more impressive is the variety of accents, usage and dialects, as Spanish-speaking immigrants arrive from places ranging from Buenos Aires to Tijuana. Mexicans are by far the largest national group, but there are sizable immigrant populations from all the other Spanish-speaking countries, particularly from the Caribbean and Central America. There's been nothing like this in the history of the language, and immigrants from every corner of the Spanish-speaking world are forging a new Latinx identity and developing different ways of expression to capture their bilingual and bicultural experiences. The popular television series *Jane the Virgin*, an adaptation of a Venezuelan soap opera, is a prime example of this phenomenon. Dubbed an 'American telenovela,' this show is set in bilingual Miami, at the intersection of English and Spanish and American and Latin American cultural practices.

In this new environment, sometimes dubbed the 'United Hispanic States of America,' Spanish is being reinvented day by day, partly through dialect mixing and partly through incorporating elements of English. A U.S. mixture of Spanish and English is evolving, often referred to as 'Spanglish'—for example, *qué cute* ('how cute') and *pero like* ('but like,' used to introduce a new point in a conversation). Spanglish is popular and contagious among the young, and is even spreading to other Spanish-speaking countries. Bilingual puns and wordplay can be found in the works of many U.S. Latinx writers such as Oscar Hijuelos, Sandra Cisneros and Junot Díaz. But many language purists object to this type of mixing. Octavio Paz, the Mexican Nobel Prize winner for literature, has harshly described Spanglish as 'abominable,' 'illegitimate,' and a 'bastard language.'

Spanglish is only one sign that Spanish in the U.S. is mutating, adapting to its linguistic environment, and therefore becoming more likely to thrive. Three generations from now U.S. Spanish will likely be a new blend, still understandable by people in Spanish-speaking countries, but further enriched by the variety of Hispanic and English influences it will continue to absorb.

Whatever new shape Spanish takes, we should recognize that it is no longer a *foreign* language in the United States. The state of New Mexico has acknowledged that by proclaiming itself officially bilingual in Spanish and English. The rest of the country, while not taking that official step, is rapidly adapting to the fact that Spanish now functions as a U.S. language second only to English.

About the author

Maria Carreira is professor of Spanish linguistics at California State University, Long Beach and Co-Director of the National Heritage Language Research Center at UCLA. Her publications focus on Spanish in the United States and Spanish as a world language. She has co-authored four college-level Spanish textbooks: *Nexos* (2015), *Alianzas* (2013), *Cuadros* (2013), and *Sí se puede* (2008). She is also a co-author of *Voces, Latinos Students on Life in the United States* (Praeger, 2014) and co-editor of the *Routledge Handbook of Heritage Language Education* (2017). Dr. Carreira received her Ph.D. in linguistics from the University of Illinois at Urbana Champaign.

Suggestions for further reading

In this book

Various languages of America are discussed in Chapters 47 (languages of the U.S.), 48 (America's language crisis), 50 (Native American languages), and 64 (rescuing threatened Native American languages). The dynamics of life in multilingual communities are touched on in Chapter 44 (countries with multiple official languages), 45 (language conflict), and 61 (bilingual education).

Elsewhere

Carreira, Maria, and Beeman, Thomas. *Voces: Latino Students on Life in the United States* (Praeger Publishers, 2014). Presents the perspectives of U.S. Latinx children and their linguistic experiences in school, at home, and in society at large. Offers an overview of the historical and current status of Spanish and Latinxs in the United States.

Commission on Language Learning. *America's Languages: Investing in Language Education for the 21st Century* (American Academy of Arts & Sciences, 2017). Reports on the status of language education in the United States and makes recommendations for improving the nation's language capacity.

Moreno-Fernández, Francisco. 'Language as a Hispanic dilemma,' *Medium* (2017), https://medium.com/@FMORENOFDEZ/language-as-a-hispanic-dilemma-6f2fd09fe9f0. Documents the state of the Spanish language in the U.S. focusing on demographics, usage, and education.

Language and technology

53

How is language used on social media?

Lauren Squires

How does language online differ from language in other contexts? What kinds of language variation exist in social media? How is social media changing language?

The internet is now an indispensable part of everyday life for much of the world. Just three decades ago, 'electronic mail' was mostly limited to the workplace, and leisure-time computer activity mostly involved command-line role-playing games and text-only chat channels. These bare-bones forms of internet-based communication have largely given way to the content-rich platforms we call 'social media.'

With each new communicative technology, people have wondered about the fate of language. Are people losing the ability to communicate face to face by spending so much time on the computer? Is the internet ruining English? It's no wonder people have these concerns, since language is a fundamental part of using social technologies. But what is really different about language on social media, compared to language in other contexts?

Social media platforms are multimodal spaces, where linguistic symbols are used in combination with other modes of communication—visual, verbal, auditory, and so on. While older internet technologies included only basic text symbols, social media can incorporate images, sound clips, and videos, as well as pictorial symbols like emoji. Still, most of what people ask about when they are asking about 'language on social media' is *written* language. Written language tends to be more static, stable, and 'standard' than spoken language, yet the language we find in social media is full of variability, and is constantly changing. In this way, language in social media is much the same as language in nearly all other contexts: it exhibits variation that reflects individual styles, group identities, and communicative purposes.

For an example of this variability, think about some stereo-typical features of 'internet language'—acronymic words like *lol*, *TY* or *IDK*; or abbreviations like *v* ('very'), *obvi* ('obviously'), or *totes* ('totally'). While such shortenings have a reputation for being used all over the internet, in fact they are used by some people but not by others. Members of some communities use *lol*, while members of others use *haha*—similar to how some people in the U.S. say *soda* and others say *pop*. Social media writing also reflects some spoken language variation. People use spelling to signal dialect differences, for instance writing the word 'that' like '*dat*,' representing the pronunciation with a *d* sound (a common feature in vernacular varieties of English such as African American English and other dialects).

Moreover, people often write one way to an audience of Facebook friends but another way on Twitter or Instagram, where their public posts may be seen by a wider, unknown audience. Or they might write differently when posting about social activism versus movies. We use different writing styles in analog media, too: I sometimes incorporate abbreviations or smiley faces in handwritten notes on student papers, but never in a formal letter of recommendation.

Language in social media is also shaped by a complicated set of factors that typically don't come into play when we're talking about spoken language. When people use social media, they draw on their knowledge of how to use their language (its words and grammar) and how to write it (its orthography), but also on their knowledge of how to use a particular media platform, plus their knowledge of how to use a particular electronic device. Consider how the keyboard on a new iPhone is different from the keyboard on a new PC computer. And consider that a new user of Twitter might not understand how to create a conversational 'thread' of tweets. Another example: while #hashtags are used on many different social media sites, they don't function identically. A single post on Instagram sometimes includes dozens of hashtags, whereas this is not even possible on Twitter, due to character constraints. Tweets might have a few hashtags, but not 29, as I just counted in one Instagram post!

This all highlights the fact that when people use language in social media, they are using language in quite sophisticated ways, incorporating multiple forms of literacy. This runs contrary to popular ideas that social media is 'dumbing down' language. In truth, social media provide spaces for people around the world to communicate in casual, personalized, quick, and efficient ways, as well as in ways that are more formal and public. All these properties are reflected in the varying language we see across social media.

People often ask what the long-term effects of the internet and social media will be on language. This is a nearly impossible question to answer, because we can't know the future. The spoken language clearly reflects technological changes (*hashtag* and *lol* did not used to be words), but technology is far from the only influence on a language. As long as language is spoken between *humans* in face-to-face contexts—and used for *social* purposes in whatever *media* that may be—it will maintain its qualities of being robustly systematic, yet ever-changing.

About the author

Lauren Squires is associate professor in the Department of English at The Ohio State University, where she teaches courses in English linguistics (including the grammar and history of English) and language and media (including digital media). Her research interests include the sociolinguistics of computer-mediated communication, language in media and popular culture, language ideologies, and sociolinguistic processing of dialect differences.

Suggestions for further reading

In this book
Additional chapters discussing written language include Chapters 16 (writing systems), 26 (origins of writing), and 56 (text messaging). Additional topics related to language and technology are discussed in Chapters 54 (language-learning technology) and 55 (machine translation).

Elsewhere
Georgakopoulou, Alexandra, and Tereza Spilioti, eds. *The Routledge Handbook of Language and Digital Communication* (Routledge, 2016).

Squires, Lauren, ed. *English in Computer-Mediated Communication: Variation, Representation, and Change* (de Gruyter, 2016).

Zappavigna, Michele. *Discourse of Twitter and Social Media: How We Use Language to Create Affiliation on the Web* (Continuum, 2012).

54

Can computers teach languages faster and better?

Trude Heift

Can you really learn a language effectively from a machine? What technology exists to help people learn languages?

Computers have undoubtedly changed the ways in which we learn and access education. However, disappointing as it may be, especially to those with high expectations of AI technologies, *faster* and *better* are not the kind of adjectives that researchers, language teachers, or even millennial language learners (who live and breathe technology) generally equate with these newer language-learning environments. Instead, *free of charge* seems to be the most commonly used description, at least among designers of online learning sites advertising for their computer-aided language materials. In fact, learning a language for free was the main motivation for DuoLingo according to Luis von Ahn, one of the two founders of the online language learning platform. DuoLingo has attracted millions of language learners since it became available in 2012 and, according to its creators, there were already more people using DuoLingo in 2014 than learning a language through the U.S. public school system.

From an educational point of view, there are clearly advantages to technology-aided learning environments that go far beyond free of charge. If not faster and better, what, then, are the clear advantages offered by language learning technologies? And what are their limitations?

One may think of the use of computer technology in language learning as a phenomenon arising in the mid-1990s with the advent of the World Wide Web. In fact, however, the idea of harnessing the capabilities of technology for language instruction was acted upon in the late 1960s by individual teachers and a few researchers at universities. For instance, the PLATO project developed in the early 1970s on a large mainframe computer included a reading course with interactive vocabulary and grammar drills and translation tests that measured students' progress. It remains clear why such capabilities were of interest, but the materials from that period reflect the structural view of language dominant in North America at that time and, therefore, the beginnings of computer-assisted language learning (CALL) are typically shown as text-based interactive programs intended to teach grammar and vocabulary.

During those years and at least for the next two decades, researchers in this area were preoccupied with the question of whether learning might be better accomplished through computer-assisted instruction than in the classroom by, for example, measuring the acquisition rate and mastery of grammar and vocabulary taught in a computer-based language learning environment compared to a teacher-led classroom. Although such comparisons are relevant in some contexts, research attempting to understand *what*, *why*, *how*, and *to what end* technology leads to successful learning outcomes is the challenge for most applied linguists working in this area today.

An important aspect of today's language learning technology, also facilitated by social media, is the participation of the users in creating and designing their own place in an ever more flexible and accessible virtual space of the World Wide Web. The precious, and in many contexts *rare*, face-to-face conversations that formed the basis of important theoretical perspectives on second language acquisition have been supplemented, diversified, and extended beyond the physical boundaries that separated learners from their target language in the past. Beyond the language classroom, the Web of today is well-populated and heavily traveled, whereby students might work and play collaboratively with their peers or remain alone at the computer—which may be at a cafe or at their home. Language technologies therefore provide an unprecedented amount and quality of target language opportunities for input, repetition, help, information, and interaction for learners who know how to use them. Many of these affordances became possible over the past decades due to technological innovations in multimedia and advances in artificial intelligence, learner modeling, and communications software, for example.

At the same time, we have also experienced shifts in teaching practices over the past decades that have emphasized learner-centered and data-driven approaches to teaching and learning, which place the learner at the forefront of the learning experience. In addition, individualization, assessment, and learner autonomy are a few of the central issues in language learning that computers have aimed to provide albeit to varying degrees of success depending on the sophistication of the technology. Nevertheless, we are far from computer technologies having reached a level of sophistication where chatbots, for instance, are capable of simulating conversations as authentic and efficacious as interaction with a human tutor.

Teachers bring passion, set focus, challenge, encourage, and build confidence—all of which contribute to motivating a learner to learn. While learning technologies, even if free of charge, might attract a student to learn a language initially and offer much value to their learning experience by also providing a level of accessibility and attention that can hardly be obtained from a human teacher, learning a language requires a purpose, dedication, and practice. In the end, learners need to be motivated to return to a language learning website or app to not only advance their second language skills but also maintain them. This might be harder to achieve in the absence of a human teacher who fulfills an important role in the language learning process and experience, and it remains speculative whether a chatbot or avatar could ever achieve that level of interpersonal interaction.

About the author

Trude Heift is professor of linguistics in the Department of Linguistics at Simon Fraser University, Canada. Her research focuses on the design as well as the evaluation of CALL systems with a particular interest in learner-computer interactions and learner language. She is co-editor of *Language Learning and Technology*.

Suggestions for further reading

In this book

For other discussions of adult language learning see Chapters 20 (language and the brain), 37 (foreign accents), 41 (history of language teaching methods), and 60 (study abroad). Other linguistic/technological topics appear in Chapters 47 (interactive map of U.S. language communities), 55 (machine translation), 65 (forensic linguistics), and 66 (the Museum of Languages), as well as 28 (Latin) and 17 (Esperanto).

Elsewhere

Chapelle, Carol A., and Shannon Sauro, eds., *The Handbook of Technology and Second Language Teaching and Learning* (Oxford 2017).

www.ict4lt.org/en/index.htm: collection of training modules in Information and Communications Technology (ICT) for language teachers.

Journals

Language Learning and Technology (http://llt.msu.edu)

CALICO Journal (http://calico.org)

ReCALL (www.eurocall-languages.org/index)

Computer Assisted Language Learning (www.tandf.co.uk/journals/titles/09588221.asp)

55
How good is machine translation?

Kevin Knight

Can machines translate human language accurately? What makes accurate translation difficult? How does translation technology work? Are some languages harder to translate than others?

Machine translation is one of the oldest challenges for artificial intelligence. The proto-computers that broke German ciphers in World War II were quickly re-targeted in the 1950s to translate Russian into English. Famed information theorist Warren Weaver put it nicely in 1949: 'When I see an article in Russian, I say to myself, it is really written in English but it has been encoded in some strange symbols. I will now proceed to decode.'

Unfortunately, machine translation development was much harder than expected. To the computer, every word is a tricky puzzle. When 'duty' means 'responsibility', it translates one way into Japanese, but when 'duty' means 'tax', it translates another way. Little words are even trickier. The word 'in' can refer to physical location ('in the room'), temporal location ('in December'), membership in an organization ('in the army'), or hundreds of other things (from 'in trouble' to 'in theory'). We can always translate whole phrases instead of words, but difficulties remain— does 'nuclear power' refer to a country with nuclear weapons, or to electricity derived from nuclear reactors? And how many whole-phrase translations are needed ... millions, billions? Worse, correct word and phrase senses are not enough. The computer also needs to assemble them together. To translate 'old men and women' correctly, we need to know if the women are also old. Probably they are. But how about 'old men and babies'? Everyone knows that babies can't be old, but the computer doesn't know that. Each new sentence contains dozens of computer-bedeviling ambiguities that need to be programmed away.

And not only that! Even if the computer processes the source sentence correctly, it still has to produce a grammatical, sensible version of that sentence in the target language. Think about how you might translate an English sentence into a foreign language whose grammar you have not yet mastered, and you may gain some sympathy for the machine.

To tackle all these challenges, researchers hit on a new idea around 1990. They created a 'monkey see, monkey do' algorithm that watches over the shoulder of a human translator and learns to imitate his or her work. Actually, the algorithm watches over the shoulders of *thousands of human translators*, exploiting the vast bilingual material they produce. Does the English word 'in' have dozens of context-dependent translations into Japanese? No problem. The machine can tabulate them all and figure out which context features predict which translations to use. The machine can also read billions of words in the target language, gathering linguistic patterns to help it generate grammatical, sensible output sentences.

System designers kept telling the computer which features to look for, and at some point, machine translation went mainstream. Google Translate began an online statistical translation service in 2006. The startup company WordLens let users point their cell-phones at street signs and menus, delivering instant visual translations. Microsoft debuted Skype Translator, an app for video-chat between two people who cannot speak each other's language. Another startup, Language Weaver, provided key technology for companies expanding into new markets, as well as for governments enhancing national security.

Translation quality steadily improved with new algorithms and more data. Then, just as quality started to plateau, a sudden infusion of new neural network technology sent accuracy higher still. Neural technology, loosely inspired by human brain function, allows the machine to come up with its own ways to exploit context. For example, the machine may figure out that there are such things as 'military' or 'automotive' contexts, and further learn different translations for the word 'tank' in those contexts, without relying on a human designer to invent those concepts. The first reported neural translation results came in 2014, and within two years, nearly all research and development had pivoted to this new method.

Is machine translation solved, then? Hardly. Systems are brittle when applied to unfamiliar genres and domains. A system trained on human translations from the United Nations will not do well on recipes or sports articles. Translation accuracy also varies by language. Spanish to English is fairly good, German to English less so. Arabic to English is a bit worse, Chinese to English is worse than that, and Japanese to English is quite bad. Furthermore, current translation technology only touches on a fraction of the thousands of languages in the world. It is easy to find a translation system for French, Russian, or Arabic, but much harder to find a system for Tigrinya, Cherokee, or Berber. Fortunately, there are promising new algorithms that let systems exploit what they learn about one language (for example, Uzbek) and apply it to a related language (for example, Uighur). It turns out that if we pool data from different languages, different language systems can learn from each other.

However, even the best systems operating on the world's most popular languages make mistakes on nearly every long sentence. Some errors reveal the machine's spectacular lack of basic knowledge—for example, the famous machine translation headline, 'Amy Winehouse found dead in his apartment.' Other mistakes result from more humdrum problems in assembling sensible, grammatical output sentences. It's one thing for a computer to read input text written by people, but it's still a challenge to accurately output new sentences that have never been uttered by anyone on Earth. Fortunately, new artificial intelligence technology is coming faster than ever before, so prospects for continued improvements are good.

About the author

Kevin Knight is a professor in the Computer Science Department at the University of Southern California (USC). He and his colleagues at USC's Information Sciences Institute investigate all aspects of computational linguistics, including machine translation. Knight is a former president of the Association for Computational Linguistics. His other research interests include deciphering historical manuscripts and generating creative language by computer.

Suggestions for further reading

In this book

For other discussions of linguistic/technological topics see Chapters 54 (language teaching technologies), 47 (interactive map of U.S. language communities), 65 (forensic linguistics), and 66 (the Museum of Languages). More on the subject of translation appears in Chapter 63 (interpreting and translating).

Elsewhere

'The great AI awakening,' www.nytimes.com/2016/12/14/magazine/the-great-ai-awakening.html. This *New York Times* article provides an accessible look at neural networks for machine translation, featuring interviews with scientists at Google Brain.

Karpathy, Andrej. 'The unreasonable effectiveness of recurrent neural networks,' http://karpathy.github.io/2015/05/21/rnn-effectiveness. Thousands of people read this early blog post by Andrej Karpathy, who encouraged them to tinker with simple neural mechanisms for reading and writing English sentences.

Kohen, Phillip. *Statistical Machine Translation* (Cambridge University Press, 2010). This textbook covers the technical basics of machine translation. Updated editions appear regularly. The author also maintains statmt.org, a one-stop shop for open-source software components (at www.statmt.org/book).

56

Is text messaging changing how I write and speak?

Joel Schneier

Why does writing on mobile devices look different than other kinds of writing? Is text messaging bad for teens? How are new terms introduced to use through mobile communication? Is text messaging ruining English?

Texting has radically changed venues of literacy and writing. And lots of people seem to be worried about its effects on how we write and speak.

Language scholars used to believe that language change and evolution only occurred in *speech*. They argued that new language features can only occur in writing if they are already widespread enough in spoken language, because writing is mostly a formal representation of language that people use in formal settings, such as school. But with the explosion of communication technologies in the twentieth century—from the telegraph, to teletype, to personal computing, to fax machines, to copiers, to mass print production, to the internet—writing was no longer limited to a formal, educational purpose. In fact, if you were to compare a telegram from the turn of twentieth century side-by-side with a text message from the turn of the twenty-first century, you would see very similar styles of writing!

For younger generations who have grown up with frequent access to the internet (via personal computers, tablets, and smartphones), a greater degree of communication between friends and family occurs through written communication, such as text messaging, or texting. Youth who have adopted texting as a way to keep in touch with their friends often use texting for more than just coordinating social plans (as their parents would). Youth often reply much faster to one another, and the content of their messages involves frequent use of emoticons and language that reflects moods and emotional states. Many text message conversations cover social and even highly personal topics, and therefore the use of emoticons and emoji, quick responses, and even non-standard writing are strategies that texters use to maintain comradery and a sense of belonging

Many unique features that are prominent in texting are often decried as 'ruining' the English language. Features such as acronyms (i.e., *lol* for 'laugh out loud'), abbreviations (e.g., *bro* for 'brother'), contractions (e.g., *txt* for 'text'), homophonic use of letters and numbers (e.g., *gr8* for 'great'), emoticons and emoji (e.g., ☺), and writing that looks like speech (e.g., *sup* for 'what's up'), are indeed strikingly different from what is considered standard written English. Parents and educators who have witnessed their children using these texting features have alarmingly worried that these features would creep into more formal writing genres—or even into speech!

So, does it? Well, we don't learn our first language through writing to begin with. We learn it through speech. Writing is still commonly learned in childhood during the early years of schooling, and then—at least for the current generation of youngsters—forms of written communication may be introduced later on. As far as text messaging goes, 88 percent of teens in the United States have access to mobile cellphones (overwhelmingly smartphones), and 91 percent of those teens use text messaging or a mobile messaging application similar to texting such as WhatsApp or Kik. That text messaging may become so frequently used and socially important to teens is critical, because language scholars have shown that adolescence is a time period when teens are transitioning from childhood to adulthood, and they may use language to reflect these social identities. Writing and sending *lit* or *sup* to friends in a text message may therefore demonstrate they are 'in' with their social group. Regional dialect can also be represented in text message form—through spelling, grammar, or vocabulary choices (e.g., *y'all*).

The frequency of media use that teens may also engage with using mobile devices also may increase exposure to new kinds of language. Just as adults may learn new words throughout their lives, being able to watch and share popular media through the same devices that teens send text messages means that many of these new forms flow through texting. Terms like *on fleek* or *lit* or even uses of hashtags in texting are examples of language features that can spread from creative individuals to Facebook, to YouTube, and then back into individual social circles via texting because they may be seen as 'cool.' And just as some features may spread from one form of media to another, these forms can spread from text messaging to speech. New words (e.g., *lit*), abbreviations (e.g., *totes*), and even acronyms (e.g., *lol*) are particularly ripe to be spoken out loud, but this is nothing new (e.g., *AWOL* or even *Scuba* are older examples of this). While some of these new features that flow from text to speech can be pronounced in a variety of ways (e.g., think of how some people pronounce *GIF* as 'jiff' while others say 'giff'), typically the pronunciation and usage in their social group will determine how the form is used.

So, to return to the question asked by this chapter—*does texting change how we write and speak?*—the short answer is 'yes,' because texting can introduce new language features like new words or phrases that serve unique purposes for communicating with your social group. However, while some of these features can flow into speech, and vice versa, it is difficult to argue or find evidence that text messaging—or any form of written language—can *completely* change how anyone speaks. After all, while the explosion of digital media and the internet has exposed people to more language through media than ever before, much of a person's language exposure still comes from the people they interact with face-to-face on a regular basis (i.e., friends, family, coworkers, neighbors, etc.). It is within these social groups that people *learn* language in the first place. So, while teens may use new words and phrases, as well as frequently reference features from text messaging and popular media in their everyday speech, they still will do so in their own voice!

About the author
Joel Schneier received his Ph.D. from North Carolina State University in Communication, Rhetoric, & Digital Media. He is currently a lecturer at the University of Central Florida in the Department of Writing & Rhetoric. His research examines how people use mobile devices to meaningfully communicate with others in their everyday lives.

Suggestions for further reading

In this book
Other chapters focusing on written language include Chapters 16 (writing systems), 26 (origins of writing), and 53 (social media). Chapters specially focusing on language change include 25 (grammar), 27 (origins of English), 28 (Latin), 29 (language change), and 49 (U.S. dialect change), as well as 9 (the 'realness' of words) and 63 (dictionaries). For more about language and technology, see Chapters 47 (online mapping of U.S. languages), 53 (social media), 54 (computer-assisted language learning), 55 (machine translation), and 65 (forensic linguistics).

Elsewhere
Kristiansen, Tore. 'Does mediated language influence immediate language?', in Jannis Androutspoulos, ed., *Mediatization and Sociolinguistic Change* (De Gruyter, 2014), pp. 99–126.

Lenhart, Amanda. *Teens, Social Media & Technology Overview 2015* (Pew Research Center, 2015).

McWhorter, John. 'Txting is killing language. JK!!!' (TED, 2013), www. ted.com/talks/john_mcwhorter_txtng_is_killing_language_jk

Tagg, Caroline. *Discourse of Text Messaging* (Bloomsbury UK, 2012).

Thurlow, Crispin. 'Generation txt? The sociolinguistics of young people's text-messaging,' *Discourse Analysis Online* vol. 1 (2003), p. 1.

Thurlow, Crispin. 'From statistical panic to moral panic: The metadiscursive construction and popular exaggeration of new media language in the print media,' *Journal of Computer-Mediated Communication* vol. 11, no. 3 (2006), pp. 667–701.

Language and education

57
Why should educators care about linguistics?

Anne H. Charity Hudley and Christine Mallinson

Can knowledge of linguistics benefit teachers? What are some sugges-
tions for teachers who want culturally and linguistically sustaining
classrooms? How can teachers value their students' home language
or language varieties while also teaching standardized forms of
English?

In schools and communities across the U.S., there are students
who communicate in a wide range of languages and varieties of
English. Yet, even as early as the preschool years, many students
have absorbed messages that the language that they use is wrong,
incorrect, dumb or stigmatized.

What's an educator to do? On the one hand, educators need
to help students prepare for a world (and standardized tests) that
aren't particularly accepting of linguistic variation. On the other
hand, they want to do so in a way that lets students continue
to be proud of who they are and where they come from, rather
than pushing them into linguistic insecurity that leads to lack of
confidence, discomfort, or silence.

Empathy matters. No student (or educator) leaves their language patterns at the door when they enter a classroom—even
classes like math and science, where language is often seen as secondary. We need to talk about this reality inside of our classrooms,
schools, and communities.

Without such discussions, educators might form negative assumptions about a student's intelligence and ability based simply on how they talk, which can result in lowered expectations, stereotyping, and discrimination. Educators sometimes also send messages, whether consciously or unconsciously, that a student's language is out of place at school.

The first strategy to change the conversation is to talk about being able to use and understand many varieties of English. The second strategy is to point out that, in fact, many famous authors have taken great care to learn and use several language varieties.

This kind of linguistic flexibility and multilingualism is a skill that's becoming more and more recognized. For example, the Common Core State Standards state that students need to 'appreciate that the twenty-first-century classroom and workplace are settings in which people from often widely divergent cultures and who represent diverse experiences and perspectives must learn and work together ... [and be] able to communicate effectively with people of varied backgrounds.'

This type of approach is not relegated to one form of teaching or one subject area. Effective education relies on effective communication, whether in English class, biology class, or a counseling session. The words that teachers and students use, their meanings, and their intentions are central to classroom interactions and dynamics. Ensuring that students, peers, and educators from diverse backgrounds understand and communicate respectfully with each other is often just as important as helping students understand the material in their textbooks. And, in fact, such respect does help students better understand their educational materials.

To do this very hard yet empowering work, educators must have specific knowledge of linguistics and the language of their students. How languages work and how people use them in different contexts matter. 'Educational linguistics' is the area of linguistics that examines learning and teaching and the role of language in these processes. We encourage you to consider taking educational linguistics courses in particular for continuing education.

Knowledge of how and why specific aspects of language—from words like 'ain't' to pronunciations such as *warsh* for 'wash'—may appear in students' speech and writing is also invaluable information for educators. When educators assess students' work, it is important to consider whether there is a possibility that differences that may be seen as *errors* might actually be rooted in the students' *knowledge* of another language or language variety. First, educators may discern whether the perceived error fits a linguistic pattern. If so, it is critical not to mark an error as 'wrong' and move on, but rather to explain the patterns underlying the difference, a process that entails showing students the details of their own language usage patterns and comparing them to the usage patterns that characterize standardized English.

Educators also have to know about bias in the materials and assessments that they use to make the sentiment of linguistic equality a reality. It is crucial for educators to know how to approach student language differences in common assessment situations including written essays, reading passages, and vocabulary tests. Language inequality doesn't only occur in the language arts, but also in math and science, or STEM disciplines. For example, one of the greatest challenges in these subjects is that word problems, questions, texts, and directions often contain unfamiliar terms, both technical and non-technical. In fact, non-technical words can often be as problematic as the more specialist terms of science. 'It's kind of like learning a language twice,' a geometry teacher once told us, because 'the vocabulary can be so intense.'

Teachers have a crucial role to play in supporting students from diverse linguistic backgrounds. Language matters not just for fostering mutual respect, but for making sure that every student, across all grades and every field of study, has an equal opportunity to succeed.

About the authors

Anne Charity Hudley is the North Hall Endowed Chair in the Linguistics of African America at the University of California, Santa Barbara and

Director of Undergraduate Research for the university. Her research and publications address the relationship between English language variation and K-16 educational practices and policies. She is the co-author of three books: *The Indispensable Guide to Undergraduate Research: Success in and Beyond College, Understanding English Language Variation in U.S. Schools* and *We Do Language: English Language Variation in the Secondary English Classroom*. She is the author or co-author of over 25 articles and book chapters. She has worked with K-12 educators through lectures and workshops sponsored by public and independent schools throughout the country. Charity Hudley is a member of the Executive Committee of the Linguistic Society of America (LSA) and has served as a consultant to the National Research Council Committee on Language and Education and to the National Science Foundation's Committee on Broadening Participation in the Science, Technology, Engineering, and Mathematics (STEM) sciences.

Christine Mallinson is director of the Center for Social Science Scholarship, professor of language, literacy and culture and affiliate professor of gender and women's studies at the University of Maryland, Baltimore County (UMBC). Her interdisciplinary research examines the intersections of language, culture, and education, focusing on English language diversity in the United States. Among other publications, she is the co-author of *Understanding English Language Variation in U.S. Schools*, and *We Do Language: English Language Variation in the Secondary English Classroom*, as well as the co-editor of *Data Collection in Sociolinguistics: Methods and Applications*, 2nd edition. Mallinson is the chair of the Ethics Committee of the Linguistic Society of America (LSA) and is a member of the editorial advisory board of three journals, *Language and Linguistics Compass, Voice and Speech Review,* and *American Speech*, for which also she previously served a 10-year term as the journal's associate editor.

Suggestions for further reading

In this book
Other chapters focusing on language-related issues in schools include Chapters 58 (teaching grammar), 59 (teaching foreign languages), and 61 (bilingual education). Additional discussions of language and inequality,

see chapters 8 (prescriptivism), 45 (language conflict), and 46 (gendered language). For more information about dialect variation, see Chapters 3 (dialects versus languages), 30 (pidgins and creoles), 49 (U.S. dialects), and 51 (African American English).

Elsewhere

Charity Hudley, Anne H., and Christine Mallinson. "'It's worth our time": A model of culturally and linguistically supportive professional development for K-12 STEM educators,' *Cultural Studies in Science Education* vol. 12 (2017), pp. 637–660.

Charity Hudley, Anne H., and Christine Mallinson. *Understanding English Language Variation in U.S. Schools* (Teachers College Press, 2011).

Charity Hudley, Anne H., and Christine Mallinson. *We Do Language: English Language Variation in the Secondary English Classroom* (Teachers College Press, 2014).

Reaser, Jeffrey, Carolyn Temple Adger, Donna Christian and Walt Wolfram. *Dialects at School: Educating Linguistically Diverse Students* (Routledge, 2017).

58

Should schools teach grammar?

Richard Hudson

What's the use of teaching grammar in school? Does it have to be a boring waste of time?

The English-speaking world has spent almost a century agonizing about whether schools should teach grammar; this crisis is undoubtedly linked in part to the demise in most schools of Latin. For instance, as the UK emerged from World War I, two reports focused on what they called 'The problem of grammar,' and between 1965 and 2013 there was no public examination in England which gave any academic credit at all for knowledge of grammatical concepts or terms. Meanwhile, grammar teaching has survived in large chunks of Europe. The United States has moved away from studying grammar though some schools still do it. To simplify, grammar is regularly taught in northern and eastern Europe, and in countries where the national language is descended from Latin. But even there it is often contentious.

So, who's right? Is grammar teaching a complete waste of time and a sure way to turn pupils off? Or is it an essential part of any child's education? Not surprisingly, it all depends what you think grammar teaching is and what you think it might achieve. It's all too easy to set the parameters in such a way that teaching grammar emerges as an unjustifiable misuse of school time—for example if it merely tries to prevent children from committing grammatical errors in writing (and fails even to do that). There's plenty of research evidence that this kind of grammar teaching is indeed a waste of time.

But there are much better ideas of what grammar is, much better reasons for teaching it, and much better ways of teaching it.

What is grammar? Grammar is the central core of any language, including the language which school children already know; so what is there to teach? The answer depends on the language. If it's the children's own language, most of the facts are already in place, so what they need to learn is how to analyze these facts and make sense of them. As any grammarian will tell you, that's not a trivial task, and it's certainly not achieved simply by learning to distinguish nouns and verbs. In fact, it may be the most daunting and exciting intellectual challenge the child ever faces.

But, of course, there are also other languages which the child may need to learn—or, at least, may need to learn *how* to learn. In these cases, the grammatical facts are new and have to be learned; but a child who understands something of how their own language works will be much better placed for learning how a new one works. And equally obviously, the experience is bound to be more interesting if links and comparisons can be made to their existing framework of ideas about grammar.

Why teach grammar? While much of the debate has assumed that the only possible reason for learning about grammar is to improve writing, there are other reasons:

- for learning other languages;
- for improving reading skills;
- for understanding the many ways in which grammar affects our thinking about the world;
- for teaching analytical skills through grammatical analysis and discussion; and
- for teaching scientific thinking (by hypothesis formation and testing).

Even if grammar teaching has no effect on writing, it could be justified against these aims.

That's an important conclusion because a great deal of research has shown that there is no effect of grammar teaching on writing, so it's widely believed that that's the end of grammar teaching. Unfortunately, the research on the other goals is less well known, though the reasons listed above may be just as vital as improvement in writing. The tide is turning even regarding writing, so reports of the death of grammar seem to have been greatly exaggerated.

How should grammar be taught? The argument so far is that grammar teaching is all about analyzing and understanding how language works, and that it has multiple goals. Given these assumptions, we can draw two conclusions about how best to teach it.

The first is that grammar should be *taught* through the study of the child's own grammar and of the language experienced by the child. What is studied could be the child's grammatical system (word classes, tenses, clause types, and so on), and (contrary to popular dogma) need not be limited to the context of what the child writes. This teaching has just one goal—understanding and analytical skill—and it can give students as much enjoyment and satisfaction as any other school subject.

The second conclusion is that this grammatical knowledge, once taught, can be *applied* in many different settings, from first-language writing through foreign-language learning and scientific investigation. All the goals listed above can build on the same array of concepts and terminology; and the more these ideas are used, the clearer and stronger they become.

This isn't how grammar has ever been taught in English-speaking countries. So is it just a pipe dream? No, there are countries where teaching roughly along these lines is a reality—and, interestingly, they are the countries that stay at the top of the Programme for International Student Assessment (PISA) rankings.

About the author

Richard Hudson is professor emeritus of linguistics in the Department of Phonetics and Linguistics at University College, London, where he worked from 1964 through 2004. He has a B.A. in modern and medieval languages from Cambridge and a Ph.D. from the School of Oriental and African Studies, London, with a thesis on the grammar of the Cushitic language of the Beja (or Bedawie) people in the northeast of the Sudan.

Suggestions for further reading

In this book
Additional issues of language and education are discussed in Chapters and 57 (teaching linguistically diverse populations), 59 (teaching foreign languages), and 61 (bilingual education). For more about grammar, see Chapters 4 (universal grammar) and 25 (origins of grammar), as well as 8 (grammatical variation), and 49 (U.S. dialect variation).

Elsewhere
Lury, Josh. *Understanding and teaching grammar in the primary classroom. Subject knowledge, ideas and activities* (Routledge, 2017). Investigative first-language grammar teaching.

Websites
http://dickhudson.com/grammar-for-writing—provides research on grammar teaching and writing

http://teach-grammar.com/geography—discusses how grammar is taught in a number of different countries

http://clie.org.uk/fl-eng—discusses grammar linking first and other languages

http://teach-grammar.com/research#comprehension—covers grammar for reading and comprehension

https://en.wikipedia.org/wiki/Linguistic_relativity—overviews grammar and thinking

http://teach-grammar.com/research#investigative—overviews grammar for analytical and scientific thinking

59

Is elementary school too early to teach foreign languages?

Gladys C. Lipton

Is there any advantage to teaching languages in primary school? Is there a risk of overloading children's brains? Aren't other subjects more important at that age?

I recently got a note from a mother whose daughter's school had a program teaching Chinese and Spanish to elementary students. 'Will it result in linguistic confusion?' she asked. It's a good question, but it's *not* a worry.

Children under the age of ten are absolutely hardwired to learn languages. In many countries they learn three or four, often at the same time—with no ill effects. In the U.S., the tradition has been not to start language study until high school or middle school—and American children are poorer for it. More recently though, Americans are recognizing what a joyous thing language learning is for children, and many schools offer different languages. The most widely used terms for such programs are 'early language programs' or 'FLES*' (pronounced 'flestar') which encompasses all types of elementary school foreign language programs' including sequential FLES (Foreign Language in the Elementary School), FLEX (Foreign Language Exploratory), and Immersion.

The *theoretical support* for FLES* comes from studies of the brain. Researchers report that it's most receptive to language learning before the age of ten, but then begins to lose this plasticity. Readers fortunate enough to have started learning a foreign language in childhood probably speak it without an accent. Does this mean that you can't learn a foreign language well if you don't start until secondary school? Not at all—you just have to work a little harder at it.

In addition to this *neurological* advantage, children exposed to the sounds and rhythms of other tongues are *culturally* flexible. Part of learning languages is getting past the notion that English is the 'right' or only way to talk, and that other languages are 'funny.' Children who take FLES* outgrow such attitudes rapidly, and don't have the inhibitions teenagers often feel when they start a foreign language. Researchers have found that children under ten not only love to imitate new sounds, they're highly receptive to and interested in other people's customs, traditions, and different ways of seeing and doing things.

Early language learning can open children's minds to other cultures, especially in the earliest grades, where songs, learning games that reflect the target culture, the arts, science, mathematics, social studies and physical education are included in language study. Often, non-verbal activities, such as handshakes, nodding, bowing, etc. can represent different aspects of the new culture.

What results can you expect from an early start in language learning? Above all, greater proficiency: students who start a language early and stick with it, achieve higher scores on Advanced Placement tests than those who start the language in their teens (see Taylor's study in the suggested reading list below). What explains this? A great deal of research has shown that success in language learning depends on three things: time on task, motivation, and frequency or intensity of learning sessions. All three flow from starting a foreign language early. Young children automatically get more exposure time; the fun of language learning motivates them; and they're likely to want to get more of it. Most early-start students are successful language learners, and they benefit greatly from effective teachers.

But, some may ask, isn't the grade school day already full? How can we squeeze in another subject, even if it's worthwhile?

Part of the answer is that, according to emerging research, time spent on languages is not subtracted from the rest of the curriculum. The interdisciplinary approach, often used by foreign language teachers, reinforces what students learn in classes other than foreign language. When a FLES* teacher works on days of the week, weather, maps, shopping, and other real-life topics in the language class, she or he is reinforcing what classroom teachers are providing instruction about numbers, dates, geography, temperature, colors, arithmetic, and money.

For all these reasons, many parents are very interested in internationalizing the schools their children attend. This can be impeded, though, by the perceived cost of establishing and continuing a foreign language program. There is certainly no magical answer to this problem, but there are many creative options. Where regular classroom teachers are fluent in a foreign language and have been trained in foreign language teaching methods at this level, they can form the nucleus of a program. Sometimes it makes most sense for one or more language teachers to travel between several classes or several schools. In some cases, video conferencing and technology can help limited language-teaching staff to cover more schools.

Even when budgets are very limited, it is highly recommended that parents, teachers, administrators, counselors, and other community members work together to formulate age-appropriate, realistic program goals and outcomes.

Many people involved in decisions may well ask, at this point, 'What are the current trends in early language learning?' The author consulted a number of people and organizations, and the composite list of trends follows:

1   *There is a need for creating opportunities for reaching parents and the public about programs teaching other languages.* This is an ongoing, urgently needed path to creating partners in planning and institutionalizing early language learning. For example, the American Association of Teachers of French (AATF), since 1999, has been preparing a National French Week packet

for teachers, including a poster and other materials, for the purpose of taking French out of the classroom and into the various parts of the school community, where students have an opportunity to show their competence in the foreign language. The American Council on the Teaching of Foreign Languages (ACTFL) has recently announced a new program for reaching the community called 'Lead with Languages.' This initiative demonstrates how knowing one or more foreign languages can help to 'boost up the ladder to success' in various careers or occupations.

2   *It is important to establish curriculum proficiency/performance language activities that are content-based or content-related.* This is an urgent trend in early language learning, in that it creates needed links between goals and outcomes. Curriculum development and updating are important functions of a school or school district early language Planning Committee. One of the major problems for this Committee is planning for effective articulation beyond the elementary school level.

3   *It is essential that the issue of teacher shortages at this level be addressed.* School boards and local communities must form partnerships with colleges and universities on the local levels, so that long range planning for staffing early language learning programs can meet the need for qualified and well-trained teachers at this level. ACTFL and AATF and other national organizations already have ongoing programs for teacher recruitment and training in place. Funding is a challenge, but hopefully local, state, and national initiatives will provide assistance.

4   *For an early language program to be effective, there must be appropriate student and program assessments at this level.* Based on carefully planned and realistic goals, there should be plans for assessing student progress, as well as assessments for program results. For further information about student and program assessments, please see the ACTFL website (www.actfl.org) and the chapter on Evaluation in Lipton's book (now distributed by AATF at www.frenchteachers.org).

5   *The rapid growth of dual language or bilingual education requires attention and support.* This appears to be the fastest growing of the several options of program models in early language learning. However, the supply of well-trained teachers does not appear to be meeting the demand for them. Perhaps the once-successful national FLES* Institutes models may help to supply teachers who are bilingual and who are trained to teach in dual language or bilingual programs and other types of foreign language programs in the elementary schools.

To return to that mother's question posed at the beginning of this piece based on research evidence: Should we teach foreign languages in the elementary school? The answer is unequivocally 'Yes!'

Acknowledgments

Appreciation is expressed to the following people for their input in the revision of this article: Jayne Abrate, Martha Abbott, Judy Ellen Ackerman, Christine Brown, Karen Kuebler, Aniko Makranczy, Nancy Naomi Carlson and Harriet Saxon.

About the author

Gladys Lipton is the director of America's National FLES* Institute, and serves as a consultant to schools, school districts and other agencies. She has directed national teacher development institutes at the University of Maryland. Her past leadership positions include program coordinator in Foreign Languages and ESOL for the Anne Arundel County Public Schools in Maryland, and director of foreign languages for the New York City Public Schools. Dr. Lipton has served as editor of the newsletter of the Northeast Conference on the Teaching of Foreign Languages. She has chaired the national FLES* committees of both the American Association of Teachers of Spanish (AATSP) and the AATF. She has also served as an associate editor of the AATSP journal *Hispania*, and as national president of the AATF. She has received many awards for her work in the profession, including ACTFL's Steiner Leadership Award and, in 2010, the award of Commandeur dans l'Ordre des Palmes Académiques, from the French government. In 2015, she was awarded the Médaille de Mérite from La Renaissance Française.

Suggestions for further reading

In this book

Other chapters discussing language acquisition by children include 13 (language deprivation), 20 (language and the brain), 30 (pidgins and creoles), 31 (signed languages), 35 (babies and language), and 61 (bilingual education).

Elsewhere

ACTFL Position Statement on Early Language Learning (2006). Available at www.actfl.org

ACTFL Report: 'Foreign language enrollments in K-12 public schools: Are students prepared for a global society?' (2015). Available at www.actfl.org

Curtain, Helena and Carol Ann Dahlberg. *Languages and Children* (Pearson, fourth edition 2010). Information about FLES research, methods, and curriculum.

Lipton, Gladys C. *Practical Handbook to Elementary Foreign Language Programs (FLES*)* (National FLES* Institute, fifth edition 2010). Offers detailed assistance in planning and supporting effective FLES* programs. Available at www.frenchteachers.org

Lipton, Gladys C. 'A retrospective on FLES* programs,' *Hispania* vol. 83, no. 4 (1998), pp. 76–87. Traces early attempts to implement foreign language programs in U.S. elementary schools.

Marcos, Kathleen. *Why, How, and When Should My Child Learn a Second Language?* (Center for Applied Linguistics, 2003). Suggestions for parents who wish to help with launching early language programs.

Portman, Catherine. 'English is not enough,' *The Chronicle of Higher Education* (April 18, 2010). Available at www.chronicle.com. Provides a strong statement encouraging elementary school foreign language programs.

Taylor, Carolyn. 'Executive summary: The relationship between elementary school foreign language study in grades three through five and academic achievement on the ITBS and the fourth grade LEAP 21,' *Learning Languages* vol. 10, no. 1 (2004), pp. 16–18.

Thompson, Paul M. et al. 'Growth patterns in the developing brain detected by using continuum mechanical tensor maps,' *Nature* vol. 404 (2000), pp. 190–193. Validates early language learning programs. Describes several different successful program models.

60
Why study languages abroad?

Sheri Spaine Long

Can you learn a language without going abroad? Isn't it easier to pick up a language by living in a country where it's spoken than by sitting in a classroom in your own country?

Are you one of those language learners who loves to be plunked into an ongoing stream of talk, soaking it up, mimicking what you hear, unruffled if you do not understand what is being said? Or do you find yourself needing more structure, wanting to know what each word means before trying it out, and being frustrated when waves of incomprehensible speech wash over you?

As a language professor, I often hear people say, 'The only way to learn a language is to go abroad.' That's not strictly true. And it's particularly not true if you are thinking that by being in another country you will automatically 'pick up' the language. I dislike the phrase 'pick up a language' because it implies that language learning somehow happens without effort. Not so.

Learning styles vary, so a good way to think about learning a language abroad is from the point of view of readiness. For most people, to parachute into a foreign culture with no previous study of the language, no preparation at all, is not only disorienting but also inefficient. With no framework to help make sense of what you're hearing, progress is slow. Readiness differs from one person to the next. For most of us, it is best to have some formal study of a language before you pull the ripcord. And once you are on the ground, it is best to enroll in a structured learning experience, a language class of some kind. You take the class to get knowledge about the language, and then use the street, pubs, and clubs of the community as your lab to practice speaking and hearing it.

The great advantage of studying and living abroad is that you can experience the language in its cultural context. Words and phrases that you hear in a sometimes 'sterile' classroom come alive, even change meaning, when you hear them coming from a native speaker over drinks in a cafe. Or when you join the crowds in a soccer game. Or deal with the local bureaucracy.

But being confronted with a foreign language is fatiguing at first. It takes constant effort to listen, concentrate, and try to make sense of what you hear; it's easier than you think to spend a long time abroad and still come home monolingual. If your goal is to learn a foreign language, try to use as little English as possible while abroad. Even a little before you think that you are ready, make a vow to yourself to communicate only in the target language, and do it as much as you can—around the clock. Don't hang around with your fellow expatriates; emergencies aside, don't stay in touch with home constantly by video chat, phone, e-mail, texting, social media, or whatever.

When a friend of mine was a junior in college, after a couple of semesters of Spanish she signed up for a program in Spain—her first experience with language learning abroad. After orientation on the first day, the instructor shifted to Spanish and told fifteen nervous Americans to take a 'no English' pledge. From then on she was immersed in a dialect of Spanish that she slowly adopted as her own. She spoke almost no English for five months. She didn't socialize with English speakers. She watched Spanish TV and movies (with no subtitles), and spent as much time as she could with locals. At first she spoke broken Spanish; but by the end of the semester, she was using the language comfortably, expressing herself at an advanced level. That was total immersion in the language and culture. She spent all of her waking hours, seven days a week, speaking or thinking exclusively in the target language.

Study abroad accelerates the learning process, provides authentic cultural context, and encourages good life-long language learning practices. Most people return from their time abroad enthusiastic about linguistic gains and new cross-cultural skills; they're likely to bring back a fresh perspective on their home culture, as well. There are a great many study-abroad programs, offered by a wide variety of providers who serve the business, health, and educational communities. There is a growing trend to enroll in short term study abroad programs. But before selecting a program, make sure that its goals are in line with yours and that the time abroad is focused on language learning. Ask questions such as: does the provider offer structured academic classes and immersion activities? Does the provider present lodging and dining situations that enhance language and cultural immersion? Does the program offer university or secondary school credit, proficiency credentials or diplomas? Time abroad is increasingly recognized as requisite for leadership and career preparation.

If study abroad is not feasible, then domestic immersion is a strong second choice. The best domestic programs mirror study abroad immersion both in spirit and practice, and can provide good language learning opportunities at a fraction of the cost of going overseas. While domestic experiences can rarely offer the same depth of cultural learning as study abroad, programs in places like Concordia Language Villages and Middlebury Language Schools can be very effective. In all such schools you'll take a pledge to work, study, sleep, eat, and socialize in the foreign language for the duration of the program. If you conscientiously keep the pledge—just as you would in an overseas environment— the combination of a structured class and total immersion really works.

About the author

Sheri Spaine Long (Ph.D., UCLA) is executive director of the American Association of Teachers of Spanish and Portuguese. She is editor of *Hispania*, the scholarly journal of the American Association of Teachers of Spanish and Portuguese. Formerly a faculty member, department chair, and study abroad program director, Dr. Long rose to the rank of (full) professor of Spanish at the University of Alabama at Birmingham. She was invited and subsequently appointed as distinguished visiting professor of Spanish at the United States Air Force Academy. Most recently Long served as professor and chair of the Department of Languages and Culture Studies at the University of North Carolina at Charlotte. Her publications include seven co-authored college Spanish textbooks as well as numerous scholarly articles, notes and reviews on Spanish literature and culture, language pedagogy, and policy.

Suggestions for further reading

In this book

For other discussions of adult language learning see Chapters 20 (language and the brain), 37 (foreign accents), 40 (adult language learning), 41 (history of language teaching methods), and 54 (language teaching technology).

Elsewhere

www.studyabroad.com—This site offers a comprehensive way to search for study abroad providers and compare options

www.nafsa.org—This site is maintained by NAFSA: Association of International Educators (formerly known as the National Association of Foreign Student Advisors), and has a variety of useful publications about study abroad and general information about international education.

www.americancouncils.org—The official site of the American Councils for International Education, it offers stories, programs, and services worldwide for study abroad.

www.amacad.org/content/Research/researchproject.aspx?d=21896— The AAAS's Commission on Language Learning published *America's Languages. Investing in Language Education for the 21st Century* (2017) that recommends promotion of opportunities for students to learn languages in other countries by experiencing other cultures and immersing themselves in multilingual environments.

The following journals focus on study aboard and contain specialized case and research studies and specific data regarding individual study abroad programs:

- *Frontiers: The Interdisciplinary Journal of Study Abroad* (www.frontiersjournal.com)
- *Journal of Studies in International Education* (http://jsi.sagepub.com)

The following organizations provide domestic immersion experiences:

- Concordia Language Villages (www.concordialanguagevillages.org/newsite)
- Middlebury Language Schools (www.middlebury.edu/ls)

61

What is bilingual education?

Phillip M. Carter

What is bilingual education? What's at stake, and for whom? What is the most effective type of bilingual education?

Imagine turning up to your very first day of school, at age five or six. You're excited to learn, maybe a touch nervous, but definitely ready to start. You walk into class, apprehensive but still smiling. You spot your teacher, who returns your smile with her own. She walks toward you, kneels down to your level, and with a big smile, welcomes you to your new school. The only problem? You didn't understand a word she said.

This exchange could easily be the experience of child in a Hmong-speaking family who moved from Vietnam to Kansas. Or of the Punjabi-speaking family who arrived recently in London. But this experience doesn't belong only to the children of immigrants. Even though the vast majority of the world's population is multilingual, children aren't always educated in their home language, or even the primary language of their community. In East Timor, a child may be expected to know Portuguese for use in school, even though the language of the home is Tetum. In Haiti, the vast majority of schoolchildren are educated in French, even though most people speak Haitian Creole. But how can you learn if you don't understand the language?

The first point to make about this situation is thus easy to make and is as obvious as it seems on its face: children don't learn content if they don't understand the language of instruction. The second point may be less obvious, but is just as important; the language selected to be used in education most often also happens to be the language of the social, economic, and political elite. This means that in multilingual societies, children from elite families have the additional privilege of being able to understand the content they are taught in school—because their home language is conveniently the dominant language of their society. Children from non-elite families, however, are faced with an additional and often unacknowledged burden of acquiring the language of the elite as they go. When no support is offered in the acquisition of the school language, this approach can be described as 'sink or swim.'

To complicate matters further, lack of bilingual education can further exacerbate inequality along racial, ethnic, and linguistic lines. In South Africa, Black children are often expected to succeed in school in languages they do not use at home; English or Afrikaans—languages spoken in the home by White South Africans—while White children are never expected to succeed in school in Zulu or Xhosa, languages used by many Black South Africans. In the United States, Latinx children who speak Spanish in the home are often enrolled in 'English-as-a-Second-Language (ESL)' programs to aid in the acquisition of English, and may therefore have little opportunity to use the language of the home at school. Meanwhile, non-Latinx children may be enrolled in Spanish as a 'foreign language' courses, which are widely seen as value-added, resume-boosting educational experiences for non-Latinx White students in the U.S.

Scholars studying education in multicultural and multilingual societies agree that the most equitable educational experience in multilingual societies is a bilingual one (for an overview, see the book by García in the suggested reading list below). Bilingual education is equitable because, if done well, it *can* give language-minority students access to a power language, without the unnecessary compromise of giving up their mother tongue, or the unfair burden of using a language they don't understand at school.

So, what exactly *is* bilingual education?

In reality, bilingual education is not a one-size-fits-all phenomenon, and can instead be thought of as an umbrella term for a range of educational structures designed to teach curriculum content (like math and history) to learners in more than one language.

Sometimes programs called 'bilingual' are not equitable. For example, *transitional bilingual education* is a program designed to use the non-dominant language for a short period of time while children 'transition' to the dominant language. The goal of this kind of program is monolingualism in the dominant language. Sometimes parents of children who speak the dominant language in the home (e.g., they speak English at home in the U.S.) want their children to develop bilingual skills, and therefore send them to *immersion schools,* where they are 'immersed' in a language considered to be 'foreign.'

Many other types of bilingual education abound. Sometimes bilingual education means teaching in two languages that are already widely spoken in a society, sometimes it means using both a power language and a minority language to teach only minority language and immigrant students, and sometimes it means using the socially dominant language alongside an indigenous or aboriginal language that is being revitalized. The shape of bilingual education programs varies school by school, district by district, and country by country, and should depend on the language backgrounds and needs of the students.

In *dual-language immersion* programs, academic content is taught and assessed in two languages over time. In the early grades, schools often use a 90/10 split, with the less-dominant language being used more. For example, kindergarteners starting a Spanish-English dual language immersion program may hear Spanish 90 percent of the time in the first year, 80 percent in first grade, and 70 percent in second grade. By the fourth grade, Spanish and English are equally split, 50/50. Some schools opt for a 50/50 split from the beginning.

All of the programs mentioned thus far are designed to keep the two languages separate, but some bilingual programs allow their students to mix their languages more freely, in acknowledgment of the fact that bilinguals rarely actually keep their languages completely separate. This kind of perspective is known as *translanguaging*.

Despite the benefits of bilingual education, the approach often faces resistance. Sometimes people say they are against bilingual education because they are against teaching children only in the non-dominant language. This common misunderstanding was used in 1996 to convince voters in California to vote for Proposition-227, a ballot initiative that severely curtailed bilingual education. Bilingual education always means *two* languages (or more), but never only one! TESOL and ESL programs, or other programs designed to teach the dominant language without teaching content in the non-dominant language, are also not bilingual education. Sometimes school districts think they are offering 'bilingual education' because they teach 'foreign languages.' The instruction of a language as a language is not bilingual education.

Bilingual education does not solve every problem in education, but linguists and educators agree that it is the best model for the most number of students. All students benefit from the cognitive and sociocultural benefits of bilingualism, while language minority students receive the educational support they need. When done thoughtfully, everyone wins!

About the author

Phillip M. Carter is an associate professor of linguistics at Florida International University in Miami. He is an expert on issues related to multilingualism, language diversity, and language contact. Carter is co-author of *Languages in the World: How History, Culture, and Politics Shape Language* (Wiley-Blackwell, 2016).

Suggestions for further reading

In this book

Educational approaches to language learning are also found in Chapters 41 (history of language teaching methods) and 59 (second language learning in elementary schools). The benefits of immersion are further discussed in Chapter 60 (study abroad). Chapter 57 (linguistics for teachers) discusses additional issues of language inequality in schools. Children's language acquisition is discussed in Chapters 30 (pidgins and creoles), 31 (sign languages), and 35 (babies and language). Multilingualism is addressed in Chapters 20 (language and the brain), 36 (hyperglots), and 38 (bilinguality).

Elsewhere

García, Ofelia. *Bilingual Education in the 21st Century: A Global Perspective* (Wiley-Blackwell, 2009).

Santa Ana, Otto. *Brown Tide Rising: Metaphors of Latinos in Contemporary American Public Discourse* (University of Texas Press, 2002).

Tetel Andresen, Julie and Phillip M. Carter. *Languages in the World: How History, Culture, and Politics Shape Language* (Wiley-Blackwell, 2016).

Zentella, Ana Celia. 'The "Chiquitafication" of U.S. Latinos and their languages, or: Why we need and anthro*political* linguistics,' in Rebecca Parker and Yukako Sunaoshi, eds., *Texas Linguistics Forum* vol. 36 (University of Texas Press, 1996), pp. 1–18.

Language application

62
How are dictionaries made?

Erin McKean

What is a lexicographer? How many of them does it take to make a dictionary? How do they decide what to put in and what to leave out? Why don't dictionaries tell us what's right and what's wrong?

As recently as a few centuries ago it was possible for one very learned person to create a dictionary single-handedly. But these days virtually all dictionaries are built by teams of talented people. For each new dictionary, and each new edition of an existing dictionary, they collect *corpora*—huge amounts of written and spoken language, from newspapers, magazines, books, plays, movies, speeches, TV and radio shows, interviews, and the internet—and sift them for evidence of how language is being used: What words haven't been seen before? What words are changing their meanings? What words are used only in particular ways? What are their histories, pronunciations, grammatical quirks?

The words of English are like stars. They are born and they die—sometimes without anyone noticing. The closest stars you can see with the naked eye, and the most frequently used words are usually easy for lexicographers to find and define. And just as astronomers need a bit of assistance from computing power to sort through the data sent by modern telescopes to learn about the stars farthest from us, modern lexicographers use computer-aided techniques to sort through word data—those corpora—to find and describe words.

And like stars, there are almost too many words of English to count. Lexicographers are constantly playing catch-up. A study published in the journal *Science* in 2011 (see suggested reading list below) found that almost 52 percent of the unique words of English aren't in traditional dictionaries, and that the number of commonly used words in English grew by 70 percent between 1950 and 2000. The same study estimated that the English language adds more than 8500 new words a year—and most traditional dictionaries are only able to add a few thousand of those to each new edition or online update.

Most lexicographers see their primary job as data collection and presentation. They try to capture as accurate a picture as possible of how people actually use a language at a given point in time.

But a lot of people in the dictionary-buying public are uncomfortable with scientific neutrality when it comes to language. They don't want their dictionaries to describe how people actually write and speak. They believe that some language is right and some is wrong, period. And they think the lexicographers' job is to tell us which is which. They want prescriptive dictionaries that omit vulgar language and condemn other words they disapprove of, like 'irregardless' or 'muchly.'

If you're one of those people, you'll be disappointed to learn that most modern dictionaries are basically descriptive. They don't prescribe what we ought to say or write; they tell us what people actually do. Like umpires, lexicographers don't make rules—they just call 'em the way they see 'em.

That doesn't mean that prescriptive views are completely left out. People's attitudes toward words are also a legitimate part of a dictionary. For example, the *New Oxford American Dictionary* doesn't forbid its readers to use the unlovely word 'irregardless,' but it clearly notes that the word is 'avoided by careful users of English.' Because people no longer use words like 'fletcherize' (meaning to chew each bite at least thirty-two times before you swallow), and because you don't talk the way people did in eighteenth-century Williamsburg, you know that language is always in flux. So if research finds a lot of good and careful writers using 'irregardless,' or creating sentences like 'Anybody could look it up if they wanted to'—using 'they' where you might expect 'he or she'—the dictionary can say with authority that it's becoming standard English—even if prescriptivists disapprove.

There's also a whole new category of dictionary—the online dictionary—where you can see word evidence as quickly as the lexicographers can, without waiting for it to make it through the editorial process. At *Wordnik* (an online dictionary I founded), automated processes sift through billions of words to select example sentences based on how well they represent the word you're interested in. The site allows users to leave comments, make word lists, tag words, and even see images from the online photo site Flickr.com and tweets from Twitter. Purely crowdsourced sites such as UrbanDictionary.com and Wiktionary.org let users put in their two cents, as well. The upside of all these sites is that they can show you much more information than a traditional dictionary, much faster (and *Wordnik* and *Wiktionary* also incorporate traditional dictionary information like parts of speech and synonyms). However, you need to use your own knowledge and employ your critical thinking skills to filter the information shown. For instance, if a word's usage is illustrated by plenty of sentences, but they're all from personal blogs, the word is likely considered more informal than one where all the sentences shown are from the *Wall Street Journal*.

So don't think of dictionaries as rulebooks. They're much more like maps. They show where things are in relation to each other and point out where the terrain is rough. And, like maps, dictionaries (especially online dictionaries) are constantly updated to show the changing topography of a language—not just with shiny new words (like 'bae' or 'airpocalypse' or 'avolatte') but new uses for old words (like 'swatting' meaning 'make a false report of a threat in order to provoke a police SWAT team response to a third party') and even new parts of words (the affix *-bro* as in 'broflake' or 'manifestbro'—used to indicate a particular kind of misogynistic male behavior). Dictionary-makers put as good a map as possible into your hands, but devising a route is up to you.

About the author

Erin McKean is the founder of the non-profit online dictionary *Wordnik*. Previously she was the Editor in Chief of U.S. Dictionaries for Oxford University Press and the Editor of *VERBATIM: The Language Quarterly*. She is also the author of *Weird and Wonderful Words, More Weird and Wonderful Words, Totally Weird and Wonderful Words*, and *That's Amore* (also about words), as well as two books about dresses (the novel *The Secret Lives of Dresses* and *The Hundred Dresses*, a field guide to dress archetypes). She has a B.A. and M.A. in Linguistics from the University of Chicago, where she wrote her M.A. thesis on the treatment of phrasal verbs (verbs like 'act up,' 'act out,' and, of course, 'look up') in children's dictionaries. She lives in California. Please send her evidence of new words you've found, by e-mail, to feedback@wordnik.com.

Suggestions for further reading

In this book

More about words and lexicography can be found in Chapter 9 (what makes a world 'real'). How languages evolve over time is discussed in Chapters 25 (grammar), 27 (origins of English), 28 (Latin), as well as Chapters 29–34 (language variation and change). Language evolution as a result of technological advances is discussed in Chapters 53 and 56 (social media and texting). The concept of language rules is covered further in Chapters 8 (prescriptivism). Other professional opportunities for people interested in language are discussed in Chapters 38 (bilingualism), 48 (America's language crisis), 63 (interpreting and translating), and 65 (forensic linguistics).

Elsewhere

Winchester, Simon. *The Professor and the Madman: A Tale of Murder, Insanity, and the Making of the Oxford English Dictionary* (Harper Perennial, 1999). Published in the UK as *The Surgeon of Crowthorne*.
Winchester, Simon. *The Meaning of Everything: The Story of the Oxford English Dictionary* (Oxford University Press, 2003).
The two Simon Winchester books are both wonderful introductions to the greatest dictionary of the English language, the *Oxford English Dictionary*. *The Professor* recounts, with novelistic flair, the true story

of some of the personalities involved in making the *OED*; *The Meaning of Everything* has more detail and covers the entire scope of the project, which is ongoing.

Michel, Jean-Baptiste, et al. 'Quantitative analysis of culture using millions of digitized books,' *Science* vol. 331, no. 6014 (2011), pp. 176–182.

Stamper, Kory. *Word by Word: The Secret Life of Dictionaries* (Penguin Random House, 2017). A fascinating, funny read by a *Merriam-Webster* editor and one of the most popular lexicographers on Twitter.

Murray, K. M. Elisabeth. *Caught in the Web of Words: James Murray and the Oxford English Dictionary* (Yale University Press, reprinted 2001). People who are still intrigued can read this biography of James Murray, the original editor of the *OED*, written by his granddaughter, K. M. Elisabeth Murray.

Landau, Sidney I. *Dictionaries: The Art and Science of Lexicography* (Cambridge University Press, second edition 2001). This book is the best starting point for people interested in the nuts and bolts of how dictionaries are made.

63

Why do we need translators if we have dictionaries?

Kevin Hendzel

What does it take to be an interpreter? With a good dictionary, isn't translating something anybody can do?

I'm always impressed when I see someone standing behind a president or prime minister, interpreting a foreign visitor's comments into his ear. What *talent* it takes to translate one language into another—listening and speaking at the same time! You can't pick up a dictionary. And you can't just spit out words like a robot. The interpreter's job is to convey *meaning*. And since a lot of meaning is expressed by tone of voice or the nuance of words and phrases, his or her job is far more than translating word for word.

And what responsibility! Imagine a court case in which the defendant doesn't speak the language of the judge and the jury. If an interpreter gets it wrong, how can justice be done? Not everyone can move easily between two languages, but there needs to be somebody who knows how. That 'somebody' is a professional interpreter.

There's the same need for professional translators, who deal with the *written* word as interpreters deal with *spoken* language. Think about how important the choice of words or phrases is in, let's say, a business contract. Or on the famous 'hotline' between the White House and the Kremlin, which does not—contrary to what many people think—connect a bright red telephone on the

U.S. president's desk to a similar one on the desk of the Russian leader. Instead, it's an encrypted high-speed data link that transmits written, rather than spoken, messages—and it requires a translator, rather than an interpreter.

So what does it take to be a professional translator or interpreter? And let me emphasize the word 'professional.' Because simply knowing two languages isn't enough—it's just a starting point.

Beyond skill in speaking a second language, an interpreter needs to know the two *cultures* involved, the use of slang, jargon, and various dialects of the languages, and the subject matter to be interpreted. To be really good at it, he or she has to have an exceptional memory—and a lot of training in the art of interpreting.

A *translator* needs somewhat different skills. But again, strong knowledge of two languages is just the beginning, because translating can get very complicated. Think of the technical terminology translators are called on to handle. Lawyers file *writs of mandamus*. Physicians treat *hypertrophic cardiomyopathy*. Terms like these can be pretty daunting, and for translation it's not enough just to look up their dictionary equivalents in another language—you need to understand what they mean. This is why many professional translators and interpreters have advanced degrees in specific technical fields—many are trained engineers, architects, physicians and attorneys. When a translator works from one language into another, that process involves first understanding the concept in one language, and then 'interpreting' or 'describing' that concept in another language. In a nutshell, translation isn't about words. It's about what the words are about.

So how do you get into one of these professions? Well, it's best if you've already had training in a substantive field—like engineering, medicine or finance—that you'll specialize in. It also probably helps to be born somewhere like Belgium, where virtually everyone grows up with two or more languages. But even if you're not bilingual from childhood, with hard work you can get close to it; after that, becoming professionally qualified is mostly a matter of training and practice. You'll need a minimum of a master's degree, which in the U.S. requires two years of study; in Europe, three years or more. And you'll have on-the-job internships before you're turned loose on society. The final step is certification by an organization like the American Translators Association.

Yes, it takes some time. But translation and interpreting are exciting and often lucrative careers. The value of the industry for language services and technology has been estimated at $46.52 billion (globally) in 2018, with the majority of that demand in the U.S., Europe and Asia. It's also important to remember the large volume of translation performed internationally by the defense and intelligence agencies of every country, where figures are hard to come by, as well as domestically in the U.S. in support of community requirements: immigration; court proceedings; as well as hospital and emergency care interpreting. The U.S. Bureau of Labor Statistics has also rated Translation and Interpreting to be a profession that is 'growing much faster than average,' at an annual rate of 18 percent through 2026.

And the flourishing of the European Union, with easy movement of people, products and ideas across borders, generates huge demand for certified interpreters in Europe. Training programs for translators and interpreters are on the rise all over the world—and that's a good thing, because there are severe shortages of qualified interpreters and translators in every field.

Of course, advances in technology have provided us with the universal availability of automated translation such as Google Translate. Translation capabilities embedded in everything from Facebook through Twitter have also changed the landscape. But while statistical algorithms can capture a lot of the meaning though the use of advanced math, they don't 'understand' the text at all, so it's risky to rely on them in business, diplomacy, technology and law where precision counts. In other words, while these translations are most useful for 'gisting' (or getting the idea of) a text in another language, they don't replace the expertise and experience of a language professional who actually understands the language.

If you would like to learn more about the translation and interpreting professions, to investigate training programs, or to seek out professional translators or interpreters for your business or institution, one source is the website of the American Translators Association, www.atanet.org. In addition to comprehensive information on the field, this site provides a searchable online database of translators and interpreters, plus contact information for experts on many topics relating to translation and interpreting.

There have been interpreters for as long as people have spoken different tongues; and translators for as long as there has been writing. Contrary to the myth that everyone speaks English, as the world grows smaller we need translators and interpreters more than ever before.

About the author

Kevin Hendzel is a graduate of Georgetown University's School of Foreign Service and was formerly head linguist on the technical translation staff of the Presidential Hotline between the White House and the Kremlin. He served as National Media Spokesman for the American Translators Association for over a decade (2001-2012) and continues to appear on BBC, NPR, and other national media outlets as a well-known commentator on translation and interpreting issues. His translations from Russian into English include 34 books and 2,200 articles published in the areas of physics, technology, and law. He continues to work as a translator, currently specializing in national security areas. These range from nuclear weapons dismantlement and disposition programs in the former Soviet Union to U.S.-sponsored programs aimed at preventing the proliferation of nuclear, biological, and chemical weapons worldwide.

Suggestions for further reading

In this book

Other discussions of opportunities and requirements for professional use of language abilities are discussed in Chapters 2 (what linguists do), 38 (bilingualism), 48 (America's language crisis), 62 (dictionaries), and 65 (forensic linguistics).

Elsewhere

Bellos, David, *Is that a Fish in Your Ear? Translation and the Meaning of Everything.* (Particular Books, 2011). From the Greeks and Romans to modern times, this book covers the whole of human experience, from foreign languages to philosophy, to show why translation lies at the very heart of what humans can do and who we are.

Durbin, Chris. *The Prosperous Translator* (FA&WB Press, 2010). A collection of the best insight, no-nonsense advice, and witty commentary on working at the very top of the translation field, collected over twelve years from Chris Durbin and Eugene Seidel's online advice column 'Fire Ant and Worker Bee.'

Grossman, Edith, *Why Translation Matters* (Yale University Press, 2010). A delightfully insightful and exceedingly well-informed book on the nature and history of translation by one of the most important literary translators of Latin American fiction in the past century and well into the twenty-first.

64

How are endangered and sleeping languages being revitalized?

Tracy Hirata-Edds, Mary S. Linn,
Marcellino Berardo, Lizette Peter,
Gloria Sly and Tracy Williams

How are threatened, endangered, and sleeping languages being revived? What skills and resources does language revitalization require? Why it is worth the effort?

Today many of the world's languages are like rare and beautiful whooping cranes—hanging on for dear life. Saving endangered languages takes work, but it can be done. Consider Indigenous languages like Cherokee, Ojibwe/Anishinaabe, and Lakota. In the past four decades, the number of children acquiring them as first languages has declined so sharply that they could disappear in another generation. But a scene that provides hope starts with colorful preschool classrooms in Oklahoma, North Carolina, Minnesota, and South Dakota, where three- and four-year-old children sit with their teachers, reading picture books. These look like typical preschools anywhere, but the books are written in ancestral languages, the only languages used in the classroom. The hope is that as they continue to study in later grades, these children will become comfortable using their Indigenous languages to communicate and learn. Together with older speakers, children are taking threatened, endangered, and sleeping languages into the future.

Similar intensive programs, from childcare through high school classes, are achieving success among the Mohawk in New York State and Canada, the Blackfoot in Montana, the Arapaho in Wyoming, the Wampanoag in Massachusetts, the Alutiiq in Alaska, the Hawaiians, and other Indigenous communities. Work with creole languages like Gullah, a fusion of African languages and English spoken in coastal areas of Georgia and South Carolina, similarly seeks to preserve not only language, but also unique aspects of identity and culture. Language revivals are taking place worldwide. Consider Basque, being revitalized in Spain, Welsh in Wales, and Maori, which has been made an official language in New Zealand.

Limited exposure to ancestral languages makes them difficult to acquire. A language is challenging to learn if it is not heard, seen, felt, or lived as part of one's life. In endangered language communities, successful revitalization programs have found innovative solutions to this problem, expanding language use to new domains such as video and social media.

Where populations of speakers have a willingness to keep languages alive, community members, linguists, and educators are working to document, describe, and use endangered languages in ever-expanding ways. In communities where only a few speakers remain, young language learners spend time with elders doing everyday chores in the language so that they can become speakers. In places where the languages have not been spoken for years, language researchers and community language practitioners use archives and oral histories to revive languages, just as spoken Hebrew was revived from scriptures and rituals. In California's 'Breath of Life' workshops, participants learn how to locate, read, hear, and interpret archived documents and recordings, as well as how to use them for language revitalization. Regional and national workshops have also been held in Oklahoma and Washington, D.C., respectively.

Endangered languages are also the focus of formal and informal education at a growing number of universities. In the United States, Indigenous languages are being taught in colleges and universities in Arizona, Hawai'i, Kansas, New Mexico, North Carolina, Ohio, Oklahoma, and Oregon. Workshop formats provide training related to language teaching, maintenance, documentation, and revitalization in a variety of venues, including the Northwest Indian Language Institute in Oregon, the American Indian Language Development Institute in Arizona, in Canada through the Canadian Indian Languages and Literature Development Institute, in Australia through the Resource Network for Linguistic Diversity, and in China through the Sino-Tibetan Language and Linguistics Methodology Workshop. At rotating locations throughout the U.S., the Collaborative Language Research Institute (CoLang) provides trainings in documentation and language revitalization for undergraduate and graduate students, practicing linguists, and Indigenous community members from around the world.

Over the past 30 years, language revitalization has become an international movement. Supportive funding and policy measures for endangered languages have emerged in the U.S. (through the Native American Languages Acts of 1990 and 1992 and the Esther Martinez Languages Preservation Act of 2016), the United Nations (through UNESCO), and various organizations and institutions such as the Endangered Language Fund, the Foundation for Endangered Languages, and the Endangered Language Documentation Project.

Documentation and revitalization are important endeavors that provide hope for stemming the loss of languages. The number of living languages will continue to decline as their speakers pass on, but revitalization is not just about speakers, new or old—it also promotes linguistic diversity, cultural understanding, identity, ways of living, and connections to rich heritages. Languages offer a way to access, use, and transfer knowledge as part of the human experience. This is why Ken Hale, distinguished MIT linguist, likened the loss of a language to 'dropping a bomb on a museum'—impacting culture, intellectual wealth, and works of art. It is a sobering thought that most languages alive today may not continue into the next century. Thus, we need to nurture threatened, endangered, and sleeping languages ... as though they were whooping cranes.

Acknowledgment

For earlier versions of this chapter, we thank Akira Y. Yamamoto (professor emeritus, University of Kansas), active in bringing together language communities and professional communities for language and culture revitalization programs, and Kimiko Y. Yamamoto (professor emeritus, University of Kansas) who works with Native educators in developing literature.

About the authors

Tracy Hirata-Edds (Applied English Center, University of Kansas) partners with Native communities to enhance opportunities for culture and language learning/teaching, teacher training, and revitalization. Her interests include endangered languages, documentation, and language development.

Mary S. Linn (curator of Cultural and Linguistic Revitalization at the Smithsonian Center for Folklife and Cultural Heritage) researches effective grassroots strategies in language and cultural sustainability and training in community-based language documentation and archiving in Oklahoma and worldwide.

Marcellino Berardo (Applied English Center, University of Kansas) has been active in U.S. language revitalization programs and second language pedagogy. His specialties include language description and advanced second language teaching/learning.

Lizette Peter (Department of Teaching and Leadership, University of Kansas) is Associate Professor of second language acquisition, teaching, and learning. She has collaborated with several communities on endangered language revitalization initiatives.

Gloria Sly (Tahlequah, Oklahoma) initiated and guided various language programs of the Cherokee Nation.

Tracy Williams (director of the Oneida Language Department in Oneida, Wisconsin, and doctoral student, University of Arizona) has been engaged in revitalizing her language, Oneida, and is currently pursuing a Ph.D. in Indigenous language education.

Suggestions for further reading

In this book
Language extinction and rescue are discussed from various angles in Chapters 5 (languages of the world), 28 (Latin), 34 (language death), and 49 (U.S. dialect change). Also of possible interest is Chapter 50 (Native American languages).

Elsewhere
Hale, Ken, and Leanne Hinton, eds. *The Green Book of Language Revitalization in Practice* (Academic Press, 2001). Useful examples of language revitalization programs with topics ranging from designing a program to training language teachers, from one-on-one immersion to one-on-many classroom approaches.

Hinton, Leanne. *How to Keep Your Language Alive: A Commonsense Approach to One-on-One Language Learning* (Heyday Press, 2002). Effective book on how one-on-one teaching can ensure new speakers of severely endangered languages will emerge—a must have handbook for working on revitalization.

McCarty, Teresa L., and Ofelia Zepeda, eds. *Indigenous Language Use and Change in the Americas*, theme issue of *International Journal of the Sociology of Language* vol. 132 (1998). Excellent collection of articles concerning how Indigenous language groups in the Americas revitalize ancestral languages.

Nettle, Daniel, and Suzanne Romaine. *Vanishing Voices: The Extinction of the World's Languages* (Oxford University Press, 2002). Readable and comprehensive book covering causes and effects of language extinction throughout the world.

Websites

Endangered Language Fund—www.endangeredlanguagefund.org

Endangered Language Project—www.endangeredlanguages.com

First Peoples' Cultural Council—www.fpcc.ca/language

Foundation for Endangered Languages—www.ogmios.org

Hans Rausing Endangered Languages Project—www.hrelp.org

Institute for Endangered Languages—https://livingtongues.org

Living Languages Enduring Voices—https://www.nationalgeographic.org/archive/projects/enduring-voices/about/

UNESCO Intangible Cultural Heritage—https://ich.unesco.org/en/what-is-intangible-heritage-00003

65
Can you use language to solve crimes?

Natalie Schilling

What kinds of crimes involve language evidence? Do people leave 'linguistic fingerprints'? Can experts uncover language disguise?

An anonymous bomb threat is phoned in to a school; a ransom note is found at the home of a missing child; a Facebook post of cryptic authorship threatens harm to a frightened recipient. When there's linguistic evidence at a crime scene, or when language itself constitutes the crime, language scientists—linguists—can use their expertise in the examining the structure, meaning and use of language to help investigators solve crimes. Among other types of analysis, forensic linguists may conduct tasks known as 'authorship attribution' and 'voice identification.' These involve comparing anonymous writings or voice recordings to language samples of known authors or speakers to help investigators link anonymous language samples to suspects—or to clear innocent people who have been wrongly charged with crimes.

For example, in the early 1980s, a series of anonymous bomb threats was phoned in to the Pan Am counter at the Los Angeles airport. Airline executives thought that the voice on the recorded calls sounded like that of Paul Prinzivalli, a cargo handler from New York City, and Mr. Prinzivalli was jailed. His defense attorney contacted William Labov, a leading figure in the study of language variation, in the hopes that Labov could use his linguistic expertise to separate Mr. Prinzivalli's accent from that of the bomb threat caller, perhaps by demonstrating that different New York City boroughs had slightly different accents. Upon listening to recordings of both the threat and Mr. Prinzivalli, Labov immediately knew that the authorities had jailed the wrong man—and that the caller was not actually from New York City at all.

The linguistic 'smoking gun' in the Pan Am case turned out to be one seemingly minor dialect feature: the bomb threat caller's pronunciation of the vowel in 'that' (the 'ae' vowel) as more of an *ey*—something like *they-ut* for 'that.' People who are native to New York City, like Mr. Prinzivalli, do sometimes pronounce their 'ae' vowel as *ey*, but interestingly *never* before *t* sounds. In other words, they might say *bey-ug* for 'bag' but never *they-ut* for 'that.' It's a very subtle pattern, and non-experts typically don't notice it, but it's a clear-cut and well documented pattern nonetheless. Labov conveyed this expert knowledge in the courtroom, the judge was convinced, and Mr. Prinzivalli was set free.

In another case, that of the infamous Unabomber, FBI agent James R. Fitzgerald compared the known writings of a key suspect, Ted Kaczynski, with the anonymous 56-page Manifesto of a serial bomber who had been mailing bombs to university professors, airlines, and others across the U.S. for nearly 20 years, beginning in 1978. Fitzgerald found many linguistic commonalities between the Manifesto and Kaczynski's known writings, including alternative spellings like 'licence' for 'license' and 'instalment' for 'installment,' distinctive words and phrases such as 'power-hungry' and 'cool-headed logicians,' and grammatical 'fillers' like 'more or less,' 'presumably,' and 'in practice.' And while neither feature alone was enough to pin the bombings on Kaczynski, the sheer number of shared features enabled authorities to obtain a warrant to search the cabin where Kaczynski lived. There they found conclusive evidence that Kaczynski was indeed the serial bomber. In addition, there was a linguistic 'smoking gun.' In this case, it was the use of the adage 'You can't eat your cake and have it, too.' Granted, this is not an uncommon saying, but the way Kaczynski phrased it was highly unusual, since its typical wording is, 'You can't *have* your cake and *eat* it, too,' not the other way around. Interestingly, it seems that Kaczynski actually had it 'right,' in the sense that he used the original wording, from centuries ago. But in terms of remaining anonymous, he got it wrong, since this phrase, along with the other linguistic clues, played a key role in his arrest, conviction, and imprisonment.

While linguists have been enormously helpful in cases like these, forensic linguistics is not without its limitations. People sometimes refer to an individual's distinctive linguistic patterns, or 'idiolect,' as a 'linguistic fingerprint,' or linguistic 'DNA.' But that's a faulty analogy. DNA is innate; it's inherited and unchanging, and one tiny sample of DNA contains all we need to know to nearly uniquely identify one individual from among billions. Language can tell us a lot about a person, but it is acquired, not inherited, and it changes over the course of an individual's lifespan, as well as across situations. And no single language sample, no matter how lengthy, ever represents *everything* about an author's linguistic history, habits, and choices. Language is a behavior, not a trait, and so forensic linguistics is less like genetic analysis and more like other types of forensic behavioral analysis—for example, gait analysis (the analysis of walking and its associated body movements). You have a habitual way of walking, and investigators can use your typical 'gait' to pin you down on closed-circuit camera. But if you know they're looking for you, you can change your gait—but only to an extent. Similarly, criminals can change their way of talking or writing in an attempt to evade detection. However, they still leave behind valuable language clues, and forensic linguistics can go a long way toward piecing them together to help solve crimes.

About the author

Natalie Schilling is a professor of linguistics at Georgetown University in Washington, DC. She has authored and co-authored books, articles and chapters on a wide range of topics connected to the study of language variation and change. Her publications include *Sociolinguistic Fieldwork* (2013, Cambridge University Press), *American English: Dialects and*

Variation (with Walt Wolfram, 3rd edition, 2016, Wiley-Blackwell), *The Handbook of Language Variation and Change* (co-editor, with J. K. Chambers, Wiley-Blackwell, 2nd edition 2013), and *English in America: A Linguistic History*, an audio-video course with The Great Courses. She has served as a forensic linguistic expert in cases involving authorship attribution, speaker profiling, and possible false confessions. She regularly teaches forensic linguistics, to audiences ranging from university students to FBI agents, to incarcerated individuals. Composite characters based on Dr. Schilling have appeared in two TV series—once in the CBS series *Criminal Minds* (Alex Blake, FBI agent/Georgetown linguistics professor) and once in the Discovery Channel's miniseries *Manhunt: Unabomber* (Natalie Rogers, a linguist at Stanford University).

Suggestions for further reading

In this book
Opportunities and requirements for professional use of language abilities are discussed in Chapters 38 (bilingualism), 48 (America's language crisis), and 62 (dictionaries). Other linguistic/technical topics appear in Chapters 47 (interactive map of U.S. language communities), 54 (language teaching technology), 55 (machine translation), and 66 (the Museum of Languages), 28 (Latin), and 17 (Esperanto).

Elsewhere
Jessen, Michael. 'Forensic phonetics,' *Language and Linguistics Compass* vol. 2, no. 4 (2008), pp. 671–711.

Schilling, Natalie and Alexandria Marsters. 'Unmasking identity: Speaker profiling for forensic linguistic purposes,' *Annual Review of Applied Linguistics* vol. 35 (2015), pp. 195–214.

Shuy, Roger W. 'Language in the American courtroom,' *Language and Linguistics Compass* vol. 1 (2007), pp. 100–114.

Solan, Lawrence M. and Peter M. Tiersma. *Speaking of Crime: The Language of Criminal Justice* (University of Chicago Press, 2005).

66
How can you keep languages in a museum?

Jill Robbins, Pat Barr-Harrison and
Gregory J. Nedved

Are there museums that celebrate language? How would you do that
in a museum? What kinds of things might be displayed?

In recent decades, the celebration of language through various
exhibitions and museums has shown increasing popularity. One
such place is the National Museum of Language (NML). In 2008,
the museum opened to the public in College Park, Maryland. What
a unique institution! Everyone is familiar with museums where
you see (and sometimes touch) physical objects like airplanes,
paintings, bleached bones, and antique coins. But language, you
might think, is mainly sounds and words and books. Don't libraries already exist to store and display them? What would a language
museum do? And why? Language is a subject most of us want to
know more about: how it developed, how languages differ, how the
body works as a language machine. NML's purpose is to answer
such questions by making clear why language is important, what
we know about language, and how we know it. NML lets you
explore linguistic knowledge enjoyably.

From 2008 to 2013, the museum offered exhibits that very
much fulfilled the dreams of the museum's founder, the late
Dr. Amelia C. Murdoch. Its longest running exhibit, 'Writing

Language: Passing It On, compared alphabetic writing systems (e.g., Greek) and pictographic writing systems (e.g., Japanese). How could one forget the museum's awesome language tree, which allowed visitors to trace their language roots? Another exhibit, 'Emerging American Language in 1812,' celebrated the 200th anniversary of the War of 1812 by looking at the English language of the time. This exhibit included a colorful exhibit on Noah Webster and an 1812 spelling game. Its third exhibit, 'Glimpses of French in the Americas,' introduced the exceptionally diverse universe of French dialects and creoles in the Western Hemisphere. What else could one see at our museum? The world's only International Flag of Language (created by the museum to represent languages past, present, and future) hung there. You could take an 1812 spelling test or review rare foreign language sacred texts. Children, frequent visitors to the museum, could practice writing characters in Chinese, guess the origins of Native American words, translate their names into other languages, or play an online language game.

The museum made the strategic decision in 2013 to close down its brick and mortar facility and go virtual. But we have carried on Dr. Murdoch's dream by finding new ways of making language exciting and relevant to the public. As part of NML's Virtual Museum strategy, we formed a partnership with the Dictionary of American Regional English (DARE). Our newest virtual exhibit provides an interactive way for visitors to learn about how young linguistic field researchers travelled around the United States in the mid-1960s to collect words and audio recordings for the DARE dictionary. The graphic-novel style stories in the exhibit, 'DARE Fieldwork: The Adventure Begins,' are intended to inspire today's young people to become involved in language research. A simulation game places you in the role of a linguistic field worker and lets you try to overcome the kinds of challenges they faced in collecting data on variation in American English.

As part of our Moveable Museum strategy, NML lends out display items (e.g., our International Flag of Language) to other museums. The museum has continued to hold the Amelia Murdoch Annual Speaker Series and has even expanded its language camps by developing an add-on world language component to local recreation programs.

Our ultimate goal remains to return to a brick and mortar facility. As we pursue that dream, and display language at its very best, NML welcomes the ideas and participation of everybody to whom language is important—and that includes you. To learn more about our museum, visit www.languagemuseum.org.

About the authors

Dr. Jill Robbins is a former president and currently chief technology officer of the National Museum of Language. She develops online learning materials for English learners and language teachers at Voice of America. She is co-author of several textbooks for learners and teachers of English as a Second Language, including a contribution to the 2019 volume, *Learning Strategy Instruction in the Language Classroom*.

Dr. Pat Barr-Harrison is Director of Outreach for the National Museum of Language (NML). She served as Supervisor of Foreign Language for Prince George's County, Maryland, as well as vice president of the NML. She has been president of the National Association of District Supervisors of Foreign Languages in the U.S. (NADSFL) and of the Greater Washington Association of Teachers of Foreign Languages (GWATFL).

Gregory J. Nedved has served at the National Museum of Language in numerous capacities since 2008 (his position at the time of this publication was museum president). He has over 25 years of experience as a Mandarin Chinese instructor, translator and interpreter for the Department of Defense (DoD). He is the author of the 2016 book, *Presidential Foreign Language Trivia*.

Suggestions for further reading

In this book

The National Museum of Language covers a range of subjects similar to that of this book. A sampling of chapters that may be of special interest to eventual museum goers includes Chapters 5 (world language survey),

34 (language death), 47 (languages of the U.S.), 54 (language teaching technology), 63 (interpreting and translating), 64 (language rescue), and 65 (forensic linguistics).

Elsewhere

Comrie, Bernard, ed. *The World's Major Languages* (Oxford University Press, 1990). An authoritative presentation of the most interesting facts of the major languages of the world.

Crystal, David. *The Cambridge Encyclopedia of Language* (Cambridge University Press, second edition 1997). An invaluable comprehensive, indeed essential, reference treating all aspects of language.

McWhorter, John. *The Story of Human Language* (The Teaching Company, 2005). An outstanding series of 36 lectures (30 minutes each, available on DVD, videotape, or audio CD) on the history and development of language.

Wade, Nicholas, ed. *The Science Times Book of Language and Linguistics* (The Lyons Press, 2000). A collection of very readable essays. The topics, organization, and style correspond to the approach of the National Museum of Language.

Index

CPSIA information can be obtained
at www.ICGtesting.com
Printed in the USA
FSHW011708120719
59861FS